THE CIVIL SERVICE IN AN ERA OF CHANGE

The Civil Service in an Era of Change

Edited by
PETER BARBERIS
Manchester Metropolitan University

Dartmouth

Aldershot • Brookfield USA • Singapore • Sydney

Published by
Dartmouth Publishing Company Limited
Gower House
Croft Road
Aldershot
Hants GU11 3HR
England

Dartmouth Publishing Company
Old Post Road
Brookfield
Vermont 05036
USA

British Library Cataloguing in Publication Data
The civil service in an era of change
   1.Civil service - Great Britain 2.Civil service reform -
Great Britain
   I.Barberis, Peter
   354.4'1'0009045

Library of Congress Cataloging-in-Publication Data
The civil service in an era of change / edited by Peter Barberis.
     p.   cm.
   ISBN 1-85521-805-4 (hardcover)
   1. Civil service--Great Britain. 2. Bureaucracy--Great Britain.
   I. Barberis, Peter, 1948-
JN425.C56   1997
354.4'006--dc20   96-35394
                                        CIP

ISBN 1 85521 805 4

Printed and bound by Athenaeum Press, Ltd.,
Gateshead, Tyne & Wear.

Contents

Preface and acknowledgements

This volume is largely the product of a one day workshop which took place in April 1995. The workshop was held under the auspices of the Joint University Council Public Administration Committee (JUC/PAC) and took place in the commodious and uplifting Mary Ward House, the premises of the National Institute for Social Work (now the offices also of the JUC/PAC). Most of the chapters here are revised versions of papers given at the workshop, the exceptions being those by Peter Barberis and by Tony Butcher. Conversely, one of the presentations from the workshop finds no place here – that of Hugh Taylor, an under secretary in the Cabinet Office. Conspiracy theories may be laid aside: the absence of a chapter from Taylor is the result neither of editorial injunction nor of the hand of higher authority in Whitehall, simply the 'exigencies of the service'. It must be reckoned as a casualty of the unceasing and near intolerable pressures under which senior mandarins work. Let us hope that it is the nation's only such casualty!

The JUC/PAC now stands as the principal independent body devoted specifically to the dissemination of ideas about contemporary public policy and administration in Britain. It deserves congratulations and thanks for that and for the many activities it organizes, of which the April 1995 workshop is but one example. Thanks are due also to the NISW for the use of their premises to host the workshop. As editor, I should like to thank the other contributors for producing material according to schedule and for their patience in dealing with any ensuing (minor) queries. Last but certain-

ly not least I should like to thank Sara Phillips, with whom I have communi-
cated only through the medium of technology. Not for the first time she has
contrived a final product to camera-ready specification, notwithstanding the
antediluvian methods of the editor. This she did while making her contribution to another line of production – the infinitely more precious one of
human stock. Oh that the value of all our labours could so match the efforts
therein expended!

Peter Barberis
Manchester
June 1996

Notes on contributors

Peter Barberis is Reader in Politics, Manchester Metropolitan University. He is the author of *The Elite of the Elite: Permanent Secretaries in the British Higher Civil Service* (Dartmouth, 1996); the editor of *The Whitehall Reader: The UK's Administrative Machine in Action* (Open University Press, 1996); and co-author (with Timothy May) of *Government, Industry and Political Economy* (Open University Press, 1993). He has written various articles and other published contributions on the civil service.

Tony Butcher is Senior Lecturer and Head of Department of Social Policy and Politics, Goldsmiths' College, London. He has published extensively on British government and on the civil service. He is the author of *Delivering Welfare: Government of the Social Services in the 1990s* (Open University Press, 1995) and co-author (with Gavin Drewry) of *The Civil Service Today* (Blackwell – 2nd edn., 1991).

Richard Chapman was, until his retirement in 1996, Professor of Politics, University of Durham. He previously taught at Carleton University and at the universities of Leicester, Liverpool and Birmingham. Before that he was a civil servant. From 1977 to 1991 he was Chairman of the Joint University Council Public Administration Committee. His writings on the civil service include *The Higher Civil Service in Britain* (Constable, 1970); *Leadership in the British Civil Service* (Croom Helm, 1984); and *Ethics in the British Civil Service* (Routledge,

1988). He has also edited a number of volumes, the most recent being *Ethics in Public Service* (Edinburgh University Press, 1993).

Susan Corby is Senior Lecturer in Industrial Relations, Manchester Metropolitan University. She has published on the topic of industrial relations in the civil service. Between 1981-89 she was an assistant general secretary of the Association of First Division Civil Servants.

Alan Doig is Professor of Public Services Management and Head of Curriculum Quality and Design, Liverpool Business School, Liverpool John Moores University. He is also Co-Director of the Unit for the Study of White Collar Crime, Liverpool Business School. He has written widely and is the author of *Corruption and Misconduct in Contemporary British Politics* (Penguin, 1984); *Westminster Babylon* (Allison and Busby, 1990); and is the co-editor (with Fred Ridley) of *Sleaze: Politics, Private Interests and Public Reaction* (Oxford University Press, 1996).

John McEldowney is Reader in Law, University of Warwick. His publications include *Public Law* (Sweet and Maxwell, 1994). He is the co-author (with Leigh Hancher) of *The Electricity Industry Handbook* (Chancery, 1992) and (with Owen Lomas) of *Frontiers of Environmental Law* (Chancery, 1992). He is also the co-editor (with Paul O'Higgins) of *The Common Law Tradition* (Irish Academic Press, 1990) and (with Patrick McAuslan) of *Law, Legitimacy and the Constitution* (Sweet and Maxwell, 1985). He has contributed to various edited collections in the field of public law. As a public lawyer he has acted as a UN consultant to the People's Republic of China and has been visiting Professor at the University of Nagoya, Japan, lecturing and researching on the public law of the UK.

Andrew Massey is Reader in Public Sector Management, University of Portsmouth. He has published widely on the civil service, most notably in his book, *Managing the Public Sector: A Comparative Analysis of the UK and the USA* (Edward Elgar, 1993). He is also the author of *Technocrats and Nuclear Politics: The Influence of Professional Experts in Policy-Making* (Gower, 1988).

Barry O'Toole is Senior Lecturer in Politics, University of Glasgow. He is the author of the definitive history of the FDA, *Private Gain and Public Service: The Association of First Division Civil Servants* (Routledge, 1989). He is also the co-editor (with Grant Jordan) of *Next Steps: Improving Management in Government?* (Dartmouth, 1995). Elsewhere he has published widely on industrial relations in the civil service and on ethics in government. He is the editor of *Public Policy and Administration*, the journal of the Joint University Council Public Administration Committee.

1   An era of change

Peter Barberis

Introduction: a special era?

Since its emergence as a recognizably modern central state bureaucracy Britain's civil service has been in more or less constant flux. This may seem surprising. The immediacy, the vividness of current and recent changes are apt to blind us to what has gone on before. It is easy to assume that there existed a lengthy period of suspended animation stretching from the heady days of the Northcote-Trevelyan report and its aftermath during the second half of the nineteenth century until the shake up of recent years. Such a view would accord with the picture painted by the Fulton Committee (1968, para. 1) in its famous assertion that the civil service was essentially the product of the Northcote-Trevelyan philosophy. This was sound-bite politics before the age of sound-bite, but no music to the historian. It was too much (or too little) for one member of the Fulton Committee, Lord Simey, who issued a brief note of dissent arguing that Whitehall *had* changed. The notion of continuous, albeit gradual, change is supported by various monographs dealing with developments from the late nineteenth century onwards (Fry 1969; Roseveare 1969; Chapman and Greenaway 1980). The testimonies of civil servants and others drawn from almost any period over the last hundred years or so are replete with references to change of one sort or another, sometimes with the lament that 'things ain't what they used to be' (West 1908; Guillemard 1937; Dale 1941; Salter 1961; Leith-Ross 1968;

Delafons 1982; Part 1990). In reality, things have never stood still.

For all this, there are good reasons, quite apart from chronological prox-
imity, for giving special attention to the changes of the last 15-20 years. We
cannot be sure: the dust has not settled and never will. Yet even with dust in
the air it is sometimes clear enough when significant things have been happening. What, then, makes a special era special? And what are the reasons
for thinking that the present era of change is one of these special eras?

Taking the first of these questions, there are perhaps four factors. First,
we are usually talking about changes on a number of fronts – the structure
of an institution such as the civil service; the way it works; its personnel; or
the role it plays. There may be important changes in one dimension alone,
though usually changes of any significance in one will be accompanied by
shifts elsewhere. Second, some periods of change become defining moments
when the institution takes on a new or different character. Such transformation implies some fundamental reorientation, as distinct from mere embell-
ishment or facade. Third, there is an assumption about time scale. Other
things being equal (which they never are) the longer the period of time the
greater the magnitude of change that can be expected. Most institutions will
change to some extent given a period of, say, fifty, sixty or seventy years.
But this would hardly qualify as a defining moment, or special era. So we
are talking about changes within a generation – twenty years or so. From
this a fourth factor may be inferred – participants and others from the recent
past will find it difficult to recognize the institution as being the one with
which they were associated. Of course, highly significant changes are sometimes only so perceived in lengthy retrospect. Contemporaries and recent
contemporaries may just as easily assimilate and take for granted the
changes they see around them as they are to exaggerate their importance.
Still, where sentiments of estrangement are expressed it is likely (though far
from certain) that something significant has been going on.

How do changes over the past twenty years stack up in the light of these
four factors? Some idea may be gained by comparing the main characteristics of the civil service today with those of the 1970s. Table 1 summarizes the
respective characteristics. Of course the contrasts are not quite so sharp in
reality as they are portrayed in Table 1. But many would agree that these are
the main features and that the contrasts indicated do betray the essentials of
the more concrete, observable changes that have taken place. Some of the
changes are interconnected – indeed perhaps all of them are in some ways.
They have quite a broad span. They are multi-dimensional if not all-
enveloping, so reflecting the first of the four factors specified above. Do they
constitute a fundamental transformation, giving the civil service a new or
different character? This is more difficult. But the terms used by some writers do imply an underlying, qualitative transformation of Whitehall's inner
soul, not just the facade. The emergence of a 'new public management' has

Table 1 **Then and now: the main contrasts between the civil service in the 1970s and the 1990s**

1970s	1990s
Approx. 750,000 civil servants	Under 500,000 civil servants
Fewer ad hoc bodies (QUANGOs) outside and adjacent to the civil service; no executive agencies	More ad hoc bodies; over 100 executive agencies
Recruitment largely centralized through Civil Service Commission	Recruitment by Recruitment and Assessment Services (RAS) on behalf of and directly by departments and agencies; Civil Service Commission abolished in 1991 (though commissioners remain)
Uniform, service-wide pay and conditions of service	Pay and other conditions determined by departments, agencies (within cash limits)
National pay bargaining under Whitley Council system	Whitley system continues, but heavily supplemented by departmental and individual contracts, including performance pay
Predominantly career civil service; 'jobs for life', virtually no fixed term contracts	Career civil service less predominant; more movement in and out of the service; fixed term contracts more common
Little *overt* accountable management; few if any performance targets	Measurable performance targets; agency framework agreements; 'business plans'; decentralized 'cost centres'
Detailed 'bureaucratic' procedural rules and constraints; but codes of behaviour based more on 'common understanding'	Less detailed rules for procedure, more entrepreneurial; but 'common understandings' now enshrined in written codes

been widely acknowledged (Hood 1991b; Butler 1992a; Hughes 1994; Zifcak 1994). For some it constitutes a new paradigm (Overman and Boyd 1994; Hood 1995). The advent of executive agencies has been seen in terms comparable to that of the Northcote-Trevelyan report (Massey 1993, p. 51; O'Toole and Jordan 1995, p. 3). The decentralization and greater delegation implicit in their creation may mark a shift away from the Weberian hierarchical model of bureaucracy, associated as it was with a constitutional, representative vision in which the civil service is 'a neutral machine wound up and kept ticking by an elected government, supported by a parliament representing the people' (Dowding 1995, p. 3). Some have gone further, envisaging the end of the 'Whitehall paradigm' (Campbell and Wilson 1995). By this they mean a 'professional civil service (which) provided politicians with both fearless advice... and a smoothly running machine for implementing decisions once they had been made' (Ibid. p. 5). In a rather different sense Chapman (1991, p. 5) has said that 'the British civil service, as a distinct institution of the public service, identifiable primarily through certain characteristics or qualities rather than through an authoritative and/or legal definition, no longer exists'.

Needless to say, some of these interpretations are highly contestable. Not all would agree with the emphasis given by these writers or with the conclusions drawn. There is no consensus as to where exactly it is all leading. The genesis of recent reforms and the ways in which they were conceived and implemented are further matters of contention (Barberis 1995). Yet it would appear that some fairly important shift of direction has been taking place within the last twenty years – the third factor identified above. Rather less certain, though, are the perceptions of recent contemporaries. It is doubtful if many among those who have left Whitehall since the 1970s would find it beyond recognition were they to return today. On the other hand, a good number of former senior officials have, in different senses and with varying inflections, alluded to changes of substance which were in train at the end of their careers or which have since become apparent (Wass 1985; Heiser 1994; Quinlan 1994; Holland 1995). The current Head of the Home Civil Service has described agency chief executives as a new breed of civil servants (Butler 1990, p. 8).

Hindsight may impart some 'flattening out'. Events and changes which loom large now may in time assume more moderate proportions. Nevertheless, there are *prima facie* grounds for thinking that the recent and current period of change may be a special era in the history of the British civil service. It is useful, therefore, to identify some of the landmarks in this period of change. This will be the focus of the next section of this introductory chapter. It is followed by an account of each of three major reports of the 1990s: that of the Treasury and Civil Service Committee (TCSC) into the role of the civil service; the Nolan Committee on Standards of Conduct in

Public Life; and the Scott inquiry into the sale of arms to Iraq. The chapter concludes with a résumé of the rest of the book.

The civil service since the 1970s: the landmarks of change

Only the briefest sketch of events is necessary here. They have been chewed over, digested and regurgitated many times before (Pollitt 1993; Fry 1995; Pyper 1995; Theakston 1995). The story is familiar enough. Such immediate enthusiasm as there had been for the spirit of Fulton seemed to have ebbed by the late 1970s, both within and perhaps also outside Whitehall. The Heath government's white paper *The Reorganisation of Central Government* (Cabinet Office 1970) had promised much – a more rational, systematic and indeed holistic approach to government, no less. This had been the implicit message not only of Fulton but also of the Plowden Committee (HM Treasury 1961). The Public Expenditure Survey Committee (PESC) had been set up in the light of the Plowden Report and, later, the Wilson government had responded to Fulton by creating the Civil Service Department (CSD) and the Civil Service College (CSC). The creation (by amalgamation) of giant departments, or super ministries, in the late 1960s and early 1970s was presented as an exercise in rationalization and rationality of structure. The Central Policy Review Staff (CPRS) and Programme Analysis Review (PAR) were introduced in 1970 as instruments of more systematic (and sensible) policy making. The Administrative Trainee Scheme (1971) was an attempt to broaden the base of recruitment without diminishing its quality, while the Open Structure sought better use and promotion of talent within the civil service.

All this fell well short of the Fulton vision. Instead of providing the springboard for sustained onslaught, these reforms of the late 1960s and 1970s began to calcify and even to recede – or so it began to appear. The English Report (Expenditure Committee 1977) was, in effect, a post-Fulton progress audit. For good or ill, it found little substantial progress about which to report. It was more a post-mortem. There had been no follow through from the 1970 white paper which, to this day, remains the one and only 'official' attempt since the Haldane Committee (Ministry of Reconstruction 1918) to apply first principles to the broad structure and workings of central government. Two of the giant departments created by the Heath government had disappeared, either partially dismembered (DoE) or dissected (DTI), though the latter was to be reinstated under Thatcher. PAR had run its course long before it was formally wound up in 1979 (Gray and Jenkins 1982). So too had the CSD and the CPRS, disbanded in 1981 and 1983 respectively (Chapman 1983; Greenaway *et al* 1992, pp. 139-63; Blackstone and Plowden 1988). By the late 1970s and early 1980s the planning philosophy of PESC had given way to the expenditure 'survey' with an emphasis upon control and retrenchment (Thain and Wright 1995, pp. 482-4).

The wheels of change seemed to be grinding more slowly at the end of the 1970s than at the beginning of that decade. Perhaps Whitehall was taking stock, quietly consolidating in preparation for the next burst of activity – or perhaps not. In any event, things changed when Margaret Thatcher came to office in 1979. Her radical instincts and those of some of her ministers secured the launch in 1979 of the Rayner scrutinies, the introduction of Management Information for Ministers (MINIS), the Financial Management Initiative (FMI) in 1982 and, in 1988, the Next Steps programme. Not all was plain sailing. Relationships between certain ministers (including Thatcher herself) and some of the most senior officials were sometimes strained. Thatcher wanted from them something more or at any rate other than they were accustomed to give in pursuit of the government's political objectives. She had scant regard for the sensibilities of the traditional mandarinate. She forced the issue on pay, pay bargaining and the making of top appointments. On the latter she exercised rights of intervention which had belonged to all her predecessors of the last sixty years but which had been used only sparingly. Civil servants were on the defensive, something that had seemed improbable in the 1960s and 1970s. Some fought fire with fire – such as Clive Ponting who deliberately leaked confidential information in an effort to expose what he considered to have been unethical behaviour by his minister (Norton-Taylor 1985; Ponting 1985). And then, when he was prosecuted under the Official Secrets Act, he succeeded, in spite of the judge's promptings, to convince the jury that there are circumstances in which a civil servant may have an alternative and higher loyalty than that solely to his or her minister.

The government tried to draw a line under the Ponting Affair by reasserting, in the Armstrong Memorandum, that the loyalty of the civil servant is to the departmental minister. It held the maintenance of strict confidence to be necessary not only to trust between officials and ministers but also to the efficient conduct of government (HM Treasury 1993, (Personnel Management) 4.1 Annex A, para. 8). Such qualms as may be felt by the individual civil servant were to be dealt with 'in house', behind closed doors. But it was no longer possible to hold the line. This was partly because other developments – most notably the creation in 1979-80 of the new select committees – had already brought increasing numbers of civil servants to wider public attention. In part, too, the Thatcher and later the Major governments brought things upon themselves. When in a tight corner, ministers were showing a greater readiness publicly to expose civil servants in order to deflect hostile probings. During the Westland Affair a mid-ranking official at the DTI was allowed to take some of the blame for the leaking of an embarrassing letter despite strong suspicions that the leak had been prompted by No. 10 Downing Street. This helped to save the prime minister, though the whole affair claimed the resignations of two ministers, one voluntarily (Michael Heseltine), the other enforced (Leon Brittan). That was in 1986. The following year Sir Robert (now Lord) Armstrong, Cabinet Secretary and Head of the Home Civil Service, was sent to an Australian court to defend the government's attempts to prevent publication of the book *Spycatcher*, written by former secret service officer Peter Wright. Armstrong did not want to go. He was clearly ill at ease in trying to discharge a task for which he possessed neither the experience, the training nor the aptitude. It was simply not the job for a senior mandarin.

All this began to raise questions about what should be the proper role of senior civil servants. Instead of answers there seemed only uncertainties. Yet these uncertainties took none of the steam out of reforms which, as the 1990s unfolded, were to give the appearance of 'permanent revolution'. John Major's accession to the premiership in November 1990 brought no slacking in the pace of change, perhaps even an acceleration. His first twelve months in No. 10 saw the creation of many more Next Steps agencies, together with the launch of two substantial initiatives – the Citizen's Charter and Market Testing. By the end of 1995 there were 109 executive agencies employing 69 per cent of the entire home civil service (Cabinet Office 1996, p. iii). There were forty main charters covering most key services and promising, among other things, the setting and monitoring of explicit standards, effective remedies for the citizen when services fall below those standards and full information about how public services are run, what they cost, how well they perform and who is in charge of them (Cabinet Office 1995b, p. vi). The latter rests in tandem with the white paper *Open Government* (Cabinet Office 1993b). Programmes of market testing have been introduced though, as yet, they have not turned the structure of Whitehall upside down. In fact market testing is a procedure, a method by which government determines whether a particular task should be carried out by government or by private contractor on behalf of government or indeed whether a whole tranche of work should be privatized once and for all (O'Toole and Jordan 1995, p. 16).

Privatization and contracting out have provided fertile ground for party political exchanges. Other aspects of change in the civil service have nourished wider controversy, too. The whole ethos of the 'new managerialism' is seen by some as either an unwelcome intrusion or else as having been bought at too high a price. Specifically, critics feel that it has displaced some of the traditional values – values which are worth preserving and whose diminution has been to the undoubted detriment of the service. Civil servants have, it has been asserted, been consumed in a headlong rush to become more cost-conscious, to meet performance targets increasingly linked to pay. In so doing they have been too readily inclined to bend the knee to the whims of ministers rather than risk their career prospects by offering less palatable home truths. In short, the civil service has changed not only in structure but also in the way it works and in the role it plays. The existence in office of the Conservatives for nearly a whole generation may have given added emphasis. Ministers may have become blasé. Some of them, it has been said, are less likely to listen to professional advice which fails to fortify their prejudices (Plowden 1994, pp. 102-9). They look to civil servants as technicians of implementation, especially those in the Next Steps agencies. And when things go wrong, the 'technicians' can take the blame, as in the case of the Child Support Agency or the Prison Service (O'Toole 1995). Meanwhile the Whitehall mandarinate in the core departments is increasingly unsure of its role. Top officials have and will probably continue to have a vital role (Barberis 1996, pp. 88-92). But there is no denying the uncertainty. Again, during the 1990s the Cabinet Secretary and Head of the Home Civil Service has on occasion tried to play a role that many consider inappropriate. In 1993 he, together with the current and former Permanent Secretary to the Treasury, was called upon publicly to defend the propriety of payments made from official funds in order to meet a proportion of the legal expenses incurred by chancellor of the exchequer Norman Lamont in connection with allegations about and the subsequent ejection of a 'sex therapist' from one of his own private properties. A year later he was asked 'independently' to investigate allegations of impropriety by the then chief secretary to the Treasury, Jonathan Aitken.

In both cases Sir Robin Butler duly discharged his assignment, willingly or unwillingly but probably unwillingly. In the Aitken affair he later admitted that his investigation had been less than thorough. This was perhaps also an acknowledgement that he was less than ideally placed properly to perform the task he had been given. It was not a question of personal inadequacy, rather the unsuitability of one in his position to conduct an inquiry about a cabinet minister. After all, the cabinet secretary is there to serve the cabinet, not to unearth embarrassing evidence about its members. The suspicion was that Butler had been used by the government as a 'shock absorber'.

In themselves the Lamont and Aitken affairs were political storms in teacups. But the controversy surrounding the mopping role played by Sir Robin Butler reflects a wider concern about the duties of officials and their working relationships with ministers. This, together with the perceived impact of the managerial reforms, has given added zest to the debate about the civil service. In its white paper *The Civil Service: Continuity and Change* the government declared its adherence to the key principles of 'integrity, political impartiality, objectivity, selection and promotion on merit and accountability through Ministers to Parliament' (Cabinet Office 1994a, para.

1.3). These, it said, would be as important to good government in the future as they had been in the past. We do not know to what extent this affirmation of principles represented the heartfelt sentiments of ministers, as distinct from words put in their mouths (force-fed?) by Sir Robin Butler and his senior colleagues. Enshrined in a white paper, they represent the government's official position – this notwithstanding the fact that the same white paper heralded further managerial reforms the like of which are said by critics to have undermined many of Whitehall's traditional values.

A few months later the government issued a further white paper, *The Civil Service: Taking Forward Continuity and Change*. The traditional values were restated with greater emphasis and amplification (Cabinet Office 1995a, paras. 2.1-2.7, pp. 3-5). This the critics found welcome but not wholly convincing. For some, the necessity to state and restate the virtues of these traditional characteristics was itself a sign that they had been placed under increasing strain and that they could no longer be taken for granted. For others, any attempt formally to enshrine such values in cold script was futile if by so doing it was hoped to condition behaviour in a complex entity like the civil service. Others again thought it better to have a set of signposts, however vague, than not to have any at all, especially when the way forward seemed to be in some doubt. Nowhere were these differing sentiments better illustrated than in connection with perhaps the most significant feature of the 1995 white paper – the government's agreement to adopt a civil service code. This was part of a much broader agenda of issues which were to stimulate three major inquiries in as many years during the first half of the 1990s: the TCSC inquiry into the role of the civil service; the Nolan Committee on Standards of Conduct in Public Life; and the Scott inquiry into the sale of arms to Iraq. The latter two went well beyond the civil service. Yet they had much to say about the Whitehall bureaucracy and about the context in which it operates. Each of these inquiries warrants some consideration.

The TCSC inquiry: the role of the civil service

The TCSC issued two reports on the role of the civil service – an interim report (TCSC 1993) and a final report (1994). The latter, published in November 1994, was therefore the culmination of some two years' deliberation. In a way the title of the report was misleading. The Committee did not, in the final analysis, consider the role of the civil service in any prescriptive sense. It did not examine different possible models, though it received much evidence, oral and written, some of it suggesting that the role of the civil service had changed. In the end, it accepted the government's view that the new managerialism was compatible with traditional civil service values. But it also stressed the need for greater vigilance in maintaining those values in the face of 'devolution of authority within the civil service and the disappearance of traditional structures of control' (TCSC 1994, Vol. I, para. 5). The new managerialism had not been a threat and need not be a threat, but it was a potential threat to those values which the Committee, like the government, wanted to preserve.

The TCSC judged the government to have been complacent in assuming that the ethics and standards of conduct necessary to uphold the traditional values of objectivity, impartiality, fairness and so forth were well enough understood not to need spelling out in a written code. It considered the Armstrong Memorandum to be out of date and inadequate, a view it took also of *Questions of Procedure for Ministers*. The latter had first been published in 1992, though it had existed in earlier versions since the 1940s. Only four of its 134 paragraphs dealt directly with the permanent civil service. The TCSC thus recommended a civil service code, intended partly to provide officials with a benchmark, partly to help protect them from being forced to act at variance with their proper role. In connection with the latter, it wanted to give aggrieved individuals an ultimate right of appeal to a new civil service commission, to be established on a statutory basis. For all that it had fought shy of such a written code, the government in the event accepted this idea. It adopted with only minor amendments the TCSC's prototype. The government may have decided that it would make little material difference and that a timely concession would be less trouble than continued resistance. It almost certainly preferred the TCSC's brief, thirteen paragraph version to the much lengthier and more detailed model being pressed by the Association of First Division Civil Servants. A civil service code was duly introduced. The civil service commissioners were given an appellate role, though there was to be no statutory commission.

Although the suggested civil service code received considerable publicity, the TCSC cast its net further and wider. A report of the Committee of Public Accounts (PAC), published a few months earlier, had expressed concern about the 'delegation of responsibilities, streamlining and... more entrepreneurial approach to work' (PAC 1994a, para. 2). It had talked about 'a departure from the standards of public conduct which have been mainly established during the past 140 years' (Ibid., para. 1). While sharing these concerns the TCSC maintained its earlier broad support for the logic of the new managerial and operational reforms. In particular, it believed that the 'benefits of delegated authority for pay and personnel management could outweigh the drawbacks' (TCSC 1994, Vol. I, para. 262). It wanted agency chief executives to be directly and personally responsible to select committees in connection with their annual performance agreements. It agreed, though, that ministers should remain accountable for agency framework documents and for the instructions given to agencies (paras. 152-71). In saying this the TCSC recognized the confusion that had arisen over the question of accountability. It was not satisfied with the government's attempts to distinguish between 'accountability', which cannot be delegated by ministers, and 'responsibility' which could be delegated (para. 132). Here one of the things for which ministers have tried to hold civil servants routinely responsible is the failure to meet published performance targets. The TCSC thought that target setting should be replaced by annual performance agreements which would require a process of formal negotiation and concurrence by the agency chief executive as well as the minister (para. 169). It was highly critical of market testing, partly because of the government's refusal in some cases to allow 'in-house' bids, partly because the process cast a constant shadow over the work of many people, so adversely affecting performance (paras. 172-95). At the same time, it wanted annual performance assessments to apply to permanent secretaries.

The TCSC report held public attention for a little longer than might otherwise have been the case. For, a month before its publication, the prime minister announced the setting up of a special committee under the chairmanship of Lord Nolan to enquire into standards of conduct in public life.

The Nolan Committee

The immediate prompt to the creation of the Nolan Committee was the revelation that two Conservative back bench MPs had indicated a willingness to table Parliamentary questions in return for payment. This was the 'cash for questions' scandal. But the establishment of the Nolan Committee reflected broader misgivings about standards of conduct in public life. The Committee was given the following terms of reference:

> To examine current concerns about standards of conduct of all holders of public office, including arrangements relating to financial and commercial activities, and make recommendations as to any changes in present arrangements which might be required to ensure the highest standards of propriety in public life.

This covered ministers, MPs, MEPs, civil servants and members and officers of all public bodies. The Committee was given a three year 'rolling brief', allowing it to issue a succession of reports and to monitor progress on the implementation of its recommendations. It issued its first report in May 1995.

The Nolan Committee received oral testimony from one hundred witnesses in addition to nearly 2,000 written submissions. It noted the results of a Gallup survey, conducted in November 1994. This showed that 67 per cent of those polled believed that 'the ethical and moral standards of British politicians have been declining in recent years' (Nolan 1995, p. 108). Nolan was not certain whether there had been a decline but accepted that the public believed there to have been a decline. This itself was taken to be a matter of considerable concern. Nolan did not think that it could be explained away as the product of mass media publicity, though there was acknowledged to be a less clear distinction than in the past between right and wrong, between the acceptable and the unacceptable (paras. 4-6).

In order to establish a broad benchmark, the Nolan Committee enunciated seven principles of public life, namely: selflessness; integrity; objectivity; accountability; openness; honesty; and leadership (i.e. setting a good example) (p. 14). To turn these principles into reality Nolan made three types of recommendation, based around: codes of conduct; independent scrutiny; and education and awareness of obligations. In its first report, the Committee concentrated upon three areas: MPs; ministers and civil servants; and quasi (non) governmental organizations (QUANGOs). In the circumstances, most of the public attention focused upon MPs and upon QUANGOs – in particular Nolan's call for MPs to declare the financial rewards they received from all relevant consultancies and other outside interests. Nolan wanted a code of conduct for the guidance of all MPs and the creation of both a Parliamentary Commissioner for Standards of Conduct and a Committee for Public Appointments, the latter to concentrate upon QUANGOs. Both were duly established, though the House of Commons agreed to the disclosure of financial rewards only after a number of government back benchers either abstained or voted with the opposition.

Nolan was largely satisfied with standards of conduct among civil servants. Indeed arrangements for the acceptance of paid employment by top officials upon leaving Whitehall were suggested as the model for ministers. These arrangements require senior mandarins (and now ministers) to seek the approval of the Advisory Committee on Business Interests before accepting any paid position within two years of leaving office. This followed concerns about office-holders in effect using their positions to secure lucrative jobs with organizations with which they had dealings while discharging their public duties or, worse still, as a deferred reward for favours rendered. Certain Conservative ex-ministers had been accused of taking lucrative positions with companies they had helped to privatize.

The Nolan Committee was by no means wholly sanguine about the civil service. Like the TCSC, it acknowledged that 'with greater delegation and more movement in and out of the civil service, there is a need for ever greater vigilance about standards...' (Nolan 1995, para. 47). Standards of conduct, Nolan believed, had received 'far less attention than the need for efficiency and effectiveness in the delivery of services' (para. 43). In particular, Nolan reported 'a perception that reward and promotion may depend... on commitment to Ministerial ideology inconsistent with the impartiality of a civil servant' (para. 48). This, Nolan said, would be wholly unacceptable. It was therefore suggested that performance pay should be structured so as not to undermine political impartiality. While supporting the introduction of the Civil Service Code following the TCSC report, Nolan wanted a strengthening to protect 'whistle-blowers' who observed unethical practices in areas which were not within their remit. This the government accepted and a revised version of the Code came into operation in January 1996.

Other recommendations of the Nolan Committee in connection with ministers have a bearing upon civil servants. Most importantly, Nolan wanted a rewriting of *Questions of Procedure for Ministers* so as to make the prime minister the ultimate custodian of standards among ministers – in effect an adjudicatory role where the integrity of a particular minister had been called into question (Nolan 1995, para. 13). But the government was prepared merely to declare that ministers 'can only remain in office for as long as they retain the Prime Minister's confidence' (Cabinet Office 1995c, p. 3). Again, *Questions of Procedure for Ministers* had stated that ministers have 'the duty to give Parliament, including its Select Committees, and the public as full information as possible... and not to deceive or mislead Parliament and the public' (Cabinet Office 1992b, para. 27). The government now proposed to say: 'Ministers must not *knowingly* mislead Parliament... They must be as open as possible... *withholding information only when disclosure would not be in the public interest*' (Cabinet Office 1995c, p. 32 – additional wording indicated in italics).

This last amendment seemed to confound the spirit of Nolan, sowing seeds for suspicion when many were looking at least for some reassurance about the integrity of ministers. It was made in the light of controversy surrounding the Scott inquiry into the sale of arms to Iraq. This involved, among other things, allegations that ministers and civil servants had hoodwinked Parliament and the public. The controversy was in no way diminished when finally Lord Justice Scott reported in February 1996.

The Scott inquiry

It is necessary to provide some account of the events which precipitated the setting up of the Scott inquiry and of the politics surrounding the ensuing report. Any such account must signal some of the complexities involved, without knowledge of which it is impossible to make sense of the affair.

In 1980 war broke out between Iran and Iraq. It continued for eight years. During the whole of this period and thereafter, the export of arms and defence related goods from the UK to either of these countries was supposed to be strictly controlled. In 1984 these controls were reaffirmed and strengthened by the then Foreign Secretary, Sir Geoffrey (Lord) Howe. The Howe guidelines stipulated that approval would not in future be given for the export by British firms of any defence equipment which would significantly enhance the military capability of either side. Moreover, the British government would 'continue to scrutinise rigorously all applications for export licences for the supply of defence equipment to Iran or Iraq.' (HC Debs 1985, 6 Series, vol. 84, written answer col. 450).

Although Britain remained impartial as between the warring countries it was the Iranians who had, in the recent past, given the greater offence to western policy. By the late 1980s there were allegations that British companies had been exporting to Iraq components and other equipment for military purposes. It was further alleged that such exports had been surreptitiously encouraged by officials at the DTI and by the Minister for Trade, Alan Clark (*Sunday Times*, 2 December 1990). By this time one company – Matrix Churchill – was under investigation by HM Customs and Excise. In February 1991, three senior executives of Matrix Churchill were charged with having deceived the government as to the intended use of certain machine tools for which it had sought export licences. In the meantime (August 1990) Iraq had invaded Kuwait and, from January 1991, the Gulf War had brought western (including British) troops into armed conflict with Iraqi forces. There was a political and public outcry. Had a British firm assisted in the manufacture of weapons that were now being turned upon 'our boys'? If found guilty, the three Matrix Churchill executives faced prison sentences of up to seven years.

In their defence the three executives claimed that the government had quietly acknowledged the strong likelihood of the machine tools being used for munitions manufacture and that the company had, in the person of Alan Clark, been actively encouraged to proceed with the export. The fact that the tools exported could be used for civil as well as military purposes (i.e. 'dual use') would provide cover in the event of subsequent probings.

The plot thickened as it transpired that one of the executives, Paul Henderson, had, between 1978-88, supplied information about Iraq to British intelligence agencies. In order to develop their case, it would be necessary for the defendants to secure the disclosure of certain official documents which would, it was claimed, expose the government's complicity. These documents the government was unwilling to make available. Ministers in four departments signed Public Interest Immunity (PII) certificates, effectively preventing disclosure on the grounds that the public interest would thereby be jeopardized. The issue of these so called 'gagging orders' formed the basis of further allegations that ministers were now prepared to allow innocent people to go to gaol rather than expose the government's connivance. It later became apparent that one minister, Michael

Heseltine, had had serious reservations about signing a PII; that he had specifically asked for his reservations to be conveyed to the court judge; but that the Attorney General, Sir Nicholas Lyell, had not conveyed Heseltine's reservation. Further questions were to arise about the extent to which the other ministerial PII signatories had been properly briefed by their civil servants and by the Solicitor-General.

In the event counsel for the defence made a successful application to the trial judge for the PII certificates to be set aside in connection with some (though by no means all) of the documents. This elicited a number of previously withheld documents, though those emanating from the intelligence agencies were disclosed only in 'heavily redacted form' (Scott 1996, Vol. I, para. A1.11, p. 4). The cross examination of witnesses proceeded, including that of two DTI officials. But it was the evidence of the minister, Alan Clark, which brought the trial to an abrupt halt. He contradicted certain of his earlier evidence, rendering untenable the prosecution case. The three Matrix Churchill executives were in the clear, though the political fallout was to increase in intensity. Now Whitehall was on the defensive, ministers and civil servants alike. Quickly the government announced the setting up of a full and independent inquiry under Lord Justice (subsequently the Vice Chancellor Sir Richard) Scott. The terms of reference were:

> Having examined the facts in relation to the export from the UK of defence equipment and dual use goods to Iraq between December 1984 and August 1990 and the decisions reached on the export licence applications for such goods and the basis for them, to report on whether the relevant Departments, Agencies, and responsible Ministers operated in accordance with the policies of HM Government; to examine and report on decisions taken by the prosecution authority and by those signing public interest immunity certificates in R v Henderson and on any other similar cases that he considers relevant to the issues of the Inquiry; and to make recommendations.
> (HC Debs 1992, 6th Series, vol. 214, written answer col. 76)

The prime minister promised that all papers requested by Scott would be made available and that ministers and civil servants would co-operate fully. Scott was given the freedom to decide how to conduct his investigations and how to publish both his report and the evidence collected.

Scott chose to set up his inquiry on an *ad hoc*, non-statutory basis rather than under the terms of the Tribunals of Inquiry (Evidence) Act 1921. Among other things, this meant the absence of formal *sub judice* rules, so allowing free public comment as the inquiry proceeded. He also chose to set aside certain of the key recommendations of the Royal Commission on

Tribunals of Inquiry (Salmon 1966). Most notably, Scott declined to give individuals advance notice of allegations made against them or of the evidence offered in support of such allegations. This Scott justified (1996, Vol. I, para. B2.29, p. 37) on the grounds that there were no prior allegations against particular individuals and that, if damaging evidence were to emerge, then those implicated would be given due notice and invited to make their responses. Similarly, Scott declined to permit those giving evidence the opportunity of being directly represented and examined by their own counsel. Scott held that all witnesses were given adequate opportunity to offer whatever evidence they wished, including supplementary evidence in the light of the hearings. Full legal representation and defence cross-examination would, furthermore, prolong the duration of the inquiry.

These deviations from the 'Salmon principles' gave government ministers, their supporters and others the opportunity to criticize the conduct of the inquiry, hence to question its conclusions. Long before the report was published ministers and (especially) ex-ministers began to 'rubbish' the inquiry. Civil rights groups expressed their concern. To many it seemed odd not to say iniquitous that, in denying legal representation to witnesses, there was a barrister to conduct cross examination, in effect on behalf of the 'prosecution'. Partly in response to these concerns Scott allowed certain individuals to see and comment upon an unpublished draft of the report. We do not know and may never know to what extent criticisms were toned down in deference to the heavy pressure that was almost certainly brought to bear during this process.

The Scott inquiry lasted over three years. A myriad of documents were scrutinized, including written submissions from 278 individuals of whom 81 attended oral hearings. The duration of the inquiry was a further point of contention among critics, though it perhaps vindicated Scott's decision not to allow defence counsel cross-examination. It was later claimed that proceedings had been distended on account of recalcitrance by government departments and other agencies in making certain documents available. By the time the report was published many minds had already been set, the battle lines drawn and hardened.

The government's handling of the report's publication added to the political drama. It prevailed upon Scott to give certain ministers eight days' advance access prior to publication of the final report. (Technically it was a report to the President of the Board of Trade.) A handful of senior opposition figures were offered sight of the report under strict supervision three hours prior to publication, while other MPs and civil servants (including those implicated) were given one hour. The report was in five volumes, totalling some 1,800 pages. The government was thus well prepared and quick off the mark, claiming that Scott had exonerated ministers from the more serious charges. Certainly Scott accepted that there had been no con-

spiracy, either in conniving at the export of arms or in risking the imprisonment of innocent people. This may have helped to save the two ministers
whose resignations were most vehemently sought by opposition parties,
namely Sir Nicholas Lyell and William Waldegrave. The latter had been a
junior minister in the Foreign Office and had been accused of having
deceived Parliament into thinking that the Howe guidelines had not been
changed when in practice they had. Whatever doubts they had, government
back benchers were not inclined to rock the boat. Lyell and Waldegrave sur-
vived. But it became increasingly clear that the government's summary of
the Scott Report had been a highly selective one. Scott himself took the
unusual step of saying so publicly.

In truth the Scott Report provided ammunition for protagonists of all
shades in judging the extent to which individual ministers were culpable,
even if there were to be no ministerial resignations. Many passages in
Scott's lengthy report were convoluted, replete with heavy qualifications
and apparent contradictions, especially about ministerial motives and inten-
tions. But Scott seemed clear that ministers had failed to inform Parliament
about a relaxation in the granting of export licences; that this failure was
deliberate; and that it had been driven by a fear that the ensuing outcry
from any public acknowledgement of the fact would be detrimental to
British trading interests (Scott 1996, Vol. I, para. D4.42, p. 495). If nothing
else, this highlighted the dilemmas of those involved at the sharp end of
policy and decision-making – not only ministers but civil servants as well. If
these were the overriding thoughts in the minds of ministers, then they
could hardly be ignored by officials. But in the light of the TCSC report
about the role of the civil service and the Nolan concern for standards of
conduct, this was not what the critics wanted to hear. If ministers were wont
to engage in chicanery was it or was it not for senior civil servants at least
somewhere along the line to assume counsel for the moral high ground?
Was there no one in Whitehall who could put their foot on the ball, so to
speak, and take in the broader picture? Were civil servants as guilty as ministers and had they indeed been putting ministers up to some of their tricks?

All these questions kept alive some of the broader issues that had been
simmering for ten years and more. Do civil servants have a higher duty over
and above the immediate, routine loyalty to their ministers? If so to whom
or what – and how exactly is it to be discharged? Can and if so when can
officials legitimately say 'no' to ministers? The answers to these and other
questions remain as elusive as ever in the light of the TCSC Report, the
Nolan Report and the Scott Report. These uncertainties and the climate of
suspicion in which they have flourished in recent years were given further
substance by the testimonies of a number of senior officials, including that
of the Head of the Home Civil Service. The modern craft of government
seems to rest on the assumption that 'truth' is something negotiable, some-

thing almost incidental to the primary objective of contriving an outcome that will 'stick' – and doing anything necessary to ensure that it does. This is nothing new. Scott was also very critical of what he saw as Whitehall's excessive and obsessive secrecy. Yet there is now more openness – enough occasionally to allow that which has been made to stick later to come unstuck.

Scott made few concrete recommendations, aside from those in connection with export controls, prosecution procedures and PII certificates. He made many highly critical observations, not only about excessive secrecy but also about co-ordination within Whitehall (including intelligence agencies), accountability to Parliament and the obscurity surrounding the respective responsibilities of ministers and civil servants. The latter was underlined in the immediate aftermath of the report. For while ministerial resignations were averted, up to twenty officials were said to have been singled out for possible disciplinary action (*FDA News* May 1996, p. 5). They would probably keep their jobs. But here again was grist for those who believe that ministers are increasingly inclined to deflect blame on to officials. Officials, by contrast, were permitted to make public statements in their own defence following publication of the Scott Report only on condition that such statements were first vetted and that they neither incriminated ministers nor contradicted government policy. This, of course, reflects the classic civil service anonymity and accountability exclusively through ministers. Officials stand four square behind the minister, at least in public. In return the minister faces the music, at least to the extent of answerability, even if this need not mean accepting culpability when it is clear that the minister personally has not been at fault. To an increasing number of observers, though, it seems that ministers now want to transfer to civil servants some of the burdens of accountability without passing over any of the accompanying prerogatives. Critics can moan but it is ministers who ultimately determine and operate the 'rules of the game'.

Outline for the rest of the volume

Much of this is probably inevitable in a unitary system of government with a dominant executive. It is partly on account of this that there have been growing demands to change the system, including calls for a written constitution. Not only have there been multi-dimensional changes within the civil service: some of these changes have implications and connections on a much wider front. This is reflected in the contributions to this volume. In the next chapter Richard Chapman touches upon a number of themes developed by other contributors. He now dispenses with the question mark with which he had earlier raised the prospect of the end of the civil service. Not all would agree that the era of change has gone quite so far, but he develops his argument persuasively and with conviction. He also cites the characteristics identified by the government and by Sir Robin Butler as providing the core values of the civil service – integrity, impartiality, objectivity, selection and promotion on merit and accountability through ministers to Parliament. Save for the last, these characteristics are, Chapman insists, little different from those that would constitute good management practice in any organization. The civil service has been robbed of its distinctiveness. It no longer exists – at least not as a discrete entity and as distinct from an aggregation of particular departments and agencies. The decentralization of recruitment, the delegation of pay bargaining and of much else beside have brought a critical fragmentation and loss of coherence. By contrast, Chapman upholds the virtues of a unified civil service. Such a service received its strongest endorsement and practical application during the middle decades of the present century under the leadership of Sir Warren Fisher (Head of the Civil Service, 1919-39) and Sir Edward Bridges (Head of the Home Civil Service, 1945-56). The tradition bequeathed by Fisher and Bridges received hostile treatment from the Fulton Committee and from the managerial reformers of the 1960s onwards. But many now see at least some wisdom in their ways and virtue in the high standards of conduct they upheld and entreated others to follow. Today's penchant for written codes is almost certainly a sign that good behaviour can no longer be taken for granted. As Chapman points out, the socialization and on the job training of days gone by may have been less important for the particular job (one of Fulton's complaints) but it did inculcate certain attitudes of mind and (unwritten) codes of behaviour.

Each of the three subsequent chapters deals with a specific area of change partly responsible for some of the concerns expressed by Chapman. In Chapter 3 Andrew Massey examines Next Steps executive agencies. He does so against the broader background of the so called 'new public management' which, he says, is often founded upon 'best practice research'. But context is what matters. Such research and, in consequence, the new public management has often been insensitive to the peculiarities of a multicentric public sector. Massey notes the wide variety of agencies and patterns of relationships with sponsoring departments. He distinguishes between the administrative autarky and the administrative cypher, replete with performance indicators, monitoring procedures and increasingly sophisticated 'contract management'. With these patterns and mechanisms the system is, he believes, 'more open, better managed and accountable to ministers than at any time since the growth of a large welfare state'. But, in consequence, many decisions about resource allocation have been removed (mainly by ministers) from the electoral and Parliamentary arena. Ministerial control has been enhanced but the ability of senior officials to exercise independent judgement has been diminished. Constitutional checks have been weakened and the *potential* for abuse increased. Yet Massey finds little firm evidence so far of agencification having *on its own* brought about any serious diminution of the public service ethos. Tony Butcher (Chapter 4) finds some positive benefits having accrued from the Citizen's Charter. Customer orientation has been a key factor here, though not the only one. Butcher shows high levels of customer satisfaction in connection with the Benefits Agency and with the Inland Revenue. There is nevertheless cause for concern about the use and misuse of performance targets. Moreover, staff morale has been adversely affected by other civil service reforms, most notably by the uncertainties of market testing. There is thus every danger that the customer orientation of the Citizen's Charter may be negated by other, adjacent developments. One such development is in pay bargaining and industrial relations, the subject of Chapter 5 by Susan Corby. She reminds us that the fashion for fragmentation, decentralization and delegation is not peculiar to the civil service. Whitleyism is still alive, but substantially diminished. A career civil service remains predominant, though is no longer taken for granted; collectivism has been eroded and the role of the unions diminished; and service-wide negotiations have given way to delegated arrangements involving over 150 bargaining units. So far variations have been minimal. There is the likelihood of continued control from the centre, not least via cash limits. Nevertheless, Corby shows that staff transfers may become more difficult to manage and that the unity and collegiate ethos of the civil service may have become impaired. If so, this may bring a new cast of mind – one in which officials assume less the grand, impartial, public spirited mantle of the 'philosopher guardian' and adopt instead (if only out of fear) more the narrow, whimsical, plaudit seeking tendencies of the apparatchik who defers only to gratify the minister.

In Chapter 6 Barry O'Toole reminds us of the idealized glories of Plato's philosopher guardians. These are they who, in Plato's words, 'are to be found full of zeal to do whatever they believe is for the good of the commonwealth and (are) never willing to act against its interests'. 'Gold and silver,' Plato says, 'they will not need, having the divine counterparts of those metals always in their souls... whose purity it is not lawful to sully by the acquisition of mortal dross'. It is heady stuff, for sure – though never more than an ideal for the modern polity. Still, O'Toole contends that many (not all) British mandarins of the late-nineteenth and early/middle twentieth century decades (including Fisher and Bridges) loosely resembled this Platonic ideal. O'Toole, like many others, doubts whether there now prevails quite the same sense of public duty. What does it matter? For some, it marks a welcome release from a stuffy, self-righteous and often arrogant elitism. For others, though, the elitism of yesteryear did at least serve to sustain the 'gold standard' of public duty, trust and correct conduct. The Fulton Report may well have laid the groundwork for a fundamental change in administrative culture. Barry O'Toole is not mollified by government lip service to 'civil service values'. Nor does he think that the new civil service code is an adequate substitute for the internalization of public spiritedness – at least not in itself and in a climate of enthusiasm for enterprise, entrepreneurship and 'can do' management. These concerns are shared by Alan Doig who, in Chapter 7, focuses upon some of the consequences. Casting his net beyond the civil service, Doig identifies instances of fraud and improper conduct. He takes to task all (including the head of the home civil service) who have put their trust in an 'organic and adaptable' ethos of public service. He berates the Nolan Committee for its reliance upon the tradition of 'personal responsibility'. Like Chapman and O'Toole he does not doubt the desirability of personal responsibility – simply that it is on its own inadequate in an era in which risk taking has replaced risk avoidance. The new public management has been nourished in the climate of Thatcherism and the aftermath of Thatcherism, leaving 'a downside of greed, acquisitiveness and personal ambition'. According to Doig, stronger measures are needed to prevent fraud and misconduct, so increasing the likelihood of detection and punishment. The Committee of Public Accounts (PAC), the National Audit Office (NAO) and the Audit Commission have, he says, provided leads which should be followed.

The PAC, NAO and the Audit Commission are permanent, 'standing' bodies. Perhaps they are more appropriate than judicial review or *ad hoc* inquiries in pointing the way towards systematic, structural reform. This brings us back to Nolan and, in particular, to Scott. The background and broad outlines of the Scott Inquiry have been set out above. In Chapter 8 John McEldowney examines one of the central concerns of the inquiry – the issue of public interest immunity (PII) certificates in criminal cases. He analyzes the law on PII certificates with particular reference to the role of the Attorney General. The ramifications are complex and wide-ranging. McEldowney thinks that ministers are not bound unconditionally to sign PII certificates – only where necessary in order to uphold the public interest. As matters stand, it is for the Attorney General to distinguish between the public interest and the interests of the government of the day. But the Attorney General is a party politician and a member of the government – an overlapping of roles in which the British constitution seems to specialize. As McEldowney says, the Matrix Churchill trial and the Scott Report raised issues that test to its limits the efficacy of the British constitution. Not the least of these issues is accountability, the focus in Chapter 9. There has never been a neat congruence between the doctrine (such as it is) of accountability and its practical application. In recent years, though, there has been an increasing incongruence. It has become increasingly difficult to maintain the notion that ministers alone are accountable to Parliament for their own actions and for those of their departments and that officials are accountable

2 The end of the British civil service

Richard Chapman

Background: definitions of the civil service

Since 1931 students of public policy and administration have used, as the basis for their understanding of the British civil service, a definition in the Tomlin Royal Commission Report. It is a classic definition in the sense that it was widely adopted in textbooks and by subsequent official enquiries into the civil service (such as the Priestley (1955) Royal Commission and the Fulton Committee (1968)). The Tomlin Report defined the civil service as 'those servants of the Crown, other than holders of political or judicial offices, who are employed in a civil capacity, and whose remuneration is paid wholly and directly out of moneys voted by Parliament' (Tomlin 1931).

This definition, as many students have learned, requires a certain amount of qualification and explanation. This was ably provided in *Central Administration in Britain*, a valuable textbook published in 1957 (Mackenzie and Grove 1957). Mackenzie and Grove pointed out that 'servants of the Crown' is a phrase of little use in deciding marginal cases (such as regional hospital boards) whose statutory position in that respect was uncertain. Furthermore, if it was held that a particular public corporation was a 'servant of the Crown' it apparently followed that its employees were 'servants of the Crown', though it did not follow that its employees were civil servants. Just how fine a distinction this could be, and also how confusing, first attracted the attention of scholars when the Post Office became a public corporation in 1969, when, for almost all purposes, its employees ceased to be civil servants – although they continued performing the same functions and the change in status of the organization hardly affected the general public at all.

'Holders of political office' can be defined by reference to the House of Commons Disqualification Act 1957. However, until that Act was passed the phrase could be defined only by reference to the practice of the House of Commons in interpreting clauses in the Regency Act of 1705 and in later Acts which excluded the holders of certain offices from sitting as members of the House of Commons: offices which were not excluded were then political offices. The phrase 'holders of judicial office' also presented difficulties because the courts have had to decide when an employee was bound to act judicially.

While 'employment in a civil capacity' is quite definitive in a negative way, as it covers employment other than in the armed forces, 'remuneration paid wholly and directly out of moneys voted by Parliament' was probably the most important part of the definition. A 'servant of the Crown' may be remunerated 'directly but not wholly' if he or she worked for a government department part-time. Thus someone working one day a month for a retaining fee may, in law, be a 'Crown servant' that day, but could scarcely be called 'a part-time civil servant'. 'Directly' is also important because it excludes servants of the Crown (such as those working for the British Council) who are paid by moneys issued indirectly as a grant-in-aid and not from the normal form of parliamentary appropriation.

Despite these qualifications, the definition from the Tomlin Report was useful. In the absence of the sort of neat definition that can be found in other countries in a Civil Service Act, the definition stood the test of time – until comparatively recently.

When analyzed systematically the point could be emphasized that the British civil service was a peculiar institution for a number of reasons. Officials did not normally have written contracts, presumably because they were servants of the Crown, though they had implied contracts. Defining the civil service became a useful example of how the so-called unwritten constitution worked in practice. Most British students of public administration, though not necessarily foreign students, knew what civil servants were and did not confuse them with local government officers. Civil servants were known to have modest privileges, or benefits, as a result of being servants of the Crown – they had a day's holiday to celebrate the birthday of the monarch, they had attractive non-contributory pension arrangements and, in general, they held their jobs 'for life'. As the textbooks on bureaucracy put it, following Max Weber's characterization of the ideal type bureaucracy, employment in such a civil service was 'based on technical qualifications and (was)... protected against arbitrary dismissal' (Blau 1956, p. 30).

The British civil service in the early and middle years of the twentieth century built upon the advantages that resulted from these characteristics. No one contributed more to this process than Sir Warren Fisher, who regarded the civil service as the fourth service of the Crown, after the armed services. Fisher did much to encourage a sense of belonging to the service and emphasized the need to maintain the highest possible standards. His approach was continued by Sir Edward Bridges who, when he was head of the home civil service, also tried to develop a sense of belonging and of loyalty to a distinctive service.

Following the creation of the Civil Service Department in 1968, the publication *Civil Service Statistics* also at first accepted the Tomlin definition, though from 1972 the wording was modified. In 1972 it read: 'A *Civil Servant* is a servant of the Crown (not being the holder of political or judicial office) who is paid wholly and directly out of money voted by Parliament and who works in a civil capacity in a department of government' (Civil Service Department 1972, p. 12). This was further modified in 1976 by adding the sentence: 'However, some civil servants work for Crown bodies which are not government departments, such as the Manpower Services Commission and its two Agencies or the Health and Safety Executive, and are paid out of grants-in-aid to these bodies' (Civil Service Department 1976, p. 12).

By 1994, the definition as it appeared now in *Civil Service Statistics* had been changed again, this time presumably to adjust to the creation of Next Steps agencies, especially those with Trading Fund status. This, the current definition, omits all reference to what had previously been regarded as the key financial clause; there is no longer any reference to pay being drawn wholly and directly out of money voted by Parliament. It states that 'A *Civil Servant* is a servant of the Crown working in a civil capacity who is not: the holder of a political (or judicial) office; the holder of certain other offices in respect of whose tenure of office special provision has been made; a servant of the Crown in a personal capacity paid from the Civil List' (HM Treasury 1994, p. 18). This is, on the face of it, comprehensive, though much less specific than earlier definitions. All officials working in the central administration come within its ambit; but recent explanations and changes have tried to clarify what it means in practice.

Recent explanations and changes

Since the creation of Next Steps agencies, following the publication of the Ibbs Report (Efficiency Unit 1988), there has been discussion about whether a civil service as such can still be said to exist as a recognizable and discrete service – as distinct from, say, an aggregation of employees of particular

government departments and agencies. This is stimulated by the characteristics of work in agencies, which operate on business-like lines, where staff
increasingly have contracts with pay and conditions of service that vary
from agency to agency, and where staff are given targets to achieve, with
incentives including pay related to the achievement of their targets. Sir
Robin Butler, Head of the Home Civil Service, says he is quite clear that the
civil service as a distinct entity still exists, though it is a service that is 'unified but not uniform' (TCSC 1989, Q.320). The 1994 white paper, *The Civil
Service: Continuity and Change*, is also confident on this point. It asserts that
'The importance of the Civil Service as a coherent entity, rather than simply
the sum of the staff of individual departments performing specific roles, has
been recognised for more than 150 years', and it goes on to quote Butler's
key principles. These are 'integrity, impartiality, objectivity, selection and
promotion on merit and accountability through Ministers to Parliament'
(Cabinet Office 1994a, para. 2.7).

Other recent publications have also focused on this issue. Sir Peter Kemp,
known as 'the architect of Next Steps' (Finkelstein 1993, p. 7), has written
about 'moving away from the model of a single service monolith to one
where a loose federation of many smaller agencies, units and cores predom-
inates' (Kemp 1993, p. 8). However, he believes there is 'no such thing as a
single "public service" ethos' (Kemp 1993, p. 33) and that 'there has never
been any real unity' (p. 44). Instead, the 'unity of the civil service rests on its
being a body of professionals, like doctors and lawyers, rather than on any
harder commonality' (Ibid.). Similar sentiments were expressed in the
report by Sylvie Trosa, *Next Steps: Moving On*. Recognizing that agencies are
semi-autonomous bodies, she says that: 'Financial, management and personnel rules will become more and more different; the only element of unity
which will be left, besides ethical standards, will be the uniform tag of being
a civil servant' (Trosa 1994, para. 2.17). One of her conclusions on the agencies was that: 'typically, the main protagonists either want to maintain a
complete uniformity of rules or alternatively argue that the unity of the
Civil Service is an obsolete preoccupation, contradictory to the requirements
of good management practice ... (however) it seems that the solution can
neither be uniformity nor complete diversity, but a mixture of both' (para.
4.5.4).

William Waldegrave, the then minister responsible for the Office of
Public Service and Science, explained how he saw the future of public service in the context of reforming Britain's bureaucracies. He did not define
the civil service, nor did he discuss the problems associated with various
definitions, but he explained recent changes as he saw them. Agencification,
he said, 'involves the separation of the Civil Service into a number of smaller, increasingly specialised units known as Next Steps agencies'
(Waldegrave 1993, p. 18). This, the result of recent reforms 'will leave us

with a smaller... public service... (which is likely to) consist of a comparatively small core, and a series of devolved delivery organizations' (p. 23). Furthermore, he saw the new ethos of public service, an ethos based on the principles to be found in the Citizen's Charter, as being grafted onto 'unshaken, unchanging, unchallenged uncorruptibility and political impartiality'. These principles are explicit standards of service which are set, published and prominently displayed at the point of delivery; full, accurate and up to date information about how public services are run, what they cost, and how well they perform; value for money; regular and systematic consultation with service users; accountability; and well published and readily available complaints procedures (Waldegrave 1993, pp. 19-24).

If these are the identifiably distinctive features of the civil service, one wonders either whether they are in any way different from the best standards of employment elsewhere or, alternatively, how employment elsewhere has been able to continue with any sense of propriety and self esteem if its standards are so deficient. In other words, Butler's list of key principles hardly differentiates the civil service from good management practice elsewhere – except, of course, for the reference about accountability through ministers to Parliament. Even on that criterion, however, there must now be some doubt, because ministers are differentiating between policy, for which they say they are responsible, and 'operational matters', which are apparently the direct responsibility of officials to parliamentary committees, the media and, presumably in theory, the public.

Practical arrangements: recruitment, grading and pay

Until about the middle of the nineteenth century, ministers were entirely free to choose their own staffs and there were practically no common standards in government departments. However, following the recommendations of the Northcote-Trevelyan Report, published in 1854, a Civil Service Commission was established. Its creation marked the beginning of the central organization of the civil service. In 1870 competitive examination was made the normal method of entry to almost all the important government departments. At the same time, the Treasury was given 'power to approve rules respecting the age, health, character, knowledge and ability of candidates, the times at which examinations were held, the fees, the number of vacancies and the grouping of situations' (HM Treasury 1952, p.3). This established Treasury control over general personnel questions in the civil service. Together, the Civil Service Commission and the Treasury (within whose ambit the Commission operated) became the focus for the civil service and it was from these institutions and the standards they upheld that the world-wide reputation of the British civil service developed. Indeed, a new recruit joining the civil service in, say, 1953, was presented with a small handbook explaining what the civil service was and what was expected of its members. Among other things, it explained how, from the middle of the nineteenth century, there 'developed slowly a tradition and a code of behaviour which belongs to the whole Civil Service and not to any one Department or to any one grade or class of civil servants' (HM Treasury 1952, p. 4).

This handbook was written with pride in the service which it explained. It outlined practical details that the new entrant might find useful. For example, deductions from pay could be authorized, free of charge, to pay contributions or subscriptions to such organizations as the Civil Service Benevolent Fund, the Civil Service Nursing Aid Association, the Civil Service Sanatorium Society, the Civil Service Insurance Society, and the Civil Service Sports Council (HM Treasury 1952, p.15). The handbook also included a long quotation from the report of the 1928 inquiry into the Francs case which had stated what was expected in relation to the 'Civil Service tradition'. The quotation, written in fact by Fisher as head of the civil service, included a few sentences which are relevant to the present discussion:

> A civil servant is not to subordinate his duty to his private interest; but neither is he to put himself in a position where his duty and his interests conflict. He is not to make use of his official position to further those interests; but neither is he to order his private affairs to allow the suspicion to arise that a trust has been abused or a confidence betrayed.
> (HM Treasury 1952, p. 32)

> Practical rules for the guidance of social conduct depend ... as much upon the instinct and perception of the individual as upon cast-iron formulas; and the surest guide will, we hope, always be found in the nice and jealous honour of civil servants themselves. The public expects from them a standard of integrity and conduct not only inflexible but fastidious, and has not been disappointed in the past. We are confident that we are expressing the view of the Service when we say that the public have a right to expect that standard, and that it is the duty of the Service to see that the expectation is fulfilled.
> (HM Treasury 1952, p. 33)

These statements from the Treasury's *Handbook for the New Civil Servant* do not seem to fit the civil service as it appears to an outsider today. Four examples will illustrate this.

First, consider the new arrangements for recruitment. One of the significant reforms of the nineteenth century was to introduce open competitive examinations on a service-wide basis, with the recruitment responsibilities in the hands of the Civil Service Commission. This was a key factor in reducing (indeed, virtually eliminating) corruption and partisan political influence in the executive operations of government – features now widely regarded as consistent with the highest aspirations of democratic government, and especially well suited to the British political and administrative culture. Since 1991, however, the Civil Service Commission has not existed. Instead, there is an agency called Recruitment and Assessment Services, which contracts to do recruitment for departments; and a small Office of the Civil Service Commissioners. The Office of the Civil Service Commissioners consisted in 1991 of only about twenty people (Civil Service Commissioners 1991). It was reduced further, to a core staff of eight, by 1994-95 (Civil Service Commissioners 1995b). Among their duties the commissioners at first monitored, in a 'light-handed and economical way', more than 3,000 devolved units of recruitment, known as 'accountable units' (Civil Service Commissioners 1991). This they did to ensure that they were recruiting according to the principles, laid down by the minister, for fair and open competition. However, under the 1995 Civil Service Order in Council the Commissioners' monitoring responsibilities were replaced by a duty to audit departmental recruitment systems. The subsequent annual report from the civil service commissioners explains that the auditors will use a 'top-down' approach. They will concentrate on departments' and agencies' recruitment systems and 'will reach down to the level of individual competitions only if they decide there is a need for a spot check' (Civil Service Commissioners 1995b, p. 20). The recruitment principles were subsequently embodied in the Commissioners' Recruitment Code (Civil Service Commissioners 1995a). But by the mid-1990s there was already evidence of confusion in recruitment so far as candidates are concerned, inefficiencies in commercial agencies that have been awarded contracts to administer the arrangements, and corruption in the form of dilution of the high standards for which the former Civil Service Commission was justly proud. In the light of this experience, questions may be raised about the role of the audits (which are *post-hoc*, compared with the original administrative responsibilities of the commissioners) and about the appointment of the auditors who are not the commissioners themselves but 'independent consultants' (Civil Service Commissioners 1995a, p. 22).

The second example concerns the lack of unity in the civil service. Sir Robin Butler has said that we now have a civil service that is unified but not uniform. However, this sense of unity that he believes still exists seems to have been largely undermined by the fact that, since December 1994, 353,000 civil servants, 62 per cent of the total, now work in agencies or other organizations operating on Next Steps lines (OPSS 1994b). These agencies, units and offices are being positively encouraged to develop their own team spirit and loyalties. Staff, we are told, now often think of themselves as belonging to a particular department or agency, not to a wider civil service. They work in units which, far from displaying a team spirit with a common civil service ethos, compete with each other, issue contracts to each other and, in so doing, charge what are thought to be business-like rates for their services. In other respects the agencies are not completely independent entities. They have been created by executive decisions, no legislation being required. Nevertheless, conscious efforts are now made to stimulate feelings of enterprise and initiative in them, often by developing new logos and corporate clothing. There can be no doubt that these have resulted in a fundamental change from previous arrangements which contributed to the identity of a more uniform civil service.

Thirdly, one of the ways in which enterprise, initiative and a more business-like style has been encouraged is by devolving to the lowest possible level details about such matters as staff grading, pay and conditions of service. This also involves decision making on such matters as performance-related pay. The Civil and Public Services Association has recently estimated that the end of national pay bargaining will increase the number of officials who will be required to administer the various delegated pay systems by seventy-five fold – to some 3,000 staff – and that by the end of the century there will be about 150 different pay bargaining units in existence (Civil and Public Services Association 1994). If there is to be so much scope for variations in grading, pay and conditions of service, it seems difficult to understand how the civil service can still be regarded as unified.

Fourthly, there is the matter of changing the civil service culture. This, of course, was what the Fulton Committee hoped their recommendations would do. The Committee wanted to change the philosophy of the generalist, make the civil service both more management conscious and more professional and to restructure its organization. The Thatcher government advanced towards these aims by emphasizing enterprise, initiative and a more business-like style of management and by such expedients as promoting or appointing staff who were thought to be 'can do' types (RIPA 1987). This seems to be contrary to the expectations of officials working in a bureaucracy. Moreover, the dangers in adopting these preferred qualities have, in the past, been well illustrated by examples like Crichel Down (where the enthusiasm of officials for creating model farms was a factor in a situation which led to a ministerial resignation) and the dismissal of Sir Christopher Bullock (whose enthusiasm for his work as Permanent Secretary to the Air Ministry in the 1930s led to errors of judgment) (Chapman 1988, Ch. 4). In very recent times initiatives to introduce more business-like approaches have been aided by such measures as pay at rates similar to business and the introduction of performance-related pay.

However, there is no clear evidence that performance-related pay is an effective means of motivating staff or improving the performance of organizations. More significantly, in relation to civil servants, it introduces the factor of private interests which could easily affect the judgment of officials in their daily work. Of course the civil service should be concerned to stimulate economy, efficiency and effectiveness – whatever is meant by these highly controversial terms. Fundamentally civil servants have, as their primary task, the duty to carry out the functions allocated to ministers. It is this democratic context, where ministers in the British system of government have in the past been thought to be personally accountable, that is now in danger of being overlooked or blatantly disregarded (see below, Chapter 9). Nevertheless, the role of ministers in relation to Parliament as well as in relation to their officials is crucial to an understanding of both how the British civil service works and, more importantly, how the system of government works.

Socialization and convenience: written and unwritten rules

In the past, the most important factor for determining and maintaining standards in the British civil service, and for creating and maintaining a sense of unity, was socialization. Training was never really important. Consequently Kemp (1993, p. 44) was quite wrong in the passage quoted earlier: the civil service has never been a body of professionals like doctors and lawyers. In contrast to the civil service, doctors and lawyers have professional qualifications which are publicly known and approved by professional bodies; doctors and lawyers also have established training programmes during which they serve as interns or are articled. Indeed, civil servants, except for specialists, still largely acquire their expertise and professional insights through socialization and on-the-job training. What is often not sufficiently widely recognized is that this form of training may be less important for learning how to do a particular job than it is for learning attitudes of mind and accepted codes of behaviour and for learning what is done and what is not done in different circumstances. In practice, it is this process which creates for each civil servant the opportunity to form in his or her own mind a fairly indelible picture of the ideal civil servant.

Whilst some of the consequences of this socialization are easy to caricature and can be found in amusing stories or on the television, its real value is largely underestimated. This may be seen in, for example, processes where officials are ordering priorities, or are determining and exercising the use of bureaucratic power in individual circumstances. In practice the experience may be compared to the secluded upbringing and training of Plato's guardians (see below, Chapter 6). This was most aptly reflected by Sir

William Armstrong when, as head of the home civil service, he was questioned about his personal attitude to exercising the considerable power he had. He explained that, for him, being accountable to oneself was the greatest taskmaster and he added: 'I am accountable to my own ideal of a civil servant' (Armstrong 1969).

The line of argument being advanced here is twofold. First, the British civil service (as it was), never excelled in its provision of formal training. Indeed, there was no Civil Service College before 1970. Moreover, little serious study has been made of the value and effects of the so-called traditional on-the-job approaches to civil service training. To an outside commentator, especially an academic, this is remarkable; it is a topic well suited for research by a civil service college and such research is long overdue. Secondly, so-called reforms in the post-Fulton period have largely disregarded the significance of the socialization processes associated with on-the-job training. The significance of socialization received hardly any serious attention by the Fulton Committee, which thought that the setting up of a civil service college would be a major development towards the civil service becoming less amateur. This has now been followed by the 1994 white paper proposing a further move in the same direction: it recommended new MBA programmes for fast stream civil servants (Cabinet Office 1994a, para. 4.7).

A related matter concerns the new Civil Service Code (Cabinet Office 1995a, Annex). This, like the creation of the Civil Service College and the launching of MBA programmes, may contribute to more professional approaches and attitudes to work in the civil service. All these innovations may be commendable; they may rightly deserve the approval and support of both officials and citizens. It needs to be recognized, however, that they have their limitations; and uncritical acceptance and strong support for their implementation may provoke questions about whether they are as beneficial as may at first be thought. Two points in particular should be made in relation to these developments. First, while they may introduce more professional approaches, and in some respects may even result in more efficient and effective management, over reliance on them may be short-sighted and even potentially dangerous. Of course codes of conduct can be valuable as training aids, or as guides in difficult circumstances, or as a focus for public discussion. However, they are no substitute for thinking carefully about individual cases and they cannot be used to avoid difficult decision making.

As in other contexts, conceptualization and codification can sometimes adversely affect rather than protect the interests of citizens. Civil servants ought to be intelligent enough to administer natural justice, to recognize its significance and to decide when and how its principles should be applied. Also, some of the latest approaches to the study of public sector management, including references in the recent white papers, are based on the unproven assumption that management in business, with private sector values, is superior to public administration. However, the latest management techniques will not necessarily solve all contemporary problems of public sector management and one may question whether they really fit the public sector environment at all. For example, it must be noted clearly and unambiguously at the present time that the rigorous application of resource accounting methods and business process re-engineering, impressive as they sound and admirable as they may be for some purposes, will not necessarily lead to a more efficient public service. Other considerations may be at least as important; indeed, other considerations may be more important. It should be remembered that one of the leading figures to develop business process re-engineering has been quoted as saying, on the launch day of his practice's book on the subject: 'We always write a book to create a market' (Earl and Khan 1994, p. 23).

Much the same may be said about the advantages of written constitutions and bills of rights. They may be useful; they may be valuable; but on their own they do not necessarily advance the quality of life of citizens. Nor do they necessarily protect what citizens believe to be their most cherished rights and interests. Indeed, they may be potentially dangerous if they create a sense of security or set standards and expectations that can never be actually achieved. However, if there are such reservations about current reform measures, it should also be asked what of real value, in the civil service as it used to exist, should be preserved in the new conditions of change and reform in public sector management. In other words, does it really matter that there is no longer a civil service in the form and with the standards and reputation that previously existed?

The values of a unified civil service

The argument being advanced here is that there is no longer a unified civil service. How can there be anything resembling a unified civil service when there are no common recruitment arrangements, conditions of service, grading systems, or pay arrangements; and when officials are actively encouraged to maximize their personal benefits, and therefore their private interests, through the achievement of individual and measurable targets? The questions that seem naturally to follow are these: does it matter that the civil service no longer exists?; and what, if anything, may be done to remedy apparent deficiencies in the new arrangements?

First, consider the motivation and morale of staff. One of the most obvious lessons that emerges from research into what motivates staff is that, so long as workers are not on the breadline, pay is not the most significant motivating factor. Other factors are almost always more important. This was one of the findings of the Hawthorne experiments in the United States in the 1930s (Roethlisberger and Dickson 1939). It was confirmed by research for the Fulton Committee. Working with congenial colleagues; doing interest- ing, important work; doing intellectually challenging work – all were much more important to a sample of fast stream entrants who joined the civil ser- vice in 1956 than were the attractions of pay or leave entitlements. Moreover, had those entrants not joined the civil service, the overwhelming majority said they would have chosen other public sector employment rather than joining industry or commercial management (Chapman 1968, pp. 1-29). It therefore seems quite clear that people have been attracted to public service work because they believe it is useful and enables them to do satisfying work. It also seems that many of the officials attracted to a civil service career have been good at it – because, in the past, the British civil service has been well thought of, both in this country and, more significant- ly, abroad (where people have tended to compare our civil service with theirs).

In the light of these comments it seems very odd that so much effort has been given to introducing performance-related pay when research indicates that it is not a strong motivating factor and when there are warnings that it can instead actually demotivate staff (Richardson and Marsden 1991). Also, it seems that in some cases the criteria being applied to determine perfor- mance can be counter-productive. This may be so where, for example, Job Centre staff are reportedly given targets for disqualifying claimants from benefit as part of their performance-related pay scheme (*The Observer*, 1 January 1992). Performance-related pay may, of course, be more relevant in other forms of employment, but in the public sector where there is a bud- get limit on the amount available for incentives, the effects may result in demoralization and demotivation rather than their opposites (Richardson and Marsden 1991). The civil service that used to exist was not embarrassed about being an important part of the public service. If people are still attract- ed to work in the public sector, as some appear to be, should not its virtues and attractions be emphasized, instead of undermined and denigrated?

This, secondly, leads to comments by ministers and in official publica- tions – including the latest white papers. One of the features in ministerial statements in recent years has been continuous criticism and adverse com- parison with the private sector. For example, the white paper *Continuity and Change* says that 'Civil servants of the future will need to have ... the same commitment to performance and achievement found in the best outside organizations' (Cabinet Office 1994a, para. 5.2). The same sort of message is contained in recent statements from Treasury ministers. For example, in a speech to the Engineering Employers' Federation, Mr Jonathan Aitken, then Chief Secretary to the Treasury, said: 'We now have the smallest civil ser- vice since 1939. We want the public sector to match the private sector in efficiency' (Treasury Press Release, 15 February 1995).

Such statements by ministers are most unfortunate and lead to questions involving constitutional propriety. If something is wrong in the civil service, then ministers should take appropriate corrective action. Carping criticism and assertions that private sector management is better and more committed is worse than simply demoralizing. Moreover, it is criticism from which civil servants, who are servants of ministers, are almost unable to defend themselves, especially in public.

Thirdly, consider the roles of the most senior officials. In the past it has been known that the most senior civil servants have, on occasions, stood up to ministers in private when ministers were behaving badly. Fisher did this, so did Bridges. In more recent times, so, reportedly, did Ian Bancroft. However, since the early 1980s it has become difficult to imagine this happening (though it is impossible to know for certain, because the evidence is not yet available). What is publicly known, however, is that heads of the home civil service have accepted tasks that their predecessors might have been expected to refuse – such as defending the government's position in an Australian court of law, or investigating the conduct of ministers. Perhaps these examples are the consequence of promoting Thatcher's preferred 'can do' types of civil servant. Nevertheless, it may be hoped that what remains of the civil service will in future find defenders among its leaders. It is hoped that the new First Civil Service Commissioner, as a sort of ombudsman for the civil service, will be able to achieve an appropriate leadership role in this direction.

Fourthly, the passing of the civil service, as a service to which its members could point with pride, which was highly regarded by citizens of the United Kingdom and which overseas observers could regard as an example worth copying, was a service in tune with the values of liberal democracy. These values include justice, fairness, and impartiality. They may still be values which the public service has as its ideals; but they are less likely than in the past to be commonly found in government administration. This is because, on the one hand, they are costly and do not often result in efficiency savings to government. Officials will still have to make judgements involving these qualities, but the priorities of the environment have changed. What is economical and convenient now may be quite different from what in the past was conditioned by the end(s) of public service. On the other hand, any really business-like organization, using the term in its commercial and industrial context, has no need to bother with such qualities. There is no need for a business to be anxious about dealing with its customers in one part of the country on quite different terms from its dealings with customers in another part of the country. However, who knows what may evolve in the future, in the form of quite different governments in different parts of the United Kingdom?

Concluding reflections: reform in a political environment

As far back as historical records go, there have been civil services (Gladden 1972). Supreme administrators found it necessary to delegate certain administrative responsibilities and functions. Some of these functions were peculiar to government, though others were not. The civil service, however, acquired expertise not only in relation to the techniques officials developed and the areas of administration in which they worked, but also in relation to rulers and the political environment from which their instructions originated and towards which their accountabilities evolved. The term 'civil service' originates from the British administration in India, but it became a general term to refer to a designated group of staff working in the public sector. Even today it only has a precise meaning in relation to particular national political systems.

In the United Kingdom, as in many other developed countries, civil servants do not change when a government changes and, as a consequence, they acquire specialist knowledge and expertise in how the system of government works. Moreover, as confidential advisers to government, especially in relation to the most important functions of the state and as the recipients of sensitive personal information about citizens and private companies, civil servants hold positions of trust. Whilst contractual obligations may ensure that some safeguards are ensured when firms are engaged to do government work, such formal safeguards may not be quite the same as the understandings appreciated by civil servants in the United Kingdom. A country without a basic document called a constitution has to give more significance to customs and conventions, which are mainly learned through socialization. To disturb these traditional and often sensitive elements in the British system of government without the care and attention that would be given to any other major constitutional change is to fail to appreciate the values of the civil service in the British political system.

The British civil service, as defined by the Tomlin Royal Commission, clearly no longer exists. The best evidence of that is the way the definition of a civil servant has had to be so radically changed. Supporting evidence of the consequences is also unquestionable. There are no common standards for recruitment or conditions of service; incentives are set that undermine the qualities previously thought crucial in public service; there is demoralization, increasing corruption, increasing absenteeism and, not surprisingly, lack of respect for officials. Ministers, themselves, have failed to defend the civil service; and leaders of the service appear to be can-do yes-men. The 1990s has been the decade when the civil service, like the Royal Institute of Public Administration, was killed. However, the future is not all gloomy. In the public sector, reform results from pressure; pressure comes from the political environment; and when the state of public sector institutions has worsened somewhat further there will be new reforms acceding to new requirements. How this will occur is not yet clear. Perhaps a new royal commission will look at the civil service, in the aftermath of the Scott and Nolan inquiries; perhaps it will be asked to report in a hurry, even by the year 2000 – or perhaps, as an economy measure, the Northcote-Trevelyan Report will simply be republished and its recommendations reimplemented.

3 The British agency model of government*

Andrew Massey

Introduction

Charles Goodsell begins his book, *The Case for Bureaucracy: a public administration polemic*, with some memorable lines:

> To make the case for bureaucracy. What a ridiculous idea! The author must be an earthbound Screwtape or just plain mad. Only the devil himself would make a case for evil. Only a lunatic would come to the defense of the indefensible. (Goodsell 1994, p. 1)

Yet that is precisely what Goodsell attempts to do. He sifts the different perspectives and approaches to the reform of public administration in the USA, describing the attacks and misrepresentations as 'The Great Falsehood about American Government' (Ibid. pp. 165-84). His analysis suggests that, whatever its faults, bureaucracy is essentially benign and that the assaults upon it by the public choice theorists, reinventing government gurus, politicians, cartoonists and journalists are both malign and misinformed. Far

* A large section of this chapter first appeared in Public Policy and Administration, Volume 10, Number 2, 1995. I am grateful to the editor for his permission to reproduce it here. The non-attributed views of civil servants quoted in this chapter were gained from extensive interviewing and are reported in Massey 1995b; 1995c.

from being an 'alien' force:

> bureaucracy is very close. It is public institutions operating
> within our communities. It is public employees living in our
> neighborhoods. It is programs mandated by government offi-
> cials for whom we personally voted. It is collective action in
> our behalf. In a meaningful sense, then, bureaucracy is *ours*.
> That is why the case for bureaucracy is so important.
> (pp. 183-4)

The more astute reader will also observe that Goodsell uses the term
'public administration' in preference to 'public management'.

In many countries criticism of the bureaucracy is not new. There have
been many attempts at reform in both the UK and USA over the last thirty
years, some ending up as mild tinkering, others being of a more fundamental nature. The difference inherent to the current reform is that some
observers have detected a paradigm shift. That is, a change in the 'entire
constellation of beliefs, values, techniques and so on shared by members of
a given community' (Kuhn 1970, p. 175). In part this is reflected in the new
nomenclature, such as the use of the term 'management' instead of 'administration', but it is also a deeper, cultural change led by the New Right and
their allies' assaults upon the public sector, categorized by many observers
as New Public Management (NPM) (Dunleavy and Hood 1994).

This chapter addresses these issues from the perspective of Britain's Next
Steps and other agencies. It attempts to place NPM within the context of a
postbureaucratic reform paradigm, before discussing its applicability to the
principles of Next Steps. It then explores the future role of core departments
in the UK.

The postbureaucratic reform paradigm

The frenzy of change in Britain's public sector (in common with other countries) shows little sign of abating. In reviewing the US experience, Overman
and Boyd (1994, p.75) discuss the view that a postbureaucratic reform paradigm (PRP) may have evolved with the transformation of administrative
bureaucracies into managerial structures. The alleged new paradigm is:

- anticipatory;
- strategic;
- results directed;
- based on executive leadership (rather than explicitly
  political leadership);

- market orientated;
- customer driven;
- entrepreneurial.

There are clear links here with best practice research (BPR) as epitomized by the work of Osborne and Gaebler (1992). Indeed much of the operationalization of the PRP has been instigated as a result of BPR.

Osborne and Gaebler are prone to provide checklists of traits or steps by which to recognize or implement the 'reinvented' government. These are frequently located within the PRP and include, for example, advice on:

> 'The advantages of competition':
> the most obvious advantage of competition is greater
>   efficiency: more bang for the buck...
> competition forces public (or private) monopolies to
>   respond to the needs of their customers...
> competition rewards innovation; monopoly stifles it...
> competition boosts the pride and morale of public
>   employees.
> (Osborne and Gaebler 1992, pp. 80-4)

The examples they provide to illustrate these points are often anecdotal, rather than evidence of sustained empirical research and it is difficult to accept what at times appears to be little more than a 'wish list'.

Using another list they advocate the transformation of 'rules driven government' into 'mission driven government' and argue that:

- mission driven organizations are more efficient than rule driven organizations;
- mission driven organizations are also more effective than rule driven organizations: they produce better results;
- mission driven organizations are more innovative than rule driven organizations;
- mission driven organizations are more flexible than rule driven organizations; and
- mission driven organizations have higher morale than rule driven organizations.

(pp. 113-4)

Furthermore, they argue that these organizations give every employee an incentive to save money, free up resources to test new ideas, give managers the autonomy they need to respond to changing circumstances, create a predictable environment, simplify the budget process, save millions of dollars on auditors and budget officers and free legislatures to focus on the important issues (pp. 122-4). Much of this has formed the criteria under which the most recent set of American and British reforms have taken place.

These are strange lists, however, to have been taken seriously by so many people. The efficacy of their case surely depends upon the type of organization under discussion; its political, social and cultural location; the manner in which it is held accountable (if at all); the type of rules or missions written and applied; the quality of the people employed within it, and so on. In short, context is what matters. Yet it is a sophisticated discussion about context which is singulary lacking in *Reinventing Government* and in much of the 'Best Practice Research'. Osborne and Gaebler's book is well-written, clear and entertaining. It presents a compelling case and to argue against their goals of greater efficiency and effectiveness is as churlish as to argue against democracy itself. Yet their use of illuminating stories and anecdotes to illustrate the folly and costs of bureaucracy is redolent of Leslie Chapman's (1978) *Your Disobedient Servant*. Amusing tales should not provide the basis upon which one reinvents the machinery of government.

Grant Jordan's (1994a) magisterial rebuke of this bland, pseudo-analysis ought to have been required reading for those involved with President Clinton's National Performance Review, especially as many of the mistakes made by the Grace Commission were repeated – for example the lack of consultation with serving officials or with Congress (Ingraham 1995). Those on the European side of the Atlantic ought to have known better. Even the most cursory reading of Osborne and Gaebler demonstrates a lack of sound empirical evidence. And that which is based upon solid experience is of limited applicability and dubious methodology. In short, it may work for Vandalia, Ohio, but the political and administrative context of small American counties cannot easily be replicated elsewhere. If there are any universal laws of management they remain awaiting discovery.

Overman and Boyd's analysis (1994, pp. 76-80) of Best Practice Research is also critical and closely resembles that of Jordan. They argue that it does not learn from experience, does not listen to all practitioners (it tends towards an 'in-crowd' of reforming managers), it does not accumulate practice wisdom and its practices are not transferable. It lacks the scientific approach required of good social science in that it is not theory testing research, is insufficiently critical and insufficiently probing. By implication, therefore, the successful operationalizing of the postbureaucratic reform paradigm, through the use of lessons gained via BPR, must be viewed sceptically. This, it must be stressed, is not to reject the PRP itself, simply some of the methods by which it has been implemented.

Pretensions to universality are among the flaws in New Public Management, which itself remains controversial (Dunleavy and Hood 1994, p. 9) and which attempts to make the public sector less distinct from the private sector by:

- reducing bureaucratic rules and hierarchies;
- ensuring budget transparency and identifying the costs of inputs and outputs;
- the use of a network of contracts rather than fiduciary relationships;
- disaggregating organizations and their functions, introducing purchaser/provider distinctions;
- increasing provider competition; and
- increasing consumer power through enhanced scope for exit and redress.

(Hood 1994, p. 130; Dunleavy and Hood 1994, p. 9)

We can see from this list that the NPM may usefully be considered to be a sub-set of the alleged postbureaucratic reform paradigm, as outlined above. It uses BPR as part of its tool kit for implementing reform and its contribution to increased efficiency and effectiveness must be viewed critically.

NPM to Next Steps

All this is by way of an introduction to the current state of agencies in Britain. There are several types of agency and these include Next Steps executive agencies, Non-Departmental Public Bodies (NDPBs), NHS Trusts, regulatory agencies and other *ad hoc* bodies. It is not surprising, given the agencification of government as a concomitant of NPM, that Grant Jordan also excoriates aspects of agencification in general and the inexorable increase in Next Steps agencies in particular. There is much in what he says when, for example, he argues that there was originally little idea in the Cabinet Office of what Next Steps agencies would look like and that the commitment to a managerialist overhaul of the machinery of central government drove the reforms toward a championing of the virtues of organizational plurality (Jordan 1994b, p. 140). The Ibbs Report (which recommended the establishment of Next Steps agencies) and the more recent *Continuity and Change* white papers (Cabinet Office 1994a; 1995a) are all strong on assertion, but follow the tradition of Best Practice Research in that they lack empirical evidence to support their managerialist assertions.

There is no accepted definition for what constitutes an agency within the British system of government. Of the many types listed above, all display a remarkable disparity in their structures, size, accountability, powers and functions. Aside from the difference between executive and judicial agencies, and those which perform both roles, there exists no single set of accountability procedures. That is, while all the agencies are nominally accountable to a sponsor department – and through that to a secretary of state and to Parliament – there is, in practice, as illustrated by Figure 1, an enormous gap between those agencies which most closely resemble a cypher model and those which are closer to a state of autarky.

Figure 1. The British agency model: a simplified continuum

Autarky	*Cypher*
Fully autonomous agencies	Purely executive agencies

Next Steps agencies
(a sub-continuum within the larger)
Judicial agencies
Large Statutory
and Royal Charter NDPBs

Source: Massey, 1995d, p. 76

A useful way to begin to define the agency model is to adapt the Treasury's (1995) guidance for executive NDPBs which outlines the principles underlying the financial and management framework under which they should operate. It extracts the essence of the Next Steps principles and contains therein the British rationale for furthering the agency process.

The principles encourage sponsor departments to ensure their NDPBs:

- operate within a clear strategic control framework, with responsibility delegated to the maximum extent practicable, while maintaining the appropriate arrangements for propriety and accountability to Parliament;
- have clear aims and objectives which are consistent with the Government's priorities and are reflected in their business and financial plans;
- increase the focus on results by ensuring that, wherever practicable, executive NDPBs have agreed performance indicators and targets by which achievement will be judged; and
- promote over time further improvements in efficiency and effectiveness.

(HM Treasury 1995, para. 8)

This incorporates what the Treasury calls a 'strategic approach' to managing agencies. Each agency is expected to possess either a framework document or its equivalent in the form of a management statement or a comprehensive financial/management memorandum which sets out its main aims and objectives, the relationship with its sponsor department and arrangements for financial planning and control (para 10).

Wherever possible, management responsibility is delegated to the maximum extent practicable. All agencies (that is Next Steps agencies and executive NDPBs) are required to have corporate plans which adopt targets for financial performance, efficiency and quality of service. There is a commitment to greater accountability and operational transparency through the publication of annual reports and accounts to allow ministers, Parliament and customers/citizens to 'judge the body's achievements against its agreed performance targets' (Ibid.).

Agencies may partly be defined, therefore, as the concrete manifestation of a reform process which is determined to utilize private sector management techniques in the public sector; shift an overemphasis away from policy and towards a greater concern for service delivery; reduce the centralization of government; free-up resources through greater efficiencies and new delivery systems; develop accountability through small, identifiable units with named individuals in charge; and reduce ministerial (and senior civil service) overload. On occasion, the process of establishing agencies and the periodic (usually quinquennial) reviews of executive NDPBs and Next Steps agencies will lead to the privatization of a body as a result of the prior options process.

This is only a partial definition as it neglects the earlier reasons for establishing agencies in the form of executive NDPBs, some of which were established as unincorporated associations – for example, under the auspices of the Board of Trade prior to 1832 and predating the first Companies Act. The analysis of the Pliatzky Report (Prime Minister's Office 1980) advanced the term 'Non-Departmental Public Bodies' and the concomitant definitions of executive bodies, advisory bodies, tribunals and other bodies, because the organizations which were the subject of the report are non-departmental, but not non-governmental. (Yet neither are they quasi-autonomous in the sense that tribunals have full judicial independence, while executive NDPBs are fully accountable to Parliament through their sponsoring secretary of state).

Executive bodies are defined as those bodies which:

> normally employ staff and have their own budget, but in a few cases bodies are included which exercise administrative or regulatory functions in their own name but are supported by staff supplied by the sponsoring department
> (OPSS 1995, p. v).

They are seen to:

> carry out a wide range of operational or regulatory functions,
> various scientific and cultural activities, and some commercial
> or semi-commercial activities.
> (Prime Minister's Office 1980, para. 1)

This type of agency is normally set up under a specific Act of Parliament, an administrative action (such as forming a company under the Companies Act) (Prime Minister's Office 1980, para 11), an Order in Council or the issuance of a Royal Charter. They are established because ministers have made a policy decision to carry out certain functions and because these are best performed at arm's length from central government (Ibid., para. 14). They reflect the belief that the nature of the work is purely executive in character and does not require ministers to take a day-to-day interest in it, although they retain a strategic interest. These bodies most often resemble Next Steps agencies in their relationship to the sponsor department, in their structures and in the nature of the work they perform (for example, the Housing Corporation).

Other NDPBs are single-purpose organizations and are established because it is argued their work is more effectively carried out by an NDPB rather than a multi-function government department, for example the Housing Action Trusts. Finally, some NDPBs are established:

> as a self-denying ordinance on the part of Government and
> Parliament, in order to place the performance of particular
> functions outside the party political arena.
> (Prime Minister's Office 1980, para. 14)

Examples include the Health and Safety Executive, the Equal Opportunities Commission and the Commission for Racial Equality. A number of NDPBs are established for a combination of these reasons.

All executive NDPBs, like Next Steps agencies, are part of the machinery of government and are wholly or partly funded out of public moneys. The duties they perform are carried out at the behest of ministers with the approval of Parliament. As such they are subject to the same managerial and efficiency reforms as the rest of the government's administrative structures. They do not all operate within the same political and social context. Two simple juxtapositions suffice to illustrate the enormous scope of these bodies:

> the Housing Corporation/the British Museum;
> the United Kingdom Atomic Energy Authority/the Health and
> Safety Executive.

Recent guidelines have sought to apply Next Steps principles (of the sort outlined in the aforementioned Treasury document) to all executive NDPBs (Prime Minister's (unpublished) policy statement, 2 April 1990; HM Treasury/OPSS 1992).

The restructuring of central government departments, including some free-standing departments like the Intervention Board and the Inland Revenue, into agencies or departments run on agency lines ensured that, by July 1995, over 60 per cent of all civil servants were working in agencies and other organizations operating along Next Steps lines. In addition to this, a further set of agency candidates had been announced by ministers. It is clear that a large proportion of the British public sector is now run along agency lines.

The Fraser Report identified four groups of agencies:

- those fundamental to mainstream policy;
- those which are essentially executive;
- those which provide services to other agencies or departments derived from their specialist skills; and
- agencies not linked to any of the main aims of a department, but nonetheless report to its Minister.

(Efficiency Unit 1991, Annex A, p. 22)

The rapid growth in the number of Next Steps agencies means that there are many which no longer fit neatly into these categories, but either straddle two (or more) or, as with the Intervention Board, must be placed in a miscellaneous grouping. Given the disparate nature of Next Steps agencies and NDPBs there are, accordingly, differing relationships with ministers. It may be seen, therefore, that the definition of the agency model must necessarily be flexible and imprecise in order to encompass the wide variations in size, function and structure.

Figure 1 above illustrates one way of analysing agencies. A propensity to seek autonomy is an aspect of most bureaux and affects the way they seek to shape policy. Indeed, it is evident in many organizational structures, including nearly all professions (Massey 1988). In short, those units of government freed from routine central control will attempt to secure even greater freedom.

In many cases, of course, this is precisely what is sought in setting them up. For example, universities, the Commission for Racial Equality or the Health and Safety Executive could not perform their duties if subjected to tight ministerial control over their activities. Neither could judicial agencies carry out their role if the public ceased to perceive them as being independent bodies, staffed by disinterested officials able to reach just decisions impartially.

There is a need, however, to distinguish between these agencies and those which have been established to fulfil an executive role and which are given an arm's length structure in order to reduce ministerial (and departmental) overload, rather than to establish them as free-standing autonomous organizations. In short, it is important to distinguish the administrative autarky from the administrative cyphers.

The cyphers are those with a purely executive function. They serve to carry out routine day-to-day functions, such as disbursing grants according to centrally defined criteria from which they may not deviate, or carrying out the mechanical servicing of plant and machinery. They are hived off from the central machinery of government because their activities are so routine and mundane they may operate away from the gaze of the centre, accounting only for the efficiency and honesty with which they conduct themselves and for the public money with which they are entrusted. Several Next Steps agencies and executive NDPBs are in, or close to, this category (Massey 1995b; 1995c).

The definition may therefore be refined to state that agencies are:

> central government bodies, established in a variety of ways, in order to carry out functions for which ministers have made provision as a policy decision, but which they have decided is best delivered at arm's length. These functions include executive, judicial, and advisory actions, and encompass service delivery, licensing, policy advising, regulatory and coercive (policing) elements.
>
> Agencies exist at the will of the government, but their ability to act independently of it is curtailed to a greater or lesser extent according to: (a) their political importance; (b) their social role; (c) the prevailing political context in which they operate; (d) the ideology of their senior managers.
> (Massey 1995d, p. 77).

The sponsor departments

In recent years some departments have sought to operate their Next Steps agencies more along the lines of NDPBs, while others have sought to apply Next Steps principles more formally to their NDPBs. For their part, Next Steps agency managers have sought greater autonomy from their sponsor departments, while NDPB managers have highlighted their perceived need for continuing to be kept separate from the sponsor department. Nearly 40 per cent of NDPB managers in a recent survey reported that they operated along Next Steps lines prior to the launch of the Next Steps initiative. Indeed, both NDPB officials and their sponsor department officials argue that the sort of autonomy bestowed upon Next Steps agencies was modelled on executive NDPBs and in many cases predated the Financial Management Initiative (FMI), with some of the new financial and reporting practices coming later (Massey 1995c).

One of the primary aims of the agency creation process is to reduce ministerial overload by shifting much routine departmental activity out of the sponsor departments and into agencies. Another goal is to increase the accountability of career officials through the creation of identifiable units of administration charged with carrying out a limited set of policy commitments according to clearly defined procedures. Yet the implementation of these goals may itself present problems. The main difficulties lie in coordinating a system that has been fragmented, ensuring that ministerial policy directives are being fulfilled without retreating to the centralized oversight the system is specifically attempting to reform.

In some cases departments have seen the bulk of their activities and staff move into agencies, carrying with them the technical expertise of the department in service delivery. Agencies have also assumed the ability to advise ministers on the routine problems facing policy implementation and upon the need to formulate policy in such a way as to ensure its successful implementation. There is a careful distinction here between the right of ministers to initiate new policy and the duty of officials to advise on the best way to frame the statutes and regulations in order to ensure it is carried out.

When the agencification process is combined with privatization, market-testing and contracting-out, departments have to develop new ways of keeping ministers informed about their responsibilities. These include a heavy emphasis on financial and management reporting by agencies, the use of performance indicators, the use of ministerial advisory boards (containing officials from departments, agencies and the agencies' customers), and the cultivation of new skills in writing and overseeing contracts among senior departmental officials.

In some cases the departments may become complex letting agencies, overseeing the delivery of services determined by ministerial policy decisions, by a mix of government agencies and private sector organizations. The slimming-down of central departments will inevitably bring a reduction in their number. Those which remain will increasingly assume more coordinative and oversight roles, rather than a delivery role. This makes access to senior departmental officials and to ministers by agency managers an important aspect of the new system.

A majority of Next Steps agency chief executives have direct access to ministers as and when they require it. For executive NDPB managers this has been less necessary, given the nature of their activities. But senior officials in the large statutory and Royal Charter bodies – those most nearly representing the autarky model – do obtain access when they seek it. Those who rarely or never gain access are in small, purely executive agencies of the cypher model (Massey 1995b; 1995c). Meetings with ministers are used to discuss future policy and as part of the general process of accountability. Chief executives of the larger Next Steps agencies meet ministers on a routine weekly basis as part of their departments' senior management systems (Ibid.). For NDPBs such meetings are less frequent, although there are routine links with senior officials in the sponsor division of the sponsor department. Even if the nature of their business is such that they do not require frequent meetings with ministers, the senior managers of agencies most closely fitting the autarky model tend to have an almost automatic right of access to ministers if that is what they seek.

As an example, the chief executive of one of the larger Next Steps agencies argued that the relationship between the different constituent parts of the department to which his organization was attached had evolved into a federal one. He met the secretary of state every three weeks formally to review his agency's business and to keep the minister up-to-date but, given the nature of that business, declared: `I probably meet him once a week on something else'. The chief executive of an executive NDPB with a large budget argued, however, that he rarely saw the need to meet ministers, given that the nature of his work was routine and that it took place within narrow boundaries set by ministers when they established the strategic policy governing his organization's activities (Massey 1995b; 1995c).

There is considerable variation in the way agencies relate to their sponsor departments. This reflects the differences between departments as well as those in size and function between agencies. Agencies representing a large proportion of their sponsor's business, such as the Prison Service, the Benefits Agency or the Employment Service, will have a qualitatively different relationship with their parent department than do smaller, purely executive agencies, or those agencies which have a regulatory or quasi-judicial function, such as the Health and Safety Executive or the Commission for Racial Equality. The policy role of the larger agencies will also be important as the process of administration itself has a policy impact of which ministers must be regularly apprised. An example here would be the activities of the Child Support Agency, or some of the urban development corporations.

Chief executives of the larger Next Steps agencies therefore deal directly with their secretaries of state on a regular, often weekly, basis. Among the rest, a significant minority – some 40 per cent of the total – structure their contacts via a senior official in the department known as the Fraser figure (after a recommendation in the Fraser Report), while approximately 30 per cent use a ministerial advisory board to co-ordinate their dealings (Massey 1995b). About a quarter of Next Steps agencies use a combination of these methods or some *ad hoc* arrangement which meets the requirements of their parent department or which reflects their status as agencies which are themselves government departments (Massey 1995b, Appendix 3). For executive and other NDPBs the relationship is even more *ad hoc* and flexible.

A majority of agencies report that they are content with the role of their sponsor department, although a sizeable minority believe it still interferes too much in their business. This is even more widely felt within the agencies of some departments, especially the Ministry of Defence (Massey 1995b). About a quarter of the chief executives believe their sponsor is still over-resourced and needlessly replicates agency functions, especially in providing policy advice to ministers. This is a view which tends to reflect the push for autonomy experienced in devolved bodies. It also partly reflects the experience of agency officials who have worked in sponsor departments and who feel able to identify areas they believe to be unnecessary and which ought to be hived off or closed down (Ibid.).

Officials who remain in sponsor departments display a sophisticated array of views regarding the relationship between agencies and departments. The most frequently expressed views reflect the wish to push as many of headquarters' activities as possible out both to Next Steps agencies and to executive NDPBs. They view the relationship as having been transformed into one of purchaser/provider as between departments and their agencies, a relationship reinforced by the market testing programme. In some cases this leads to tensions over the cost of central overheads charged to agencies (Massey 1995b, Ch. 4).

Departmental officials answer the charge of duplicating agency functions by arguing that ministers need to retain enough in-house expertise to be an 'intelligent customer'. The belief, held by a large number of departmental officials, that there will be many more agencies privatized in the near future, leading to the loss from the public sector of their skills and experience, has provoked a number of departments to retain their ability to be an intelligent customer. This they have done by establishing in-house contract teams and some discrete units which 'shadow' agency functions. Sponsor department officials see their residual role evolving into a series of core functions. Of these, the most important will be the general accountability to Parliament for those activities for which the department and its agencies are responsible. In particular these include the formulation of strategic policy goals; policy advice support to ministers; some financial, legislative, administrative and policy activity which cannot be devolved to agencies; the maintenance and oversight of national standards of provision; the setting and measuring of targets for agencies; and agency management and coordination (Massey 1995b, pp. 24-33).

Agencies in context

The process of agencification has created a greater complexity within the machinery of government than at any time in living memory. The relationship of each discrete unit to the whole and to its minister varies according to its context; in a sense context is everything. The context includes the way in which the body was set up – as a Next Steps agency, as a statutory body, a Royal Charter body, a corporation, or as some other *ad hoc* administrative arrangement.

Those bodies with a clear defining document (either as a statute or a framework document) are the easiest to analyse, but even their relationship will vary over time and place – for example, the Child Support Agency, the Prison Service, the Welsh Development Agency, the Arts Council, the Nuclear Installations Inspectorate (part of the HSE). In short, ministers will become involved as and when they see fit, and the agencification of government has probably increased the ability and inclination of ministers to intervene more often, especially with the application of Next Steps principles to executive NDPBs and the gradual hazing of the boundary between departments and other bodies into something more akin to a penumbra.

The reforms of recent years have strengthened ministers vis-à-vis their departmental officials and those for whom they are accountable in other public bodies (Massey 1995a, p. 30). The move to an even more federal constellation of organizational structures is replete with quinquennial reviews which ask the fundamental prior options questions:

- does the job need to be done at all?
- if the activity must be carried out, does the government have to be responsible for it?
- where the government needs to remain responsible for an activity, does the government have to carry out the task itself? and
- where the job must be carried out within government, is the organization properly structured and focused on the job to be done?

(OPSS 1994a, p. 2).

Under this regime a plethora of accountability and reporting duties are placed on each unit. Many managers find this burdensome, but it means that the system is more open, better managed and accountable to ministers than at any time since the growth of a large welfare state. It also means that ministers and their senior officials are able to use an arsenal of management tools to trim and cut the apparatus, with piecemeal but fundamental privatization through the outright sales of agencies, through market testing and through contractorization.

A common element is the removal of decisions regarding resource allocation from the electoral and Parliamentary arena. To a certain extent this has
always happened and the cynical observer may express little concern. But
the development of agencification, when combined with contractorization,
has advanced ministerial control while at the same time reducing the ability
of ministers' senior officials to exercise independent judgement of the proposals and initiatives placed before them by non-governmental interest
groups, many of which are multinational companies based outside UK juris-
diction.

High ranking, disinterested, career officials with a lifetime of experience
are an effective check on the depredations of interest groups seeking to profit from the public purse. It may not only be the costs of defence contracts
which in the future appear to be uncontrollable. Many other aspects of service delivery by the state to its citizenry, via private sector companies based
thousands of miles away from the point of delivery, will be at the whim of
private avarice without the constitutional checks currently taken for granted.

Connected to this is the opportunity to profit corruptly. Doig (1995a) has
catalogued a litany of abuse and behaviour which, although not always of
itself illegal, nonetheless offends the fiduciary ethics of the public sector. In
many ways this may be alarmist. Certainly some of the managers recruited
into agencies from the private sector and interviewed for the studies which
inform this chapter, celebrated the new entrepreneurial spirit within the
public sector, as did many career officials. Many others did not, arguing that
the adoption of a private sector business model for the restructuring of the
public sector is ill-conceived and mismatched. To support the ethos of the
private sector, however, is not the same as to support the end of a public
service ethos for those who hold public office. Indeed there is no evidence
whatsoever that agencification has led on its own to any lessening of the
ethos of the civil service.

Just as Jordan argues that there is no empirical evidence to support the
case for New Public Management, so there is no empirical evidence with
which to damn agencification on fiduciary grounds. On the contrary, as
already argued, it has tended to enhance both the accountability of officials
and of their organizations, while augmenting the power of ministers,
although the latter is not something everyone would wish in such a centralized executive-dominated polity.

It is the threat posed by agencification combined with contractorization
on a global scale that concerns some observers. The loss of sovereignty over
policy is a potential (but so far not an actual) threat to the public sector – a
loss not to supranational governmental institutions, however tenuous their
democratic links, but to interest groups and private sector providers with

vested interests other than those of the citizenry.

Conclusion

The agency model of government is now common throughout the Western world. In Britain its enthusiastic adoption with the Next Steps initiative has combined with a longer history of executive NDPBs. Both have informed each other and in turn been reformed through the use of modern management techniques and fundamental quinquennial reviews. The result has been a federalization of the machinery of government that has both strengthened the role and power of ministers, while providing a foresight of developments which may in turn come to threaten that domination in terms of policy ownership.

The agencies themselves are disparate and have varying degrees of autonomy over their operations and of influence upon the policy process. These variations are dependent upon the political and social context in which they are situated, allowing some agencies to attain greater degrees of autonomy, while others remain administrative cyphers. Even those with a genuine arm's length relationship with their ministers retain their semi-independence for so long as it is in the perceived political interest of ministers to sustain such an arrangement.

4 The Citizen's Charter: creating a customer-orientated civil service

Tony Butcher

Introduction

A key feature of civil service reform during the 1990s has been the growing emphasis on the customer orientation. Although traditionally associated with the private sector, the term 'customer' is increasingly used to describe the users of the services delivered by government departments and Next Steps agencies. Thus the Benefits Agency's list of objectives refers to an 'efficient customer-orientated' delivery service, while the Employment Service cites the 'customer-centred attitude' of its staff. Even the Inland Revenue refers to the 'customer' in its leaflet setting out the standards of service that taxpayers can expect from local offices. Government departments and executive agencies have been required to become more sensitive to the demands of the users of their services. Charters and the use of performance targets are just two manifestations of the growing attention being given to the customer orientation within central government.

This concern with the users of public services and the quality of the services that they receive from government departments and their executive agencies is not new. An occasional paper published by the Cabinet Office in the late 1980s identified the essential elements of a 'service to the public' strategy, emphasizing the importance of providing 'quick, efficient and courteous service' (Cabinet Office 1988, para. 1.3). More recently, the improvement in the quality of outputs has been described as the 'touchstone' of the success of the Next Steps programme launched by the Thatcher government in 1988 (TCSC 1994, Vol I, para. 145). Indeed, in its inquiry into the first year of the programme, the Treasury and Civil Service Committee (TCSC 1989, para. 54) maintained that it expected the success of the Next Steps initiative to 'be judged in large measure by the extent to which it improves service to customers'. Ministers and senior civil servants have also stressed that the improvement of service lies at the heart of the Next Steps programme (see, for example, Common *et al* 1992, p. 120). Speaking about the creation of executive agencies within the Department of Social Security (DSS), one senior official maintained that the DSS stood to be judged by the extent to which there was 'an observable and, indeed, measurable difference in the quality of service we give' (TCSC 1989, Q. 280).

This emphasis upon customer sensitivity was significantly bolstered by the launching of the Citizen's Charter by the Major government in 1991. Designed to raise the standard of public services and make them more responsive to their users, it signalled a clear political commitment to the customer orientation in the civil service. In the words of the Cabinet minister responsible for its early implementation, the Citizen's Charter was a policy about relationships with 'customers' (TCSC 1994, Vol. II, Q. 2507). The Charter has been seen as 'a natural extension' of the Next Steps programme (Painter 1995, p. 17). As the first director of the Cabinet Office's Citizen's Charter Unit put it, the Charter is 'the next stage after Next Steps. Next Steps gets management sorted out and we are now saying with greater clarity what we want managers to deliver' (quoted in Hennessy 1991).

Although the Citizen's Charter is seen as having raised public service standards to 'the status of a central theme of the 1990s' (Painter 1995, p. 23), it is important to realize that it has a number of different themes. Thus Deakin (1994, pp. 51-2) distinguishes four main policy agendas associated with the Charter: the 'constraining public bureaucracy' agenda, which includes the market testing and contracting out of services; the 'state and citizen' agenda with its concern for more information, effective complaints procedures and greater responsiveness to consumer needs; the 'new management' agenda with its emphasis on the delegation of responsibility; and the 'cost cutting' agenda with its concern for economies. Thus the Citizen's Charter initiative draws together a number of different strands in the Conservative government's public service reform programme (TCSC 1994, Vol. II, Q. 2504).

The focus of this chapter is on the Charter's 'state and citizen' agenda – the attempt to strengthen the position of the consumers of public services – with special reference to government departments and Next Steps agencies. The chapter will first describe the main principles of the Citizen's Charter and the rationale behind the customer orientation which lies at the heart of the Charter initiative. The next part of the chapter will provide an overview of the development of the initiative in central government departments and Next Steps agencies. An examination of the implementation of the Charter's customer ethos will then focus on developments in two important central government organizations – the Benefits Agency and the Inland Revenue. Finally, the chapter will look at some of the criticisms of the Citizen's Charter programme within the context of central government and the civil service.

The Citizen's Charter and the customer orientation

The Citizen's Charter programme spells out six key 'principles of public service' which every citizen is entitled to expect (Cabinet Office 1992a). They are:

- *Standards* – the setting and publication of explicit standards for services and the publication of actual performance against these standards.
- *Information and openness* – information and openness in the provision of services.
- *Choice and consultation* – the provision of choice wherever practicable, together with regular and systematic consultation with the users of services.
- *Courtesy and helpfulness* – courteous and helpful service from public servants.
- *Putting things right* – redress and well publicized and easy to use complaints procedures.
- *Value for money* – the efficient and economical delivery of services within the resources the nation can afford.

As several commentators have made clear, the Citizen's Charter is, despite its title, essentially about promoting the responsiveness of public services to their customers and not about enhancing the rights of citizenship (Stewart and Walsh 1992, p. 507). In the words of one observer, the Charter is about empowering 'citizens as consumers by means of rights to receive information on services and performance, to assert choices and preferences, to complain and to receive redress' (Prior 1995, pp. 89-90).

Thus the Charter programme emphasizes service to so-called 'customers'. According to one minister who was actively involved in the early stages of the programme, the underlying aim of the Citizen's Charter was 'to encourage those who work in public services to think about what they do in relation to how it affects the customer, the user of services'. The government was 'trying to get away from the old doctrine that the man or woman in Whitehall knows best, we actually think the customer knows best what he or she wants' (Select Committee on the Parliamentary Commissioner for Administration 1992, Qs. 3 and 36). In the words of the deputy director of the Citizen's Charter Unit, the Charter was trying to make the concept of the 'customer' a reality (Goldsworthy 1993, p. 141). As she states (p. 140):

> The Citizen's Charter is... about the outward face of the organisation: the relationship between public services and their users. The Charter puts itself in the shoes of the recipient of services and asks "What can I as an individual expect from this organisation?", "Does this represent my full and fair entitlement?", "Have I received what I was told to expect?", and "What is the organisation going to do for me if it fails to deliver the standards that I as an individual have been told that I can expect?"

Thus the Charter's emphasis on consumerism – consultation, courteous and helpful staff, well publicized and readily available complaints procedures – is a recognition of the importance of the customer in the delivery of public services. This concern with getting 'closer to the customer' is a view of consumerism which has been described as 'an orientation towards the consumers of goods/services rooted in a sense of public service with its concomitant moral obligations towards the public'. It is an approach which is concerned with making 'things better for the consumer' by taking the point of view of consumers and attempting to improve services in the light of those views (Connelly 1992, p. 30; see also Peters and Waterman 1982).

A key feature of the Charter's customer orientation is its emphasis on the availability of more information through the publication of service standards and performance. The provision of such information is an important manifestation of the Major government's wider attempts to replace traditional methods of political accountability within the public sector with consumer accountability, thereby increasing the influence of consumers of services – the customers – over the quality of public services (Oliver 1991, p. 25). In the words of its architect, John Major, the Charter was about 'giving more power to the citizen' (Cabinet Office 1991, p. 2). According to one minister, the publication of standards of service – together with more consultation with the users of services and more effective and accessible complaints procedures – is supposed to 'bring about greater clarity about people's entitlements to services and will create pressure for improvements in the quality of service' (Select Committee on the Parliamentary Commissioner for Administration 1992, Q. 1). As a government report marking the first four years of the Charter programme argues, the publication of performance information makes public services 'more accountable to their users: the public can see their strengths and weaknesses and seek changes where improvements are needed' (Cabinet Office 1995b, p. 34).

The Citizen's Charter, government departments and Next Steps agencies

As Prior (1995, p. 87) points out, the Citizen's Charter was not really a charter, but rather 'an agenda for the future development of charters in a wide range of services'. It was to be followed by a programme of action across the public service. Central to the development of this programme was the establishment of a Citizen's Charter Unit in the Cabinet Office soon after the launching of the initiative. Responsible for examining draft charters, the Unit has thirty staff and is currently directed by Genie Turton, a deputy secretary from the Department of the Environment. The Unit is paralleled by an advisory panel chaired by the chief executive of Boots plc, which reports to the prime minister.

Since the launching of the Citizen's Charter, a number of individual charters have been published by various government departments and Next Steps agencies. The two taxation departments – the Inland Revenue and Customs and Excise – have both published *Taxpayer's Charters*, setting out the standards of service to be expected. Customs and Excise has also produced a *Traveller's Charter*, setting out information on allowances and explaining rights. *The Redundancy Service Payments Charter* has been issued by the Redundancy Payments Office of what is now the Department for Education and Employment (DFEE). Other government departments have issued Charter Standard Statements setting out the services provided for customers. Thus, Her Majesty's Inspectorate of Pollution in the Department of the Environment has issued a Charter Statement summarizing pollution control policies and establishing performance standards. The Ministry of Agriculture, Fisheries and Food has published a document called *Commitment to Service* setting out standards for the payment of grants and a complaints procedure.

However, it is the Next Steps agencies which have been identified as the main vehicles for carrying forward the Citizen's Charter's principles in central government (Cabinet Office 1992a, p. 66). By late 1995, many executive agencies had published their own charters or equivalent statements. Thus the flagship of the whole Next Steps initiative, the giant Benefits Agency, has published a *Benefits Agency Customer Charter* outlining the services which customers should receive and how they should be treated. Other Next Steps agency charters include the *Contributor's Charter* and the *Employer's Charter* issued by the Contributions Agency, and the *Child Support Agency Charter* published by the Child Support Agency. The second largest executive agency, the Employment Service, has published a *Jobseeker's Charter* explaining what help it is able to give its customers and the level of service they can expect. In 1995 the Court Service published a *Charter for Court Users*. More than thirty other Next Steps agencies have published Charter Service Statements, including the War Pensions Agency and HM Land Registry. Companies House has published a document entitled *What You Can Expect From Companies House*, which outlines customer rights and contains named contact points at all levels within the agency.

The concept of customer service is also an important element in the launching of new Next Steps agencies. Agency framework documents and business plans are expected to reflect the customer approach. Agencies which deal directly with members of the public are normally expected to publish a Charter or Charter Service Statement setting out the service which members of the public can expect, replete with arrangements for customer consultation and complaints. Thus the Prison Service published a Charter Statement of Standards when it was launched in 1993, with a Prisons Ombudsman responsible for reviewing unresolved complaints being appointed a year later.

There has also been the development of the Charter Mark awards, introduced in 1992 and described by the Citizen's Charter Unit as 'the Oscar for public services'. The winners of these annual awards – who have been required to meet nine criteria, including high levels of customer satisfaction – are given the right to use the Charter Mark logo for three years. The Charter Unit also runs a number of activities designed to exchange information and ideas across the public service, including charter quality networks and seminars. A related development has been the setting up in 1993 of the Citizen's Charter Complaints Task Force, under the leadership of Lady Wilcox and including members from the public and private sectors, to review how complaints systems in the public services are working. The Task Force published its report in the summer of 1995 and issued a Good Practice Guide for use by public service managers and staff.

The Citizen's Charter in action

The concept of the customer, as manifest in the Citizen's Charter, is now firmly part of the vocabulary of central government and the civil service. How have the Charter's principles concerning customer orientation been applied in the context of the civil service? To what extent have government departments and Next Steps agencies become more customer-orientated? This section will look at the development of the customer orientation in the largest Next Steps agency – the Benefits Agency – and in a government department whose operations affect the lives of the majority of the population – the Inland Revenue.

The Benefits Agency

The Benefits Agency (BA) is the flagship of the whole Next Steps initiative. With a staff of over 66,000 civil servants, it is the largest of the executive agencies and manages the delivery of social security benefits. Its operations affect the daily lives of millions of people. Social security is a service which 'at some point or another, in some form or another, touches the whole population in ways which are uniquely personal and intimate' (Moodie *et al* 1988, para. 3). In 1994-95 there were more than four million claims for income support alone and more than ten million pensioners received payments.

The importance of customer orientation in the organization and culture of the government's huge social security operation was recognized well before the launching of the BA in 1991. As long ago as 1983, the then Department of Health and Social Security (DHSS) – responsible for the social security system – had acknowledged that it was not fully complying with its statutory duty to provide 'a prompt, accurate, courteous and humane income maintenance service'. The permanent secretary in charge of the social security side of the DHSS declared that its staff had to recognize that doing business with one of the Department's local offices 'must often seem a less agreeable experience than approaching many other undertakings' (quoted in MacPherson 1987, p. 131).

Criticisms of the quality of service at local benefit offices were reinforced in 1988 by the findings of an internal inquiry – the Moodie Report – which concluded that the service provided for the DHSS's customers ranged 'from the quite outstanding to the quite appalling' (Moodie *et al* 1988, para. 6). The Moodie Report (1988, para. 3) placed the customer at the heart of the social security system, arguing that few organizations could have greater claims to be 'a consumer organization'. Following the publication of the report, the DSS (which had been established in the summer of 1988 following the break up of the DHSS) published a set of 'principles of good service' emphasizing the need to provide a 'good service to the public' (DSS 1989). This commitment to greater customer sensitivity was reinforced by the development of a Quality Assessment Package which enabled managers to discuss the quality of the service provided to the public by the DSS's local offices and to consider ways in which performance could be improved (National Audit Office 1988, para. 2.3; Burns 1992, p. 58).

The existing customer focus of the benefits operation was reinforced by the BA's framework document when the social security benefits operation was established as a Next Steps agency in 1991. The framework document requires the Agency to develop an 'efficient customer-orientated benefit delivery service' (Benefits Agency 1991, para. 2.3.1). As the Agency has pointed out, there has been a movement away from the culture of the 'claimant' to that of the 'customer'. One of the assumptions underlying the claimant culture was that because those in receipt of social security benefit could not go elswhere, the quality of the service provided was not regarded as particularly important. The view of the BA, however, is that because its customers cannot go elsewhere for their benefits, the quality of service should be high (TCSC 1994, Vol. II, p. 226). In stark contrast to the claimant culture, one of the core values of the BA has been identified as 'customer service' (Benefits Agency 1995, p. 7).

Although the BA has focused on the customer orientation since it was established in 1991, its first chief executive described the Citizen's Charter's emphasis on customer service as 'a tremendous reinforcement' to what the Agency was already attempting to achieve (TCSC 1994, Vol. II, Q. 2191). The BA's *Customer Charter* was published in 1991, with a revised version published in late 1993. It lays out how customers should be treated – courteously, fairly and with confidentiality; and the service they can expect to receive – with promptness and accuracy (including details of the time it will take to deal with claims). It also states how the Agency will attempt to find out the views of its customers and provides advice on what to do if things go wrong (Benefits Agency 1993).

In line with the Citizen's Charter's emphasis on standards, the BA measures its performance nationally against twenty-two targets set by the secretary of state. These targets comprise claims clearance times, accuracy, financial management and customer satisfaction. Each local office also displays its local standard statements which spell out the details of opening hours, telephone access, key contact points, standards of performance, availability of advice and information and the arrangements for dealing with complaints. Local offices are required to consult customers as part of the process of producing an annual local business plan, which contains details of how the office intends to improve the quality of its service over the next year. In an attempt to ensure that such plans respond to local needs, local offices are also expected to undertake surveys and to confer with local organizations. Initiatives which have been introduced as a result of local business plans include customer panels representing local customers, which meet regularly with the local BA customer service manager and staff to discuss any problems.

Since its establishment, the BA has also commissioned an annual survey – carried out by an independent external research contractor – to examine customer opinion of the service it provides. The Agency has also developed its own Quality Award, providing its business units with a means of measuring improvements designed to make the service more customer-orientated.

As part of its customer culture, the BA is also working towards the development of a 'one-stop' service, whereby customers will be able to carry out all their business with the Agency in one place, with one member of staff and at the same time. By July 1994, a 'one-place' service had been introduced in which customers have access to the full range of Agency services in a single location. This is to be followed in 1996-97 by the development of the second stage of the 'one-stop' initiative, aiming to set up a 'one-person' service in which customers will be able to deal with one person in a local office. Eventually the BA will also establish the third stage – a 'one-time' service, where much of a customer's business with the Agency will be completed at the time of his or her first contact, thereby providing a more personal service.

In addition, the BA has improved customer service training, reduced anonymity by requiring all staff normally to wear name badges and has refurbished many local offices. Complaints procedures have also been improved. The customer service manager in each local office is expected to respond to complaints within seven days and the Agency is piloting two new complaints systems which include an independent element.

Thus the BA has introduced a number of initiatives in its attempt to develop a 'customer-orientated benefit delivery service'. There have been marked improvements in service quality. For example, the proportion of income support claims dealt with within five days by the BA rose from 65 per cent in 1990-91 to 68.8 per cent in 1994-95. The success of the Agency has been reflected in the fact that it has won more charter marks than any other organization. Two BA business units were awarded the Charter Mark in 1992, with seven awards in 1993, five in 1994 and thirteen in 1995. Customer satisfaction surveys indicate satisfaction rates of between 82 and 84 per cent. The report of the BA's 1994 national customer satisfaction survey showed that 83 per cent of customers questioned were satisfied with the service provided by the Agency, compared with 82 per cent in 1992 and 84 per cent in 1993.

The Inland Revenue

With a staff of just under 55,000, the Inland Revenue is one of the largest government departments. It administers the tax records of some 35 million people. In 1994-95 it handled over 120 million items of correspondence and dealt with about 33 million telephone enquiries. Since April 1992, it has operated fully on Next Steps lines, with its day-to-day executive responsibilities devolved to the controllers of its twenty-nine executive offices.

Like the Benefits Agency, the Inland Revenue had recognized the demands of its customers for some years before the publication of the Citizen's Charter. A *Taxpayers' Charter of Rights* had been introduced in 1986. Following the launch of the Citizen's Charter in 1991, the *Taxpayer's Charter* was published later the same year. It was very much a reworking of the

1986 document, outlining what the taxpayer is entitled to expect from the Inland Revenue, including impartial and fair treatment; the provision of clear forms and leaflets; courtesy; the provision of information and advice; the prompt and accurate settlement of tax affairs; confidentiality; minimal costs and the provision of information about complaints. The *Taxpayer's Charter* is supplemented by ten codes of practice setting out the standards of performance that members of the public can expect.

The Inland Revenue has also published standards and information on performance against them for dealing with people's tax affairs correctly the first time, dealing with repayment claims, replying to taxpayers' letters and attending to personal callers and telephone calls. All of the targets for 1993-94 were met or exceeded and, although two new targets were narrowly missed, the established targets for 1994-95 were also met or exceeded.

In addition to a concern with raising standards, there have also been improvements in the accessibility of services. All tax enquiry centres and telephone switchboards are now open for at least forty hours a week, with flexible opening hours to suit local needs. A network of mobile tax enquiry centres visits shopping precincts and other venues. Forms and leaflets have been redesigned to make them easier to read and the Inland Revenue has been the winner of eight Plain English Campaign awards. Echoing the Benefits Agency's 'one-stop' service approach, the Inland Revenue is bringing tax assessment and collection together into single taxpayer service offices, thereby offering taxpayers a single point of contact for dealing with their tax affairs.

The Inland Revenue has also undertaken surveys of taxpayer groups – employees, self-employed people, pensioners and employers operating PAYE (Pay-As-You-Earn) – in an attempt to discover what they think of services and to help improve them. A survey in 1994 revealed that 87 per cent of pensioners were satisfied with the overall service provided by the Revenue. A survey of employers in the same year showed that 84 per cent were satisfied with the service and that 38 per cent thought that service had improved.

One of the six principles of public service enunciated in the Citizen's Charter is that public services should have 'clear and well-publicised complaints systems' (Cabinet Office 1991, p. 42). Over the years, the Inland Revenue has been second only to the DSS as a source of complaints referred by MPs to the Parliamentary Ombudsman. Following an internal review of complaints systems, an independent Adjudicator, who is not part of the Inland Revenue management structure, was appointed in 1993. The Adjudicator acts as 'an impartial referee where people feel they have been badly treated' by the Inland Revenue and where they have not been able to resolve matters with the controller of the relevant executive office. The Adjudicator considers complaints about the way in which the Inland

Revenue has handled tax affairs, including complaints about excessive delay, errors, discourtesy and the way in which the Inland Revenue has exercised any discretion (Adjudicator's Office 1995a, pp. 2-4).

As Doern (1993, p. 24) points out, the Inland Revenue, in its role as an 'essentially unpopular tax collector', was traditionally inclined to 'underemphasise the fact that the vast majority of its clients were compliers with tax law'. Developments following the *Taxpayer's Charter* have begun to change this working culture.

Conclusions: a customer orientation?

The Citizen's Charter has clearly had a significant impact on the operations and culture of government departments and of Next Steps agencies. The customer orientation has the merit of 'forcing public organisations to look outward to those who use and receive their services' (TCSC 1994, Vol. III, p. 68). In the words of one observer of the Citizen's Charter initiative: 'Customers and clients are being differentiated more clearly so that service can be improved' (Doern 1993, p. 28). As we saw in the previous section, a number of important initiatives have been introduced by the Benefits Agency and the Inland Revenue aimed at developing the ethos of customer service. Other Next Steps agencies and government departments have introduced similar initiatives.

One important development has been the setting of performance targets and the publication of information about performance. Many Next Steps agencies have shown significant improvements in customer service. For example, the Passports Agency has reduced the maximum time for processing passport applications from ninety-five working days in 1989 to sixteen in 1994-95. The emphasis on defining standards of service is not only important in monitoring improvements in the quality of service. The Parliamentary Ombudsman has said that he takes account of published Charter targets also as 'indicators of a satisfactory or unsatisfactory performance' (Office of the Parliamentary Commissioner for Administration 1994, para. 6).

Departments and executive agencies are, in addition, providing more information about how services are run. Customs and Excise has attempted to make its services more accessible by offering tax clinics and evening seminars for new VAT traders. The Driver and Vehicle Licensing Agency has telephone helplines offering advice and information. A number of Next Steps agencies are also attempting to find out what the users of services want. Some agencies, including the Employment Service, conduct regular customer satisfaction surveys. The Passport Agency carries out postal surveys of customer opinion every two months. Like its DSS stablemate, the

Benefits Agency, the Contributions Agency has set up local customer panels where customers are consulted about services and about possible improvements.

Another manifestation of the development of a customer-orientated culture within the civil service has been the way in which departments and executive agencies emphasize the importance of staff courtesy and helpfulness. An important part of this approach has been the increasing recognition of the value of staff training. Thus the Employment Service (1995, p. 5) is committed to training its staff to ensure that they provide 'a professional, courteous and helpful service'. It was awarded *Investor in People* status in 1994 – the largest public sector organization to achieve this. Most civil servants who serve members of the public now wear name badges. The Contributions Agency has set up a network of customer service liaison officers. Another DSS executive agency, the War Pensions Agency, has reorganized its telephone service with the intention of introducing a 'one-stop' advice system. The Employment Service is integrating its separate networks of unemployment benefit offices and jobcentres into self-contained offices. Another innovation of the Employment Service is longer and more flexible opening hours – its jobcentres are open for at least thirty-six hours a week.

A further important consequence of the Citizen's Charter initiative is that greater attention has been paid to complaints and procedures for redress – the Charter's principle of 'putting things right'. As we have seen, the Benefits Agency has improved its complaints systems, while the Inland Revenue has appointed its own Adjudicator to deal with complaints which cannot be resolved internally. The holder of this office has subsequently been appointed Adjudicator for both the Customs and Excise and the Contributions Agency. The Customs and Excise promises to reply to written complaints within ten working days and its new complaints division also ensures that complaints are fed back to the management so that appropriate changes can be made (Select Committee on the Parliamentary Commissioner for Administration 1992, Q. 55). Some of the agency charters – including the *Jobseeker's Charter* and the *Benefits Agency Customer Charter* – pledge financial compensation in certain circumstances. For example, under its *Jobseeker's Charter* provisions, the Employment Service paid just over £89,000 in compensation in 1992-93 (HC Debs. 6th Series, vol. 244, written answer, cols. 430-2 (14 June 1994)).

Despite its positive impact on many aspects of the workings of departments and Next Steps agencies, however, the Citizen's Charter initiative has been the subject of much criticism. One concern is about the use of performance targets. Although the published results have shown that organizations such as the Benefits Agency have achieved marked successes in achieving their targets, it has been pointed out that performance might have improved as 'a direct consequence of the fact that it is a time of change', rather than as a result of deliberate change. Also, performance targets might have been set too low in order to make agencies 'a public relations success' (Greer 1994, pp. 123-4). Crucially, Next Steps agencies emphasize quantitative efficiency indicators such as clearance times for the handling of customer queries, and accuracy. They have few performance indicators which attempt to measure effectiveness, especially regarding service quality and customer satisfaction (Greer 1994, p. 74; Greer and Carter 1995, p. 92).

Concern has also been expressed about whether some of the individual charters are living up to their promises. Thus the National Consumer Council criticized many county courts for failing to meet the standards laid down by the Court Service in the *Courts Charter* (TCSC 1994, Vol. III, p. 62). A report by the Consumers' Association (1995) revealed that four out of the twenty-five Benefits Agency offices visited failed to display local service standards and, of those that did, five failed to show target waiting times. Nearly half of the offices visited did not have copies of their local charters to distribute.

The delivery of social security benefits continues to attract particular criticism. Despite its proclaimed customer orientation, the Benefits Agency has been reprimanded by the Parliamentary Ombudsman for 'instances of thoughtless bureaucratic behaviour', including the decision of a local office to restrict its public counter opening hours to five hours a day and only to accept telephone calls from members of the public in the morning (Select Committee on the Parliamentary Commissioner for Administration 1994a, Q. 155). According to the Ombudsman, many disabled persons and their families also suffered 'inconvenience, annoyance, distress and, in some cases, prolonged hardship' as a result of the serious delays in the payment of the new Disabled Living Allowance by the Benefits Agency in 1992 (Office of the Parliamentary Commissioner for Administration 1993, para. 26).

Another DSS executive agency – the controversial Child Support Agency – has been heavily criticized for long delays in deciding maintenance orders, slowness in responding to enquiries and for making too many errors in assessments. Notwithstanding its attempts to create a customer ethos, the Inland Revenue has been criticized by the independent Adjudicator for putting taxpayers to 'unnecessary expense and misery by thoughtless and inept behaviour by some Inland Revenue staff and managers' (Adjudicator's Office 1995b, p. 1).

As noted above, one of the principles of public service spelt out by the Citizen's Charter is 'regular and systematic consultation' with the users of services. Yet it has been alleged that there has been insufficient attempt to consult organizations who represent the interests of consumers. Consultation seems to have concentrated on market research and meetings with what have been described as 'insider' groups (Lewis 1993, p. 320; Price

Waterhouse 1993, p. 10; 1994, p. 13). Such criticism reflects a wider concern about the Citizen's Charter's narrow view of citizenship (Prior 1995, p. 90). One group of observers refers to 'the reduction of the active content of citizenship to the passive role of customer': the individuals questioned by market researchers 'have no right to frame the questions, no chance to discuss with others or to inform themselves before replying, no opportunity to discover how their statements have been interpreted' (see the evidence of D. Faulkner, C. Crouch, M. Freedland and D. King in TCSC 1994, Vol. II, p. 88).

Concern has also been expressed that the practices of government departments do not adequately reflect the Citizen's Charter's principle of 'better redress for citizens when things go wrong'. In a critical report, the House of Commons select committee which shadows the work of the Parliamentary Ombudsman reported in 1994 that much of the redress offered by departments and agencies was inadequate. It had 'come across unwillingness to admit fault, refusal to apologize, failure to identify and compensate all those affected by maladministration' (Select Committee on the Parliamentary Commissioner for Administration 1994b, para. 1).

Ultimately, of course, the success of the Citizen's Charter's efforts to create a customer-responsive civil service depends upon the commitment of the front-line staff who have to deal with members of the public. The morale of such staff has clearly been affected by the Major government's wider efficiency agenda, notably the market testing programme. The chief executive of the Employment Service described the Government's launching of market testing only a few months after the publication of the Citizen's Charter as having 'socked (staff) in the solar plexus', while the leader of one civil service union declared that he could not imagine 'a more stupid thing' with which to follow up the Charter (Willmore 1992). The permanent secretary of the DSS was reported as saying that market testing had led to 'serious costs in terms of staff morale... which in turn impinges on their ability (and willingness) to continue delivering the service' (TCSC1993, Vol. II, Q. 1126). In 1994, the chief executive of the DSS's largest agency – the Benefits Agency – accepted that the introduction of market testing had engendered a sense of insecurity among his staff (TCSC 1994, Vol. II, Q. 2225).

Departments and Next Steps agencies have also been affected by the continuing emphasis on the need to improve civil service efficiency and to reduce costs. It was reported in late 1994 that senior managers in the Benefits Agency – which was required to make new efficiency savings of £55 million in 1994-95 – had warned of a lack of resources to carry out the work required of them (Brindle 1994). At the beginning of 1995, the trade union representing Inland Revenue staff argued that government plans to cut up to 12,500 Revenue jobs – nearly a quarter of the total staff – by the year 2002 would 'lead to a loss of quality control and increase error rates' (Taylor and Kelly 1995). The associated closure of many local tax offices has been criticized as leading to 'the gradual removal of accessibility' for taxpayers, especially in remote parts of the country (Dolan 1995).

Such developments have clearly affected civil service morale. In 1993, a MORI poll found that the majority of Inland Revenue staff felt that managerial change was happening too quickly (Walker 1993). The following year, an independent study of Next Steps agencies found that staff morale was 'generally low' (Price Waterhouse 1994, p. 10). As the Treasury and Civil Service Committee (1994, Vol. I, para. 250) pointed out, morale does not simply matter because the government attempts to be a good employer; it matters 'because the morale of civil servants is likely to have a direct effect on the quality of service to customers'.

The Major government's commitment to civil service efficiency – strongly reasserted in the 1994 and 1995 white papers on *Continuity and Change* (Cabinet Office, 1994a and 1995a) – is a reminder that, despite the Citizen's Charter's emphasis on making public services user-responsive, the customers of government departments and Next Steps agencies are not simply the members of the public who use their services. Another key group of stakeholders are the taxpayers (and government ministers) who expect government departments and their executive agencies to provide the best possible value for money. The Citizen's Charter programme is not just about making public services more responsive to their users. It is also concerned with improving the quality of those services by making existing resources go further. In the Charter's own words, it is about 'finding better ways of converting the money that can be afforded into even better services' (Cabinet Office 1991, p. 6).

Thus the mechanisms identified for implementing the principles of the Citizen's Charter emphasize the importance of more privatization, wider competition and further contracting out as well as the publication of standards and results, information about how services are run, consultation with customers, accessibility and more effective complaints procedures. The Charter's concern with the customer orientation is just one, albeit extremely important, part of a wider approach to the reform of the civil service. The Citizen's Charter may reflect an increased concern with responsiveness to the customers of central government services, but the emphasis on the efficiency and economy of government departments and Next Steps agencies in the provision of those services is a crucial component of the Charter's wider programme.

5 Industrial relations in the civil service

Susan Corby

Introduction

Industrial relations in the civil service is changing markedly in the 1990s with implications for the half a million people working in it, the taxpayer (as over 70 per cent of its costs are labour costs) and Parliamentary accountability. Essentially the thrust of the changes is to make industrial relations in the civil service more like industrial relations in the private sector. This is being brought about in three main ways: first the government is reducing civil servants' career opportunities both by bringing in people from the private sector and by eroding job security; second it is introducing pay systems similar to those found in the private sector; third it is eroding collectivism, which could result in the reduction of union organization to a level closer to that found in the private sector. Before looking at these developments in detail it will be useful briefly to describe the background.

Up to 1980, civil service industrial relations was characterized by strong control from the centre (the Treasury and then the Civil Service Department), centralized rule making, a high level of union membership and organization and joint agreement over a wide range of matters. Consultation often merged with negotiation, through the 'Whitley' system (formal committees of officials and union representatives). Another characteristic of the industrial relations scene in the civil service until 1980 was the government's view that it should seek to be a model employer, providing *de facto* job security, relatively generous sick pay and pension arrangements, encouragement of union membership and effective grievance machinery. In addition, civil service pay was set by a complex procedure which entailed collective bargaining, constrained by and based primarily on the principle of 'fair comparison' with the remuneration of staff outside the civil service – the so called Priestley (1955) system – and with unilateral access to arbitration as the final guarantee of impartiality between government and unions. Although the government sometimes modified civil service pay settlements on grounds of public policy, this was regarded as a temporary aberration (Hepple 1982, p. 72).

From 1979, the Conservative government sought to improve the managerial efficiency of the civil service and to curb public expenditure. This had knock-on effects on its industrial relations. First, the Prime Minister, Mrs Thatcher, set across-the-board staff reduction targets. Second, cash limits replaced volume planning. The cash limit included a pay assumption which, if breached, required the additional costs to be funded by job losses, higher productivity or service reductions. Third, power was devolved from the centre to departments: both financial control (the Financial Management Initiative) and personnel management control (MPO 1983). The latter resulted in a change from the central prescription of civil service-wide management rules to framework guidance from the centre to departments. So, for instance, departments could devise their own staff appraisal systems but had to follow certain common denominators. Fourth, in 1981 the government ended the Priestley system for pay determination. This resulted in a dispute lasting over four months, ending with the establishment of a committee of inquiry. The committee's report recommended 'informed collective bargaining' with less weight than hitherto given to pay comparisons with those outside the civil service (Megaw, 1982, para 113). Finally, between 1987 and 1989, all the civil service unions concluded new pay agreements with the Treasury. These combined the tradition of comparability with greater flexibility. On the one hand, they were based on the need to recruit, retain and motivate staff and so there was provision for the compilation of data on annual pay movements in the private sector. On the other hand, they enabled departments to provide performance pay (within guidelines) and to make 'special pay additions' where there were particular recruitment and retention difficulties.

The most important development in civil service industrial relations in the 1980s was the report drawn up under Sir Robin Ibbs entitled *Improving Management in Government: the Next Steps*·(Efficiency Unit 1988), the broader significance of which is discussed elsewhere (see Chapters 2, 3 and 9). Suffice it to say that the civil service was considered too diverse in its activities, too vast to be managed as a single entity with common rules for financial and personnel management. It also found that the civil service was dominated by political and policy considerations at the expense of its ser-vice delivery functions and managerial efficiency. To rectify this, the report recommended that the executive functions of departments should be clearly designated and restructured to form executive agencies. Each agency would be headed by a chief executive, operating within a quasi-contractual frame-work document spelling out its objectives, set by the responsible minister in consultation with the Treasury and specifying the financial and personnel 'freedoms' judged necessary. But by the end of the decade, only nine agen-cies had been set up, compared to 102 by the end of 1994. Thus, the 1980s saw some changes in industrial relations: a lessening of civil service unifor-mity and some decentralization in the setting of terms and conditions. In the 1990s, however, we are witnessing more deep-rooted changes.

Before dealing with these, it is important to point out that the civil service is not unique. Throughout the public sector the Conservative government has sought to control public expenditure and to import private sector prac-tices and market mechanisms. Since 1979, the government has privatized public corporations and utilities; deregulated bus transport; introduced compulsory competitive tendering and rate capping in local government; reorganized the NHS into purchasers and providers, establishing self-gov-erning trusts; changed the arrangements for teachers' pay to bring them under closer government control, brought in the local management of schools and created grant-maintained schools. The driving force behind these changes has been the wish to improve managerial efficiency, to give greater priority to the needs of customers rather than producers, to bring in market disciplines or proxies for them and to exercise tight budgetary con-trol. These changes, although not led by are nevertheless consistent with the government's overall industrial relations objectives throughout the public sector. These include the breaking up of large organizations with uniform pay structures and detailed conditions to form smaller units responsible for setting terms and conditions. As a result, pay determination is devolved to a multiplicity of localities where public sector unions, with their centralized structures, have tended to be weak. Other government industrial relations objectives include movement from the nationwide prescription of terms and conditions to locally determined arrangements, reflecting more closely local labour markets and the unit's financial position rather than the going rate; the empowerment of managers so that they can become operators rather than administrators; the forcing of local management and union negotiators to confront the trade-off between pay and employment; and the growth of individualism and the erosion of collectivism, for instance through individ-ual performance-related pay. In short, the industrial relations developments in the civil service examined below are not exceptional when set in the con-text of the public sector. This will be seen by considering career patterns; decentralization; and the erosion of collectivism.

Career patterns

An important development in the 1990s has been the increase in the number
of people brought into the civil service at senior levels from the private sector. In the 1980s such appointments (e.g. Peter Levene, Montague Alfred)
were exceptional. In the 1990s, they are no longer exceptional. Thus up to
1990, agency chief executives were mainly drawn from the ranks of serving
civil servants (five of the first seven) and without open competition. Now
open competition is the norm (Goldsworthy 1991, p. 29). More than half the
chief executives have come from outside the civil service, although this does
not necessarily mean the private sector (Cabinet Office 1993a, p. 8). At levels
below the top, people from the private sector have been brought in, for
instance the head of training and the head of finance at the Benefits Agency
(TCSC 1994, Vol II, p. 238) and the head of the Procurement Unit at the
Treasury (Adonis 1995b). In 1995 the First Civil Service Commissioner was
drawn from the private sector and there was an open competition for a
mainstream permanent secretary (Adonis 1995c). The person appointed did
not have a commercial background but neither was he a career civil servant.
Moreover, this process looks set to continue. In its 1994 white paper, the
government said that departments, before filling posts in the senior civil service, 'should consider systematically on each occasion whether to use competition as a means of filling vacancies, either by internal advertisement
across the Civil Service or by full open competition' (Cabinet Office 1994a,
para 4.24). Indeed the government, which formally had as one of its objectives maintaining a career civil service, has changed this to a *predominantly*
career civil service (author's emphasis) (Cabinet Office 1995a, para 1.5, p. 2),
believing that people from the private sector can improve civil service efficiency.

Admittedly, the numbers coming from the private sector into the civil
service are minute. However, they are filling key posts, thus denting the
concept of a civil service career for life and reducing the promotion chances
of incumbents. Importantly, also, their presence has an impact on industrial
relations, parliamentary accountability and values. As to industrial relations, it is probably no coincidence that the Royal Mint chief executive who
sought to derecognize unions came from outside the civil service, as did the
chief executive of the Recruitment and Assessment Services, who operates
without a Whitley Council.

As to parliamentary accountability, the Trosa report (1994, para. 4.7.11)
found that agency chief executives recruited from the private sector did not
realize that, on occasion, they would have to make compromises between
efficiency preoccupations and political requirements. The Home Secretary's
dismissal of Derek Lewis as chief executive of the Prison Service in October
1995 underlines this point. It centred on issues of operational control, policy

formulation and the roles of the minister and agency chief executive (see below, Chapter 9). Similarly, Sir John Bourn, the Comptroller and Auditor General, said that private sector managers brought in to run public services often had an inadequate grasp of the importance of accountability to Parliament and were often surprised to learn that they were subject to scrutiny for their handling of public money (Willman 1994).

It is harder to gauge a change in values. Career civil servants normally subscribe to the public service ethos while those from the private sector adhere essentially to entrepreneurial values. Arguably, however, as those from the private sector come into key posts in the civil service, entrepreneurial values come to the fore. One example is the Meteorological Office's decision to keep its thirty day forecast secret so that it could be sold to corporate customers, rather than making it publicly and freely available (Cookson 1995). Looking at local offices of the Inland Revenue and the Benefits Agency and charting the intensification of work and increased managerial discretion, Fairbrother (1994, p. 6) argues that we are seeing in the civil service the 'beginnings of the creation of an enterprise or commercial culture'.

Civil servants' career patterns are changing, however, not only because outsiders are being brought into top jobs. Job security is being impaired by the growing use of casual and fixed-term appointees. According to a representative of the Civil and Public Services Association (CPSA), 43 per cent of administrative assistants in what is now the Benefits Agency are not permanent, whereas the equivalent figure ten years ago was 10 per cent. Job security is also being eroded by cuts in the number of civil servants. Between April 1992 and October 1995, 11 per cent of civil service jobs were cut – to 506,000, the lowest level since the Second World War. But staff reductions continue and the Chartered Institute of Public Finance and Accountancy forecasts a loss of 30,000 jobs in 1996/97 attributable to cuts in running costs (Parker and Kampfner 1995). These reductions are mainly occurring because of delayering, market testing and privatization. In its white paper (Cabinet Office 1995a, para 4.7, p. 17), the government said all departments with twelve or more senior staff were to carry out senior management reviews with the aim of moving to leaner, flatter management structures. It was estimated that over a quarter of senior jobs would go in 1995-96 (Adonis 1995c).

As to the market testing of civil service jobs, a process launched in 1991, David Hunt, when Chancellor of the Duchy of Lancaster, said that 26,900 civil service posts had gone between April 1992 and September 1994. Of these, 10,600 staff had transferred to external suppliers, 2,100 had gone through natural wastage and there were 3,300 redundancies, half of which were compulsory (Adonis 1995a). In a large minority of cases – over 40 per cent according to the Council of Civil Service Unions (TCSC 1994, Vol III, p. 133) – in-house bids were not allowed. The government argues that in these cases there is strategic contracting out – i.e. for strategic reasons the government wants the activity undertaken outside the civil service. This seems to cover cleaning and office services in some, but not all, departments, as well as drafting the Finance Bill.

Perhaps the privatization of executive agencies poses the greatest threat to civil service job security. Initially, when the first agencies were formed it was generally accepted that 'further immediate change was unlikely' (Goldsworthy 1991, p. 19). Now, however, every five years (formerly every three years) the parent department undertakes a re-examination of the feasibility of abolishing the agency, contracting out the whole of the agency's functions or of privatization, after which there is a ministerial decision. At the time of writing, agencies which have been or are in the process of being privatized include: DVOIT (the information technology directorate of the Driver and Vehicle Licensing Agency), the Transport Research Laboratory, the National Engineering Laboratory, the Laboratory of the Government Chemist, and the Accounts Service Agency (Cabinet Office 1994b). Others include the Chessington Computer Centre, HMSO and the Civil Service College (Hencke 1995). Privatization is not confined to executive agencies: Forward, the civil service catering organization, the information technology part of Inland Revenue and the Accreditation Services have been transferred (Institution of Professionals, Managers and Specialists (IPMS) 1995a, p. 7; Cabinet Office 1995a, para 3.8, p. 11).

Privatization and market testing/contracting out have both industrial relations and constitutional implications. Currently the public has access to information about the costs of services provided by civil servants through departmental accounting officers. If the work is privatized or contracted out, there is generally less information available to the public because of the application of the commercial 'in confidence' restriction. At the same time, the reduction of job security and career opportunities affects civil servants' commitment to their work. Indeed, according to a MORI poll carried out for the Association of First Division Civil Servants (FDA) in 1995, only one in five would recommend a young person to join the civil service. Moreover, in a climate of uncertainty with the undermining of the concept of a career for life, civil servants may feel tempted to tell ministers what they believe they want to hear and be less willing to offer frank and fearless advice. This could insidiously erode the political impartiality of the civil service. In the MORI survey, three in five civil servants agreed with the statement: 'speaking up can damage career prospects' (MORI 1995).

Decentralization

The Ibbs Report heralded the introduction of structures similar to those found in many private sector companies. Such companies have substituted a quasi-autonomous, multi-divisional organization (M-form) for a unitary organization (U-form) (Williamson 1975). The main impact of this restructuring on civil service industrial relations is the delegation of terms and conditions to departments and agencies, placed on a statutory basis by the Civil Service (Management Functions) Act 1992. This Act enables the Treasury and Office of Public Service to grant delegated authority, instead of 'discretions' as before.

Thus the early 1990s saw departments determining their travel and subsistence arrangements, in the light of Treasury guidance, with many agencies setting up bonus schemes. More radically, by the end of 1992 a few agencies – HMSO, the Agricultural Development Advisory Service (ADAS), the QEII Conference Centre and the Royal Mint – had developed their own pay and grading schemes. By April 1994, twenty-one agencies and two departments (Inland Revenue and Customs and Excise) had their own pay and grading regimes. In April 1996, all central civil service collective bargaining ended. The pay and grading of staff at senior levels (grade 5 and above) is now unilaterally determined, while the pay and grading of less senior staff is delegated to departments and agencies (Cabinet Office 1994b, p. iii), essentially for joint determination. This marks the end of a long tradition of central joint pay determination and nationally set grades according to Treasury grading guidance. It brings the civil service into line with practice in the private sector. According to the Workplace Industrial Relations Survey, carried out in 1990, national level bargaining was the most important level for pay determination for only 5 per cent of non-manuals in private sector services and 24 per cent in manufacturing (Millward *et al* 1992).

This delegation, however, is hardly cost effective. Some 150 bargaining units replace a handful and 3,000 managers are doing the work that was previously carried out by forty civil servants in the Treasury's Pay Division (IPMS 1995b, p. 1). Moreover, there are remarkable similarities between the pay awards of departments and agencies. For instance the independent pay research body Incomes Data Services (IDS 1995, p. 17) looked at the outcomes of delegated bargaining in 1994 and found 'little variation in the level of awards which ranged from 1.5 to 2.9 per cent with the majority between 2.2 to 2.5 per cent'. Similarly, another independent research body, Industrial Relations Services (IRS 1995, p. 5), found a number of common features in the 1994 pay round. These included paybill increases of around 2 per cent to 2.6 per cent, the replacement of salary scales by wider pay bands, a greater emphasis on merit pay and the adoption of unconsolidated but pensionable pay rises.

Yet it is not surprising that in practice departments' and agencies' pay and grading schemes show few significant differences. Until April 1996, the Treasury was directly responsible for authorizing each department's, or agency's, detailed plans for the initial delegation before they were tabled for negotiations with the unions. Once a delegated pay system was up and running, plans had to be submitted to the Treasury before annual negotiations could take place. Thus, a union representative at HMSO said that he had been told by the human resources (HR) director that he could not yet begin to negotiate the annual pay review because the Treasury had not cleared the paperwork (Corby 1994, p. 61). (At that time the HMSO HR director was new and, perhaps, naïvely candid). According to a brief from a civil service union research department (CPSA 1995):

> It has been obvious that, at least for this year [1995], the Treasury has remained *in control* of pay at the delegated level. As well as there being the public sector pay policy, it has been clear that the Treasury has been clearing the negotiating remits of management in delegated areas and/or the offers.

There will continue to be control from the centre, responsibility for industrial relations and terms and conditions passing from the Treasury to the Cabinet Office (Office of Public Service). Moreover, as the Treasury continues to retain control of public expenditure, including public sector pay, it will continue to have a finger in the pie.

There have been a number of studies of decentralized bargaining in the private sector, notably by Kinnie (1987) and Marginson (1988). They found tensions between the centre and the business unit – 'centripetal' and 'centrifugal' pressures, as Kinnie terms them. Kinnie also talks about the 'illusion' of autonomy and points out that the main advantage for management is the parochializing of industrial relations. The unions focus their attention on local issues, even though key decisions are taken at a higher level. Marginson shows that the centre can restrict the unit's autonomy on pay in a number of ways: by issuing broad guidelines, advising or by instructing. He found that, generally, companies tended towards the instruction of units. The Treasury's stance, therefore, is not unusual when viewed against private sector practice.

Even though variations in terms and conditions are not substantial, they may be hampering interdepartmental and agency/departmental transfers, thus undermining the unitary and collegiate ethos of the civil service. There is evidence that both management and union representatives share the view that it will become increasingly difficult for staff to transfer across the civil service as pay systems, grading arrangements and personnel practices diverge (Corby 1994, p. 59). Symbolically, the government also closed the Staff Transfers and Trawling Unit, which redeployed staff across the civil service (IPMS 1995c, p. 6).

A CPSA representative pointed out that previously each department had a single management hierarchy. Now each agency has its own management structure, in addition to that of the department, and it is often not easy to get the appropriate managers from these different organizations together to arrange transfers. He also ventured the view that management was at times reluctant to take on long-standing civil servants from another agency or department because they would 'bring "baggage" with them in terms of the traditions of the civil service'. They preferred 'new, more malleable people'.

The Cabinet Office appears to be distinguishing the new senior civil service, for whom mobility is important, from other civil servants, for whom mobility is not important, seemingly departing from the concept of a unitary civil service. However, it admits that mobility may become more problematic even for the senior civil service. It says 'some have expressed concern that variations in levels of pay... will act as a barrier' (OPS 1995).

The erosion of collectivism

Until the 1980s, the government regarded being a good employer as acting jointly with the unions (Fredman and Morris 1989). It encouraged unionization in the civil service and expanded the scope of consultation and bargaining, with the former merging imperceptibly into the latter. This changed in 1984, when the government banned union membership at the intelligence gathering centre, GCHQ. Although this only affected a relatively small number of civil servants (some 7,000) and a small number of workplaces, it suggested that the traditionally strong endorsement of union membership for civil servants may not endure. In fact, according to the Workplace Industrial Relations Survey of 1990 (Millward *et al* 1992): 'the proportion of workplaces in central government where managers said that management strongly recommended trade union membership halved between 1984 and 1990'. Similarly, in its handbook for the new civil servant, the government used to encourage entrants to join the union appropriate to their grade and to play an active part in union affairs. When it revised the handbook in the late 1980s it said: 'If you decide to join a union, you are encouraged to play an active part'. Another important example of the government's antipathy towards the civil service unions is its removal, from April 1996, of some 2,000 civil servants in grades 4 and 5 (assistant secretaries) from joint pay determination.

Generally managers in departments and agencies have tightened up in the granting of facility time, i.e. time off for trade union duties, and are having less regard for union involvement. This approach, according to a union representative in the Benefits Agency, was encapsulated when a senior manager advised a newly promoted lay union representative to 'take the opportunity to turn his back on the unions'.

Against this background, it is not surprising that the government, while continuing to claim to be a good employer, sees this in terms of equal opportunities and staff training and development (Cabinet Office 1995a, para 1.5, pp. 1-2). It does not see it as encompassing the encouragement of union membership or joint decision making.

There are also examples of restrictions to the Whitley system – i.e. the system of joint committees of the official side and the trade union side. For instance, in the Employment Service, the agency Whitley Council and the regional Whitley Councils meet every six months, instead of every four months as before. They have a smaller membership than before and the number of sub-committees has been reduced. At the Benefits Agency, the district Whitley meets when necessary, instead of monthly as before. Recruitment and Assessment Services (RAS) has no Whitley Council at any level. When the agency was formed in 1991 under a chief executive from the private sector and with no experience of Whitley, the Whitley Council was moribund. There were no consultative arrangements in existence and the two main civil service unions there were inactive. When the union branches were reconstituted and union representatives elected, management would not reconstitute the Whitley Council. Instead there are informal meetings.

There is an interesting contrast. In 1991, RAS management used the opportunity of union inactivity to dispense with the Whitley structures, whereas six years before and in a similar situation senior officials in the Ministry of Defence had positively encouraged staff to participate in the FDA branch to prevent its demise through apathy (Corby 1994, p. 60). Moreover, there are numerous examples of consultation rights being eroded. For instance, HMSO union representatives were given a morning to submit comments on changes to travel and subsistence allowances. Union representatives at Employment Service were consulted on a new personnel handbook, but this consultation proved to be a sham. The management circular to staff had already been written and, by accident, distributed the day *before* the joint meeting (Corby 1994, p. 60). Similarly, according to a survey by Labour Research (1995), a union representative at the Planning Inspectorate Agency spoke of 'a clear trend by management to keep the union at arm's length' and a union representative at the Health and Safety Executive said 'management is prepared to discuss everyday matters but is secretive on major changes'.

More subtly, collectivism is being eroded by the growing use of individual performance-related pay (IPRP). The government sees IPRP as an important tool for improving efficiency. As it said:

> By linking rewards more directly with quality of service we can bring about a more customer-focused culture and ensure that customer service is given priority. We need to be able to differ-

entiate between those who are making a contribution and those who are not. If we do not, success and failure would be equally rewarded (Cabinet Office 1992a, p. 3).

This is not the place to debate the effectiveness of IPRP. Suffice it to say that at national level, in 1992, all four bargaining groups of non-industrial civil servants agreed individual performance-related pay schemes, in addition to general pay increases. Under delegated arrangements, pay agreements in departments and agencies also include individual performance-related pay schemes. In some cases, these schemes are essentially the same as the national arrangements. In other cases, new merit schemes have been designed, for instance at Inland Revenue, HMSO, Customs and Excise, the Valuation Office and for senior staff in the Employment Service (IDS 1995). The CPSA (1995) says that there has been a growing use of what are called equity share schemes. Each box mark (i.e. performance mark) is allocated a number of shares whose monetary value is determined according to the size of the paybill, enabling management to control costs.

IPRP undermines the traditional union objective of a rate for the job, making it clear that an individual's pay is largely dependent on management discretion, not union action. The unions may agree the size of the performance budget and receive information on the performance assessment markings and performance awards, typically broken down at least into staff groups and gender. But it is management, not the unions, who assess the individual's performance and who decide on the amount of the individual's performance pay. Management is not directly encroaching on collective institutions, nor does it have as a key objective the reduction of the unions' role. Nevertheless, that is the by-product. As Kessler and Purcell (1992, p. 21) comment:

> The very mechanics of these schemes involve a fundamental restructuring of the employment relationship which can result in greater managerial control over staff. It is a system which isolates the individual from the work group and forces the personalised design and evaluation of work.

Again, the civil service is following the trend. Comparing 1990 against 1984 Millward *et al* (1992, p. 261) found that it had become more usual for non-manual employees to have some portion of their earnings dependent on their individual performance.

The unions' role is also being reduced as a by-product of the growth of so-called employee involvement initiatives, under which management deals directly with staff. This partially replaces or supplements the management/union representative link. Thus to gauge staff opinions in the

Employment Service, the agency carries out annual attitude surveys, rather than leaving it to union representatives to relay staff views. Similarly, management communicates with staff directly through team briefings, rather than leaving it to union representatives to pass on management's message. Moreover, working parties may not provide for union seats. Examples include HMSO's quality improvement projects or RAS's personnel strategy working group (Corby 1994, p. 61). Once again, the civil service is not unique in adopting employee involvement techniques. The Workplace Industrial Relations Survey found a substantial growth in such techniques since the mid 1980s (Millward *et al* 1992, p. 180). Nor is the civil service unique in operating a dual approach, i.e. collective bargaining and employee involvement techniques (Storey 1992).

Union power is also being weakened by the proliferation of bargaining units. The number of full-time officers (FTOs) of the civil service unions is not increasing proportionately to the increasing number of bargaining units and indeed some unions, because of financial problems, are actually reducing the numbers of FTOs. This gives greater scope for lay union representatives but they may not be able to cope adequately with an enhanced role. The new pay bargaining arrangements also bear upon union power through the law, making civil service-wide industrial action virtually impossible. This is because industrial action is only lawful in respect of those directly affected. So if terms and conditions are set nationally, a civil service-wide strike is lawful. If they are not and a department or agency is the bargaining agent, then those civil servants directly affected can take industrial action, but civil servants in other departments or agencies cannot lawfully take sympathy action.

The reduction in the role of civil service unions should not be overstated. Unions are setting up regional offices to be better able to meet the challenges of decentralization, arranging membership swaps and agreeing on union mergers (IPMS Bulletin 1995d). The most recent is that between the National Union of Civil and Public Servants and the Inland Revenue Staff Federation to form the Public Services, Tax and Commerce Union with 160,000 members (Bolger 1995). Nevertheless, civil service union membership has declined. Union density is now estimated at 63 per cent (Corcoran 1995) as compared to 91 per cent in 1979 (Fryer 1989), though these estimates must be treated with caution as they are not based on comparable data.

Union strength and union role are not only matters of interest to industrial relations specialists. They also have constitutional implications. Without a union to mediate an individual's employment concerns, the individual is less powerful vis-à-vis management. Where the government is the employer and the employee is a politically neutral civil servant, it is important that the employee feels confident enough to speak up, even though this may cause a minister political difficulties, especially where accountability to Parliament is at issue. The case in 1985 of Clive Ponting, who leaked information to Parliament about the sinking of the *General Belgrano* in the Falklands war, illustrates this. When Ponting was prosecuted under the Official Secrets Act, he was supported by his union, the FDA. But such a high profile case apart, the importance of an independent voice for civil servants is vital if they are to feel secure and confident and thus to offer impartial and objective advice to ministers. They inevitably feel less secure and confident in an environment where career opportunities are being restricted, where the collegiate and unitary concept of the civil service is being impaired by the decentralization of pay and grading and where civil service unionism is no longer encouraged.

6 The concept of public duty

Barry J. O'Toole

Introduction

The concept of public duty is as old as philosophy itself. Simply stated it means that the public official regards the interests of society as being above his or her personal interests and is a public servant purely out of a perceived duty to serve the public. Of course, in practice each individual will have great difficulty in setting aside personal interests; nevertheless, the idea that public servants seriously make an attempt at doing so has always been said to be a feature of British public life.

Increasingly, however, both the concept and the practice are thought by some to be 'old fashioned'. Indeed, the feeling seems to be that, in some ways, the inculcation of a public service ethos has led to increasing inefficiency in government. This chapter will explore the meanings of the concept of public duty; examine whether such a concept has been either put into practice or regarded as an important element of public service in the United Kingdom; and analyse recent ideas about its relevance in the 1990s.

The concept of public duty

Plato was the first philosopher seriously to consider the question of public service and public duty. In his *Republic* Plato sets about creating, not the ideal state (which for him was a primitive society, in which citizens would provide themselves with basic comforts), but a state which could exist in actuality and which would have the best chance of incorporating character-istics of the ideal. It would also be a state in which the worst features of con-temporary Athenian society could be eliminated. This state he referred to as a 'luxurious' state (Plato, Trans. Cornford 1941, pp. 58-61). It was luxurious in the sense that 'we must not limit ourselves now to those bare necessaries of house and clothes and shoes; we shall have to set going the arts of embroidery and painting, and collect rich materials, like gold and ivory' (p. 59). It was important to the discourse because 'the consideration of luxury may help us to discover how justice and injustice take root in society' (Ibid.). It is important, too, to the present purpose of this chapter, for reasons which will shortly become apparent.

It was for his 'luxurious' or 'inflamed' state that Plato saw the need for a ruling elite. As the state grew it would be 'swollen up with a whole multi-tude of callings not ministering to any bare necessity', such as hunters and fishermen, artists and poets, actors and reciters, dancers and producers, ser-vants and barbers, cooks and confectioners and a whole host of other spe-cialists. Not least would there be a need for soldiers, since 'If we are to have enough pasture and plough land, we shall have to cut off a slice of our neighbour's territory; and if they too are not content with necessaries, but give themselves up to getting unlimited wealth, they will want a slice of ours' (Ibid. p. 60). These soldiers Plato refers to as the 'guardians of the com-monwealth'. Their work was 'the most important of all' and they would need 'the most complete freedom from other occupations and the greatest amount of skill and practice' (p. 61).

These Guardians Plato proceeds to split into two groups, the so-called Philosopher Rulers and the Auxiliaries. All the Guardians will have under-gone a rigorous education, which would be similar to the education which Athenian boys underwent in Plato's day. In his *Republic* Plato would remove features which would not help to produce the type of character his Guardians were to have, for 'we can be sure... that if they are to have the best chance of being gentle and humane to one another and their charges, they must have the right kind of education' (p. 105).

This education is described in detail in Chapter IX of the Cornford trans-lation and to a large extent those details are not directly important to the present discussion. Those who are to be the Rulers are selected for further education (outlined in Chapters XXVI and XXVII) by a series of tests (though some of the tests will have been applied in childhood too). It is at this point that Plato begins to stress the qualities necessary in those who are to be rulers.

It is at this point, too, that Plato's ideas about public duty manifest them-selves directly. The argument is that those who are chosen to be the Rulers 'will be those who, when we look at the whole course of their lives, are found to be full of zeal to do whatever they believe is for the good of the commonwealth and never willing to act against its interests' (p. 101). The intention of the tests to select the Rulers must be 'to find out who are the best guardians of [the] inward conviction that they must always do what they believe to be best for the commonwealth' (p. 102).

To strengthen this conviction further the Guardians (both the Rulers and the Auxiliaries) would be expected to live in conditions of spartan simplicity. For Plato, it was 'only common sense that the dwellings and other belongings provided for them must be such as will neither make them less perfect Guardians nor encourage them to maltreat their fellow citizens' (p. 106). This sentiment is followed by one of the most important passages in the *Republic* about private interests and public duty:

> First, none of them must possess any private property beyond the barest necessaries. Next, no one is to have any dwelling or store-house that is not open to all.... Their food... they will receive from the other citizens as wages for their guardianship...; and they will have meals in common and all live together like soldiers in a camp. Gold and silver... they will not need, having the divine counterparts of those metals always in their souls... whose purity it is not lawful to sully by the acquisition of that mortal dross, current among mankind, which has been the occasion for so many unholy deeds. They alone of all the citizens are forbidden to touch and handle silver or gold, or to come under the same roof with them, or wear them as ornaments or drink from vessels made of them. This manner of life will be their salvation and make them the saviours of the commonwealth. If ever they should come to possess land of their own and houses and money, they will give up their guardianship for the management of their farms and households and become tyrants at enmity with their fellow citizens instead of allies.
> (Ibid.)

In addition to his concerns about material possessions Plato also made comments about familial and personal connections. A whole chapter (Chapter xvi) is devoted to the 'Abolition of the family for Guardians'. The Guardian class is, in effect, to form a single family. There is a eugenic intention here, as Cornford puts it: 'to rear children of the highest type'(p. 152). More importantly, from the present perspective there is the intention 'to free the Guardians from the temptation to prefer family interests to those of the whole community' (Ibid.). This:

agrees with [the] principle that they were not to have... any property of their own, but to receive sustenance from other citizens, as wages for their guardianship, and to consume in common. Only so will they keep to their true character; and [the present] proposals will do still more to make them genuine Guardians. They will not rend the community asunder by each applying that word "mine" to different things and dragging off whatever he can get for himself into a private home, where he will have his separate family, forming a centre for exclusive joys and sorrows. Rather they will all... feel together and aim at the same ends...
(p. 162)

Having been educated in the ways in which Plato outlines, having lived under conditions of Spartan simplicity for a number of years (until they are fifty) and having served a sort of apprenticeship in junior positions of authority those who are to be Rulers 'have come safely through and proved the best at all points in action and in study...' They are ready at last to be 'brought to the goal':

They must lift up the eye of the soul to gaze on that which sheds light on all things; and when they have seen the Good itself, take it as a pattern for the right ordering of the state.... For the rest of their lives, most of their time will be spent in study; but they will all take their turn at the troublesome duties of public life and act as Rulers for their country's sake, not regarding it as a distinction, but as an unavoidable task. And so, when each generation has educated others like themselves to take their place... they will depart to dwell in the Islands of the Blest. The state will set up monuments for them and sacrifices honouring them as divinities... or at least as men blest with a godlike spirit.
(p. 256)

Those who make only a vain show of being Guardians, not following the precepts outlined here, will bring the whole state to utter ruin (pp. 107-8).

British public administration and the concept of public duty

At a superficial level, it may be argued that the lives of many of the people who were leaders in the Indian civil service and later in the British civil service resembled those of Plato's Guardians (Chapman 1970, pp. 18-20). Large numbers of able and distinguished public servants of the second half of the nineteenth century and the early decades of the twentieth century had read *Literae Humaniores* at Oxford. Their training included Ethics, Logic, Metaphysics and Political Philosophy. Many were taught by T.H. Green, the great English Idealist, who inspired them to public service (O'Toole 1990). Before they had entered university they had spent three quarters of each year since about the age of eight at one of the great public schools. They had been taught never to mention their parents and to address each other only by their surnames. They led lives devoid of anything but Plato's 'bare necessaries' (Chapman 1970, pp. 19-20). Even today more than half of all recruits to the fast stream administrative grades of the civil service have been to Oxford or Cambridge. The question is, apart from this superficial resemblance to the Guardians, were they also imbued with a Platonic sense 'public duty'?

This is a singularly difficult question to answer. It is only relatively recently that the world of research has become noted for the numbers of social scientists who develop sophisticated methodology for the purpose of both providing and analysing empirical data to enable answers to be provided to such questions. What we have instead are the occasional personal observations of current and (more often) former public servants, though these observations are usually not particularly revealing. We have the official observations contained in various parliamentary and other authoritative inquiries and we have the scholarship of administrative historians (Chapman and O'Toole 1994). Nevertheless, these are rich sources.

It may be argued that this literature has created an 'ideal type' civil servant, moulded through education, recruitment and socialization to accept the ethical code which is embodied by the phrase 'public duty'. This code was most forcefully expounded by Sir Warren Fisher who was Head of the Civil Service between 1919 and 1939, perhaps the most important period in its history. That was the period in which Fisher was able to build upon the reforms of the last part of the nineteenth century and the first part of the twentieth century to create the unified civil service of more recent times (Chapman and Greenaway 1980, Chs 1 and 2; O'Halpin 1989, Ch. 2; O'Toole 1989). It is the values and mores of this civil service which construe that ethical code.

The most important and famous statement of the general principles of this code was made by Fisher, with others, in a report on 'certain statements affecting civil servants', published in 1928. The relevant paragraphs of the report read:

> Practical rules for the guidance of social conduct depend as
> much upon the instinctive perception of the individual as upon
> cast-iron formulas; and the surest guide will... always be found

in the nice and jealous honour of Civil Servants themselves....
[That] a civil servant is not to subordinate his duty to his private interests, nor to make use of his official position to further
those interests, is to say no more than that he must behave with
common honesty. The Service exacts from itself a higher standard, because it recognises that the State is entitled to demand
that its servants shall not only be honest in fact, but beyond the
reach of suspicion of dishonesty.... A Civil Servant is not to
subordinate his duty to his private interests; but neither is he to
put himself in a position where his duty and his interest conflict. He is not to make use of his official position to further
those interests; but neither is he so to order his private affairs
such that a trust has been abused or a confidence betrayed
(Fisher *et al* 1928, paras. 535-6, quoted in O'Halpin 1989, p. 162).

As O'Halpin notes, Fisher later commented that these standards of conduct existed 'long before' 1928. Their embodiment in this statement was to
form the basis of civil service ethics for many decades afterwards. It became
the definitive statement of the obligations of civil servants, circulated to all
departments and published in the handbook which all civil servants
received upon appointment (see above, Chapter 2).

The sentiments expressed in this formal statement of the concept of 'public duty', and its application in British public administration, were personi-
fied in Sir Edward Bridges, Head of the Home Civil Service, 1945-56.
Indeed, Fisher's most distinguished successor was in some ways more
assertive. As an exemplar he was probably more important. He was the
'arch proponent of generalist administration and the whole ethos of public
service which went with it' (O'Toole 1993, p. 3). As Chapman notes 'of those
who joined the civil service Bridges thought it fair to say that nearly all had
in common: "a disposition to find public affairs of interest; no desire or
intention to take part in political life ; and a readiness to work as a member
of a team, rather than seek personal glory"' (Chapman 1988, p. 38, quoting
Bridges).

The subordination of 'personal glory' was central to Bridges' ethos of
administration. He believed, for example, that 'A good civil servant has to
be more anonymous and unselfish in his work than those in other walks of
life... the traditional outlook of the modern civil service is one that recognises that the interests and welfare of the whole country come first...' (quoted
in Chapman 1988, p. 64). He thought that civil servants should be influenced 'by no thoughts of private advantage or advancement' and that they
should have 'no end in view but that the work be carried out faithfully and
well' (quoted in Chapman 1988, p. 314). Apparently, when addressing
potential candidates for the civil service and in other public lectures he went

so far as to quote from Trollope's *The Three Clerks* the passage in which Sir Gregory Hardlines says that civil servants:

> should look on none of their energies as applicable to private purposes, regard none of their hours as their own. They were devoted in a peculiar way to the Civil Service, and they should feel that such was their lot in life. They should know that their intellects were a sacred pledge entrusted to them for the good of that Service, and should use them accordingly. This should be their highest ambition
> (Trollope 1858, p. 130).

These are truly Platonic sentiments and Bridges believed in them passionately. Moreover, he apparently believed that others accepted and lived by them too. According to Chapman (1988, p. 63) '...it seems to have been normal to assume in conversations with Bridges that people always had uppermost in their minds a general anxiety to do what was right or what was best in the public interest'.

Of course, it would be naïve to assume that because Fisher and Bridges were devoted public servants, each with a profound sense of public duty, then all other civil servants must behave and believe as they did. This, however, is not to deny the influence they had as exemplars of public duty and public service. From this perspective, we should be grateful to the scholars of administrative history who have ensured that we will be able in future to reflect upon these and other examples.

Their example also lives on in other ways. One of the peculiar features of the British civil service is the part played by the process of 'socialization' in the education of civil servants. It is peculiar to the British civil service, not because people are not socialized into the bureaucracies of other countries, or indeed into other organizations, but because socialization is much more important in terms of communicating values, standards and methods in the British civil service than in other organizations. Socialization has been described as the process of 'learning by doing' or 'sitting with Nellie'. But it goes much further than the purely mechanical; it is about the acquisition and development of certain characteristics, values and codes. *Estacode*, the old establishment officers' guide, was essentially making this point when it suggested that it had never:

> been thought necessary to lay down a precise code of conduct because civil servants jealously maintain their professional standards. In practice the distinctive character of the British civil service depends on the existence and maintenance of a general code which, although to some extent intangible and

unwritten, is of very real influence.
(quoted in *FDA News*, February 1984)

In the case of the British civil service socialization is about the acquisition and development of an administrative ethos. It is about the administrative culture. Edward Bridges himself was essentially exemplifying this culture when he referred to the 'departmental point of view'. He found that there was:

> in every Department a store of knowledge and experience in the subjects handled, something which eventually takes shape as a practical philosophy... in most cases the departmental philosophy is nothing more startling than the slow accretion and accumulation of experience over the years... Every civil servant... finds himself entrusted with this kind of inheritance.
> (Bridges 1950, pp. 15-17)

At a more practical level this administrative culture manifests itself in a collegiate form of decision making. Richard Chapman deals with this in his book on Bridges. The civil service, he argues:

> ...may lack some of the physical manifestations of a corporate life found in a College...; but it certainly does not lack a collegiate approach to decision making. This approach ensures that anyone involved in the consequences of a decision, as well as those responsible for making a particular decision, is brought into the decision making process. It involves consulting and informing a wide network of people within the administrative system, not necessarily so that they can offer relevant advice important in the decision making process, but, often, simply, so that an agreed policy or line of action is not subsequently upset.
> (Chapman 1988, p. 287)

Again, this method of decision making is consistent with a view of public service which downplays the importance of the individual, emphasizing the contribution of the individual to the team effort and 'for the greater good'. Self-interestedness would not easily be served in such a scheme. It could be argued that socialization in the British civil service used to reinforce such an attitude. In other words, socialization was about the inculcation of a sense of 'public duty'.

The concept of public duty in the 1990s

The Fulton Report of 1968 marked a major shift in the way in which the civil service was perceived. In particular, the Report vilified the idea of 'generalist administration', the cornerstone of efficient public service as envisioned by both Fisher and Bridges. Instead the Fulton Committee advocated its much vaunted 'preference for relevance'. In place of the socialization process described above, 'training', in all its manifestations, would eliminate the perceived 'amateurism' of the service. There would be training in all of the specialist activities of the service, for example in economics or accounting or planning. More importantly, there would be 'management' training, so that civil servants could become accountable for what they did, in particular for the 'resources' they used. In other words, 'business techniques' would be imported into the civil service. It is this view of the civil service which has come to dominate thinking about how it should operate. While it was assumed that the Fulton Committee had failed in its attempts to change the administrative culture, in fact the Committee may come to be seen as having successfully laid the groundwork for the radical changes in the civil service in the years since 1979.

Superficially, the most important of these changes may seem to be related to structural matters. For example, the Financial Management Initiative, including the Next Steps programme, and the Competing for Quality or Market Testing Initiative, have set in train enormous organizational reforms. Further analysis may reveal, however, that the fundamental change has been in the administrative culture. There is a lot said about the inculcation of the so-called 'can-do' approach; less is said about whether this approach has undermined more traditional values. The question is, in the process of importing techniques which are argued to be 'business-like' have the recent reforms undermined the traditional concept of public duty?

Judging by the public pronouncements of the government the answer to this question is apparently in the negative. The current holder of the post held so eminently by Sir Warren Fisher and Sir Edward Bridges agrees with the government's assessment. So too does the Treasury and Civil Service Committee (TCSC), which has been heavily involved in monitoring 'progress' in the Next Steps programme and which published a fascinating report on *The Role of the Civil Service*. All seem to agree with the view of the Committee that: '... the Next Steps reforms are in principle compatible with the maintenance of the traditional values of the civil service' (TCSC 1994, Vol. I, para. 84). These values are stated quite clearly by the Committee (Vol. I, para. 72):

> It is our conviction that the values of impartiality, integrity, objectivity, selection and promotion on merit and accountabili-

ty should act as unifying features of the British Civil Service. They are as important today as in the last century; their importance should not diminish in the next century. We believe that the case for a permanent, politically impartial Civil Service is as compelling now as it has been for well over a century. The principle of selection and promotion on merit must represent the bedrock of such a Civil Service. The importance of the values of integrity, impartiality, objectivity and accountability is rooted in the characteristics of the tasks which the Civil Service is called upon to perform... They can and should act as a unifying force for the whole Civil Service.

In its reply to the Committee's Report, the government merely said: 'The Government agrees' (Cabinet Officer 1995a, para. 4, p. 24). Cynics, or at least those who believe in the special nature of public service, may well suggest that it is not difficult to agree with statements which could, and perhaps should, apply equally to other organizations. No mention is made of the central idea of the public service ethos, that the public servant puts the interests of society above his or her personal interests and is a public servant purely out of a desire to serve the public.

In the same reply the government also rejected the view of some, including the Committee of Public Accounts, that 'failings in integrity and probity had resulted from public service reforms' (Cabinet Office 1995a, para. 3, pp. 22-3; see also O'Toole 1994, p. 123; TCSC 1994, Vol. I, paras. 90-1). In its report the Committee of Public Accounts, whilst not condemning the recent changes in the ways in which public bodies are organized, nevertheless implicitly links those changes with a 'departure from the standards of public conduct which have mainly been established during the past 140 years' (PAC 1994a, para. 1). In other words that most august of parliamentary committees is concerned about corruption, one aspect of placing private gain above the public interest.

Corruption, however, is not just about financial impropriety. There is a second form of corruption:

> which may be generally described as "the perversion or abandonment of a standard"... and which is consistent with other dictionary definitions, for example, to make putrid, to taint, to debase, to spoil, to destroy the purity of, and to pervert...
> (O'Toole 1993, p.1).

It is this form of corruption, this 'all-pervasive, more insidious and pernicious form of corruption', which may be more evident in the British body politic in the 1990s (O'Toole 1993, p. 1). It is a form of corruption which may fundamentally undermine the concept of public duty. For while the government may genuinely believe that the values of impartiality, integrity, objectivity, selection and promotion on merit and accountability are vital to the civil service, it may be that the current reform programmes do nothing to protect those values. Indeed, it may be argued that they fundamentally undermine the idea of the disinterestedness of public service.

The traditional methods of protecting both the values and the idea of public service, which together form the attributes of 'public duty', were those outlined above. The socialization process, in which values and modes of operation were passed from generation to generation, was particularly important. It may be that this process is being undermined by the increasingly specialist nature of government structures, the importation of 'business-like' techniques which place a premium on individual achievement and by the greater emphasis on relationships with private organizations rather than on internal collegial relationships.

The Treasury and Civil Service Committee may have recognized this, albeit inadvertently, when it noted (1994, Vol. I, para. 101) that:

> We do not agree with the Government that "the standards and ethics essential to the operation of the Civil Service... are well founded and well understood". No document relating to the ethics of the Civil Service states the essential values with sufficient clarity, and none communicates a clear and simple message to all civil servants and to the wider public about the standards to be upheld.

To remedy this defect the Committee recommended that there should be a new code for the civil service and 'that it should be a condition of employment of all civil servants that they read the Code and conduct themselves in accordance with its provisions' (para. 105). Was the Committee simply recognizing that the old methods of inculcating a public duty ethic were disappearing and that new methods needed to be established?

While the government did not agree with all the criticisms of the Treasury and Civil Service Committee in this part of its report, it nevertheless congratulated the Committee on the draft code it had published and published its own revised version of that code for further consultation (Cabinet Office 1995a, para. 11, p. 26 and pp. 43-5).

The code is merely a restatement of comments made in the various white papers and other official publications (including the famous Armstrong Memorandum) or in evidence to the Treasury and Civil Service Committee. For example: 'The constitutional and practical role of the Civil Service is, with integrity, honesty, impartiality and objectivity, to assist the duly constituted Government' (Cabinet Office 1995a, para. 1, p. 43). Or again, 'Civil servants should conduct themselves with integrity, impartiality and honesty in their dealings with Ministers and the public' (para. 5, p. 43). Further, civil servants:

> should conduct themselves in such a way as to deserve and retain the confidence of Ministers and to be able to establish the same relationship with those whom they may be required to serve in... future... They should comply with restrictions on their political activities. The conduct of civil servants should be such that Ministers... can be sure that... the Civil Service will conscientiously fulfil its duties and obligations to, and impartially assist, advise and carry out the policies of the duly constituted Government.
> (para. 9, p. 44)

In addition, civil servants 'should not make use of their official position or information acquired in the course of their official duties to further their private interests or those of others' (para. 8, p. 44).

In total the code is thirteen short paragraphs in length, comprising many of the sentiments which could together form at least a partial statement of 'public duty'. That is they would if 'public duty' could be said to exist in a vacuum. The restatement of conventional wisdom, albeit in the elevated form of a 'code', may well not be a sufficient substitute for acquiring an appreciation and acceptance of public duty by other means. This is especially true given the fact that the present government has, over seventeen years, been inculcating the spirit of enterprise, enthusiasm and entrepreneurship into the management of government. It is enterprise, enthusiasm and entrepreneurship which tend to elevate private over public interests.

Conclusion

One of the main problems with the Treasury and Civil Service Committee's proposed list of underlying values is that they are almost all applicable to other organizations as well as to the civil service. The logical question must be, is the civil service any different from other organizations? In the past there would be no equivocation about the answer. Today, there is precious little evidence that the government believes in public service. The introduction of performance-related pay, the ghettoization of agencies, the contracting out of services once thought central to the activities of government and the increasing lack of anonymity of civil servants – all undermine the idea of the disinterestedness of public service. Yet they are all compatible with the values listed by the Treasury and Civil Service Committee. As in business and commercial organizations, where the values listed are equally relevant, personal gain and personal glory are at a premium; the self-effacing and collegial values of the old civil service are discounted.

This may be no bad thing. The changes wrought on the civil service may well have brought significant improvements to the work of government. Time will be the judge of this dubious proposition. Moreover, the elitism and insularity of senior officials has been challenged. Perhaps this is as it should be. After all, it is democratic representatives who should be responsible for deciding what should be the values of public servants. However, most of the changes have been pushed through without much public debate – and, it must be said, without dissension from the major opposition parties. Indeed, the changes have been implemented almost by dictat. The result has been that these changes in the ethos of public service have received hardly any attention at all, and what little discussion there has been has been ill-informed and superficial. At a time when we are told that public officials should be accountable for their actions and when it is increasingly the case that senior civil servants publicly account for their own actions, questions ought to be raised about the accountability of our elected representatives for the changes they have introduced. There is little doubt that they have destroyed what has always been regarded as one of the cherished aspects of British public life. The concept of public duty is dead.

7 People or positions? Ensuring standards in the reformed public sector

Alan Doig

Introduction: culture and concern

The UK public sector has long been considered to be free from the levels and types of fraud and corruption practised on and by public officials in other industrialized countries, such as the USA (McKinney and Johnston 1986; De Leon 1993). It is assumed also to be free from the systematic misappropriation of funds and the political penetration of administrative activity that often characterizes developing countries (Theobald 1990; Williams 1987).

At its centre is a civil service whose past and present senior officials have emphasized the importance of a culture of personal probity and high standards of conduct as the core determinants of an image that has been accepted both internally and externally as the norm and the expectation for those in public office. The development of the civil service has been particularly noticeable for the way that image has been fashioned by the seriousness with which allegations against civil servants have been treated, often triggering off major inquiries that have been the occasion for general pronouncements on standards (see above, Chapter 2). While much attention has been given to such assumptions about high standards, much less attention has been given as to how are they inculcated and policed and to their effectiveness in the reformed public sector.

Such standards are said to have derived from a long tradition and culture of public responsibility and service, underpinned by specific anti-corruption legislation, internal conduct and disciplinary rules and various types of scrutiny provided by internal and external audit, the media, the police and the public. Professor Andrew Dunsire (1993, p. 321) has wondered whether this is the product of 'the fairly stringent system of rules and audit checks, or the relative lack of opportunity and temptation in most agencies of government, or the general climate of social opinion, or the high personal and corporate moral standards obtaining in most of the public service, which is most responsible for this state of affairs'. Together these factors appear to have provided the framework and context for high personal standards of conduct.

Nevertheless, in December 1993, the Audit Commission published a report on probity in local government. It argued that providing an anti-fraud culture and environment had been 'rendered more demanding and complex by numerous recent changes to the nature and operation of local government services. Many of the changes, such as the delegation of financial and management responsibilities, while contributing to improved quality of service, have increased the risks of fraud and corruption occurring' (Audit Commission 1993, p. 2). In January 1994 the Committee of Public Accounts (PAC) took the unusual step of issuing a general report on the basis of several of its earlier reports, stating that '...it is important to ensure that proper standards are maintained in the conduct of public business... it is even more essential to maintain honesty in the spending of public money and to ensure that traditional public sector values are not neglected in the effort to maximise economy and efficiency' (PAC 1994a, paras. 3 and 6). In May 1995 the Nolan Committee issued its first report, stating that 'changes in the public sector have increased the need to take action...it cannot be assumed that everyone in the public service will assimilate a public service culture unless they are told what is expected of them and the message is systematically reinforced. The principles inherent in the ethic of public service need to be set out afresh' (Nolan 1995, para. 10).

Some twenty years ago the Royal Commission on Standards of Conduct in Public Life reported that: 'our evidence convinces us that the safeguards against malpractice in the public sector are in need of review' (Salmon 1976, p. 12). Honesty among public officials is again an issue of concern.

Setting a good example to others: firefighting and the failure to reform

Many of the assumptions or images of such standards rest on the socializing impact that tradition, continuity and incrementalism has had on those entering public life. In particular it has been seen in the civil service as setting the standard for organization and conduct. The recruitment process, the long apprenticeships, the steady immersion in the norms and workings of a complex administrative structure, the working relationships, the expectation of a lifetime in the service, the promotion criteria and, especially, the care not to step outside the mores of the Whitehall 'village' (Helco and Wildavsky 1981) – all these things in combination are thought to underline the homogeneity, longevity and cohesiveness which in turn serve to perpetuate and reinforce the standards expected of all new officials. They 'become quickly aware, if they did not know it already, that they are entering an organisation in which high standards of conduct and probity are the tradition, and the norm...It is the feeling of belonging to an organisation which places, and rightly places, enormous emphasis on probity and high moral values, which will cause its members to react instinctively in the right way when faced with temptation or conflicts of interest' (Russell 1993, p. 8).

Sir Robin Butler, the current Head of the Home Civil Service, has himself indicated that civil servants would 'pick up a sense of right and wrong in public administration through the traditional way of "apprenticeship from their seniors"' (Thomas 1993, p. 57). Furthermore, those imparting such guidance are themselves very clear about the importance of that mentor role. Sir Frank Cooper, former Permanent Secretary at the MoD, drew the attention of the Treasury and Civil Service Committee to the 'absolutely major and fundamental charge' on senior officials in departments for probity and standards. As he put it, once 'you lose integrity in any way, the rot sets in throughout the whole department really remarkably quickly' (TCSC 1984, Q. 222).

In such circumstances, it is hardly surprising that, during the twentieth century, other factors which could underpin standards have invariably been treated as supplementary to, or dependent for their effectiveness on, pervasive personal honesty and integrity. These include anti-corruption legislation, the last of the three Acts having been introduced in 1916; internal rules on code, developed incrementally since the previous century; and rules introduced in the 1930s on post-resignation or post-retirement moves to positions in the private sector. The same is true elsewhere in the public sector. For example, legislation on conflicts of interest in local government and disciplinary regulations in police forces owe their existence to early twentieth century reforms. Wider issues, from public participation to formal and informal monitoring and scrutiny, such as audit or the media, have been accorded probity or watchdog roles, but how such roles were enacted, as well as their effectiveness, have usually been imperfectly defined or pursued.

Nevertheless, questions about the inadequacies or ineffectiveness of the means and procedures to inculcate or underpin high standards of conduct were rarely tested. This reflected both the pervasive expectations of high personal standards, themselves an effective self-policing mechanism, and the likelihood of some form of official inquiry where there was concern about standards anywhere in the public service, no matter how much that concern may appear trivial in terms of today. Thus in 1956 the Home Office ordered an inquiry by a QC into allegations made by members of the Cardiganshire Police Authority against its chief constable in connection with the misuse of office and favouritism in promotions. The Minister of Housing and Local Government ordered an inquiry in 1965 into apparent conflicts of interest in Bognor Regis UDC. With reference to that inquiry, the Committee on the Management of Local Government (Maud Committee) emphasized the importance of 'people of integrity' in local politics as well as the vigilance of the press and the threat of public opinion to ensure high standards (Ministry of Housing and Local Government 1967, para. 548). In 1971 the Crown Agents, the public body responsible for providing a range of procurement, training and project services for overseas governments and commonwealth countries, was the subject of three major inquiries, including the rarely used quasi-judicial tribunal of inquiry. This followed losses consequent upon ill-judged speculative forays into the property market. The tribunal's report, issued in 1982, noted that the Crown Agents had exploited Whitehall secrecy, territoriality and inaction (Croom-Johnson 1982, paras. 19.02-19.20). This they had done initially to enhance pension funds against possible closure, but then, later, in order to make money on own-account activities and to indulge in increasingly unethical conduct. This had been the result of incompetence and errors of judgement largely, as one the earlier reports put it, having lost its way 'in a spiritual sense' when failing to follow staff rules and civil service standards.

The most fulsome appreciation of the existence and the centrality of personal standards came from the 1976 Royal Commission on Standards of Conduct in Public Life which was established primarily because of the Poulson affair. A Yorkshire-based architect, John Poulson had exploited contacts from every area in public life to obtain contracts, using the resources of his architectural practice to provide both rewards and incentives to those in public office (Tomkinson and Gillard 1980; Fitzwalter and Taylor 1981). His success came partly from developing a series of companies to offer a comprehensive architectural and design service that was especially attractive to smaller councils, partly from the recruitment of T. Dan Smith, an energetic and ambitious former North-East Labour politician, to market that service through a series of public relations companies organized by Smith but which were funded by Poulson. Together they targeted key council figures, officials and politicians, to whom jobs as consultants or other benefits were offered in return for or in anticipation of the award of design and building contracts.

The volume of Poulson's work expanded rapidly during the 1960s when councils had access to substantial capital and revenue funds for redevelopment but where there was insufficient regional planning co-ordination or central government monitoring to ensure the most effective and efficient use of those funds. Despite his success, Poulson failed to pay his tax bills and his subsequent bankruptcy at the start of the 1970s revealed the range of his contacts not only across the public sector but upward into Westminster and Whitehall. The initial response of the Conservative government was to establish the Prime Minister's Committee on Local Government Rules of Conduct under Lord Redcliffe-Maud (Cabinet Office 1974). It reported that, 'despite widespread current disquiet', local government was 'essentially honest' (Cabinet Office 1974, para. 1). But this failed to allay growing public concern over the extent of Poulson's bribery. This, together with media and police exposure of a number of similar but unrelated cases of public sector fraud and corruption, persuaded the Labour government in 1974 to set up the Royal Commission on Standards of Conduct in Public Life under Lord Salmon. Both reports made a series of sensible if mundane recommendations. While both inquiries focused on the behaviour and procedures under investigation, their recommendations went wider, implicitly encompassing what may be termed an anti-fraud or an ethical environment. In so doing they highlighted many of the factors intended to underpin high standards of conduct. These ranged from strengthening the direct enforcement of probity in public life – through means such as the law, the ventilation of complaints or allegations and the powers of those who investigate them – to promoting the more open, accountable conduct of public business.

The report of the Prime Minister's Committee proposed the introduction of a general oral disclosure and a register of interests for both councillors and officials; a national code of conduct covering financial and non-financial interests; policies on investigating complaints and publicizing local authority activities; police access (on 'reasonable grounds') to the financial affairs of individuals or organizations; new procedures on the award of contracts; the ability of the local ombudsman to report crime to the police; an extension of the exercise of discretionary powers under the 1916 Prevention of Corruption Act; the introduction of rules of conduct for party group meetings; and, finally, an exhortation for the public to report suspected corruption. The Royal Commission reiterated or expanded the Committee's recommendations in relation to local authorities, public bodies, political parties and the local ombudsman (who, it argued, should be allowed to look at contracts). It proposed a revamped, co-ordinated Prevention of Corruption Act (including a new offence of corruptly using official information for personal advantage); a reporting structure for complaints of corruption to the police; and the inclusion of MPs within the ambit of the criminal law. It also proposed reforms intended to encourage transparency of and access to decision-making; to promote awareness of conflicts of interest, including the use of registers and codes; to regulate moves to the private sector and to encourage high standards of conduct. In relation to moves to the private sector, it noted that civil service arrangements served a useful purpose in maintaining public confidence. Civil service standards, it said 'might usefully be taken as a model by other public sector institutions' (Salmon 1976, p. 42, p. 63). The Royal Commission laid particular emphasis on its belief that there was no evidence to cause 'concern about the integrity and sense of public duty'. It stressed that one of the main safeguards against corruption was 'the standard set and required by the management from the top downwards. This depends on *esprit de corps*, which can be seriously damaged by systems of regulation and scrutiny so rigorous that they inhibit leadership by management and imply that people working in the organisation are unworthy of trust' (Salmon 1976, para. 42, p. 12).

Most of the recommendations of both inquiries were never implemented, an unfortunate development since the Royal Commission had indicated reviewing areas that were later to become causes for concern, including the regulation of public bodies, the role of management, the role of internal audit and the importance of personal standards. Both Labour and Conservative governments deflected calls for reform. When in 1979 Labour MP Jeff Rooker asked Conservative Home Secretary William Whitelaw what proposals he had in mind to improve standards of conduct, the latter replied: 'to set a good example to others' (Doig 1984, pp. 345-6).

Continuity within change?

Of the handful of recommendations that were implemented, the majority focused on local government. But they were neither implemented uniformly nor tailored to local circumstances. There was little evidence of any 'local authority initiative and response to local conditions', while what was introduced was not likely 'to create an easy environment in which to interpret acceptable standards' (Parker *et al* 1986, p. 110, p. 112). Furthermore, some of the other areas looked at by the inquiries as means to underpin standards equally failed to match expectations. The intended police overview of potential cross-council fraud and corruption was not effectively implemented, while most of the efforts of dedicated fraud squads were increasingly consumed by the rising levels of private sector fraud (Doig 1995b; Levi, 1993). The national and local media never developed an effective role as a means of external reporting or scrutiny (Franklin and Murphy 1991; Doig 1992). At the same time, levels of public interest in local politics remained low, as did voting, attendance at council meetings and active membership of political parties (Lynn 1992, p. 38).

Thus, while such official inquiries have been seen as evidence of governments' willingness to react positively to allegations of fraud and corruption, condemning the particular behaviour under investigation while reaffirming the general integrity of the public sector, general public sector or legislative reform has not usually been an implemented outcome. There has been an invariable lack of interest in or formal response by governments and by Parliament to the conclusions and recommendations of such enquiries. Official inquiries may fulfil a public interest function as a response to political or public concern – the response to the attention cycle (Williams 1985). But their main purpose is to determine responsibility in terms of individuals and their motivation rather than to stimulate organizational or functional reform (Clarke 1981). Thus they inevitably end up as firefighting exercises – *ad hoc* attempts to confront, resolve and close a particular incident or set of circumstances where the individual behaviour is presented as the prime cause of fraud and corruption rather than the context in which they occurred. This is the classic 'black sheep' or 'rotten apple' argument.

Instead of reform reliance is placed in a belief that history, committed leadership, tradition and discipline develop a self-perpetuating public service culture and ethic. Such an ethic is seen as being at once both reinforced by and an integral element of organizational structures and practices with clearly defined responsibilities and supervision based on routine, precedent and procedure with an emphasis on stability, certainty, caution, uniformity, impartiality and continuity.

For political reformers in the 1980s, however, these qualities were also symptomatic of large bureaucratic public sector organizations, with procedures dominated by rigidity or incrementalism rather than creativity and enterprise. They reflected organizational views that appeared immune to political wishes, with overcentralized structures and ever increasing levels of expenditure. The short reference in the 1979 Conservative manifesto to the reduction of waste, bureaucracy and overgovernment as promising substantial savings has been elevated to a blueprint for reform. In fact it was a general phrase to deal with the cost and size of government. Unlike the Fulton Report, which proposed management reform within a given public service framework, there was no blueprint, no milestones and no goal. Sir Robin Butler, Head of the Home Civil Service, has said that he does not know what the final shape of the civil service will be: 'it is not unusual, I guess, for an organisation in the process of evolution not to know what its final state will be' (Dynes and Walker 1995, p. 99).

The process was and is a continuous reduction in the size and cost of the public sector – a Conservative version of the withering away of the state so beloved of Marxist theorists. It betrays an underlying belief that the private sector approach provides the model, if not to deliver public services then for a reduced public sector to follow for the delivery of public services. While the government sought to sell off or privatize its commercial or trading assets and activities, its approach within the public sector was initially to reduce expenditure, cut back on the growth of non-departmental public bodies (NDPBs) and, in relation to the civil service, conduct a series of reviews of administrative costs and activities. The Rayner scrutinies were followed by the Financial Management Initiative (FMI), encouraged by the Treasury and Civil Service Committee's enthusiasm for programme management expenditure and for line management budgetary control and responsibility. FMI sought to introduce a financial and management information system as the basis for continuous good management practice through cost awareness and devolved but responsible management. Its intention was to introduce more measures of achievement, targets for individual managers who would be held accountable for achieving an agreed level of performance.

The patchiness and slowness of the changes within the civil service, the ingrained Whitehall culture, the lack of ministerial interest in systematic reform, the lack of effective devolution for responsibility over costs and the reported frustration below senior management level – all this, together with the low level of financial savings, led the Efficiency Unit to produce the Next Steps report in 1988 as the vehicle to overcome the lack of urgency. It sought to alter 'cultural attitudes and behaviour of government so that continuous improvement becomes a widespread and inbuilt feature of it' (Efficiency Unit 1988, para. 1, p. 1). Its main proposals were for departments to be shrunk, focusing on policy and ministers while the bulk of the executive functions would pass to delivery agencies, not necessarily staffed by civil servants or working to civil service pay and conditions of service. This would create the organizational context for cultural change from public to private sector values. With the same intention this approach was echoed in different ways across the public sector as the 1987 General Election heralded radical organizational and structural reform – competing for quality and market testing; internal markets; devolution; compulsory competitive tendering (CCT); local management in schools (LMS); local force management; and the extended use of funding through NDPBs as well as through voluntary and private sector bodies – all to create the context for similar change (Wilson and Doig 1996).

The intended shift in culture from caution and risk-avoidance to risk-taking (Metcalfe and Richards 1990), from the anonymous application of rules to individual, responsive and dynamic management control (Willson 1991) has created 'significant amounts of organisational turbulence' (Flynn 1992, p. 67). Public officials have been required to take on, without substantial training, new, often complex, managerial roles – including inter-agency negotiation, political accountability, customer service delivery, competitive tendering, budgetary and financial management, property management, purchasing, locally determined pay and conditions and new technology. This has been taking place within a context of change which still assumes the existence of 'a culture of public service honesty' (Hood 1991a, p. 16). Yet it is one whose recipes have to some degree 'removed devices instituted to ensure honesty and neutrality in the public service in the past (fixed salaries, rules of procedure, permanence of tenure, restraints on the power of line management, clear lines of division between public and private sectors)' (Hood 1991a, p. 16).

The speed, purpose and complexity of change by and within organizations have also thrown up a number of issues concerning job security. Conversely, there have arisen issues concerning the opportunities offered by buy-outs and privatization, by the sometimes conflicting objectives of speed of delivery, by cost-cutting and by performance by results against those of due process, procedure and precedent. The development of a management culture within a public service context and the consequential changes in approaches to work, performance and integrity would, it could be assumed, also require change, rather than mere assumptions, in order to reassess and amend the public service ethical framework as part of a wider guidance given to public officials on the proper conduct of public business. As one observer has put it:

> to treat the establishment of the conditions for effective achievement of public purposes and the resolution of conflicts between efficiency and effectiveness in the public sector as questions of "managerial discretion" is either simple-minded or question-begging on a huge scale. The enormous complexity of defining public purposes and translating these into objectives and targets; of establishing machinery to integrate and co-ordinate different bodies; of monitoring the outcomes of action and inaction and the environment in which public policy operates, all require learning processes.
> (Birkinshaw *et al* 1990, p. 165)

This would be more pertinent where changes are showing up examples of behaviour, attitudes and decisions within the development of a management culture in a public service context that may have led to a 'misunderstanding among public servants about the quasi-private sector environment... (and)... inaccurate perceptions of private sector values and practices' (Harrow and Gillett 1994, p. 4). This reflects the concern expressed by the PAC about the 'number of serious failures in administrative and financial systems and controls within departments and other public bodies, which have led to money being wasted or otherwise improperly spent', as well as failures 'in key areas of financial control, compliance with rules, the stewardship of public money and assets, and generally getting value for the taxpayer's money' (PAC 1994a, paras 1 and 3).

Despite these warnings little attention had been given to standards of conduct or to the potential for conflicts of interest, corruption or fraud during this period. The Ibbs Report acknowledged that organizational and cultural change would require a redefinition of ministerial accountability and the accountability of agencies to the PAC and to other select committees. It was dismissive of the existing means of monitoring any adverse effects of change, saying that: 'Pressure from Parliament, the Public Accounts Committee and the media tends to concentrate on alleged impropriety or incompetence, and making political points, rather than on demanding evidence of steadily improving efficiency and effectiveness' (Efficiency Unit 1988, para. 9, p. 4).

The report also stated, though, that the role of the 'centre of government' included a requirement 'to set and police essential rules on propriety for the public service in carrying out its essential functions' (para. 33, p. 12). In a context in which the Treasury and Civil Service Committee (1990, para. 61) was praising departments for their 'hands-off approach' to agencies and inviting them to pursue 'cultural change' and 'a large scale re-writing of the rule-book', so ministers and senior civil servants have been downplaying their role as setters and policers of the rules on propriety.

Sir Robin Butler has indicated that standards are picked up through 'apprenticeship', specific training not being necessary, while Hayden Phillips, now Permanent Secretary at the Department of National Heritage, put his trust in an 'organic and adaptable' ethos whose 'essential principles do not change, but the ethos itself accommodates itself to movements in the society of which the Civil Service is a part' (Phillips 1993, p. 57). Other pronouncements have been similarly bland. Richard Luce, then Minister for the Civil Service, and Sir Robin Butler have talked of 'common standards' across a 'unified but not a uniform Civil Service' (TCSC 1989, Q. 320). In 1990 Mr Luce referred to the need, within the framework of the maximum possible delegation of authority, to ensure that the 'very important principles and traditions' were upheld in relation to 'the impartiality of the service, to the high standards of propriety in the Service, to the maintenance of principles of accountability within the Service...' (TCSC 1990, Q. 145).

The government itself has insisted that Next Steps offers 'all future governments an effective and adaptable Civil Service, with all its traditional values of propriety and impartiality intact...' (OMCS 1991, p. 13). Such values have, according to Sir Robin Butler, remained unscathed and unchanged during the years of change (TCSC 1993 Vol. II, Q. 102). Indeed, as late as July 1994, the government was suggesting that various initiatives, such as the Citizen's Charter, FMI and Next Steps agencies had in themselves 'promoted greater transparency' and strengthened 'accountability to both Parliament and the public' (Cabinet Office 1994a, paras. 2.26-7). It also argued that the existing Civil Service Management Code was sufficient to 'ensure that the defining principles and standards of the Civil Service (are) not relaxed and (that) they continue to be mandatory for all departments and agencies' (para. 2.33). Nevertheless, the environment from which the traditional public service ethic developed has changed substantially, as have the means believed to underpin standards. Added to the general areas of internal and external weaknesses already noted, the impact of change on issues raised by the 1976 Royal Commission has brought into question the continued assumptions about self-sustaining standards of conduct.

Attitudes, accountability and audit

The 1976 Royal Commission pointed out that 'the ethics of society at large must have a bearing on the standards observed in the public sector. Members and officials of public bodies are but individuals living in a particular society at a particular time' (Salmon 1976, para. 30, p. 10). The economic climate engendered by the Conservative government since 1979 has been one of promoting entrepreneurial activity, removing controls from commercial, economic and financial sectors, and of promoting financial gain as a reward for and as an indicator of worth and hard work. Yet it is also one in which the accumulation of wealth, the display of material success and the promotion of personal ambition has left a downside of greed, acquisitiveness and pursuit of individual ambition. Some have been prepared to use companies for personal ends and to cut corners to achieve status and capital. It has been claimed that their sense of self-importance has convinced them that the rules need not fetter their genius, believing that they are simply doing the best for their shareholders or employees. But, as one prominent City solicitor warned in the 1988 BBC Hibbert Lecture: 'with licensed greed creeps in the dry rot of corruption. For the value-system which tolerates the one will not be likely to resist the other, if that is necessary to achieve "success"' (Phillips 1988, p. 11).

This secularization of attitudes to personal gain has also been reflected elsewhere in society. The 1985 British Social Attitudes survey that noted that perceptions of right and wrong and of fairness and acceptability were affected by motive, social group or generational norms. One of the surveys found that: 'where laws or rules are known to be at odds with common practice, as in the case of tipping dustmen or evading VAT, people in all subgroups tended to come down in favour of practice; or at least they did not judge breaches of the rules very harshly' (Johnston and Wood 1985, p. 138). A 1994 survey of 1,022 interviewees by Research Surveys of Great Britain found that 'fiddling' social security payments was acceptable because need rather than greed appeared to be the cause, while 'fiddling' income tax may be determined by what individuals perceive as 'fair' (*Sunday Times* 10 April 1994, p. 5). A similar survey by *Moneywise Magazine* (April 1995, p. 56) reported that the younger the person, the lower the ethical standards, with one commentator warning of 'a worrying trend... (with) fewer and fewer sources of guidance and standards for young people to follow'.

It is not suggested that the morals of the marketplace have universally replaced the ethic of public service. Nevertheless, ambition and the opportunity for self-enrichment are powerful motivators. They may compromise the public service ethic at a time when the public sector is being fragmented, when the primacy of change and the promotion of private sector values, practices and personnel make the question of maintaining standards, both individually and organizationally, a matter of concern. A 1993 survey of NHS trust boards reported that 'a substantial minority' of members would condone otherwise unacceptable behaviour in certain circumstances (including those relating to contract information and following Standing Orders). In findings that the survey regarded as 'highly statistically significant', those with the most permissive attitudes were those who were executive directors, many of whom had 'gained the majority of their previous work experience within the NHS' (West and Shaeff 1994, p. 26). Similarly an Audit Commission report (1993, para. 69) on probity in local government noted that 'in some authorities there has been a reluctance by members to acknowledge that a problem exists... Few authorities have considered or produced strategy statements which emphasize to all employees the importance placed by the authority on probity, financial control and honest administration'. At the same time HM Customs and Excise was reporting that it was 'going through a period of unprecedented change. As well as providing significant benefits, reorganisation and delegation and new ways of doing things will need to be carried through without jeopardising the more traditional controls and safeguards that underpin the Department's commitment to integrity and honesty' (National Audit Office 1994, para. 3.2).

The Royal Commission had noted that 'the fortunes of companies and individuals have undoubtedly been increasingly influenced by the decisions of central government and other public institutions' (Salmon 1976, para. 36, p. 11). This is something that can be particularly problematical when either or both work within the public sector and where an over-reliance on personal standards without adequate controls creates an environment in which those with their own agenda or ambitions can realize them as a consequence of the pace of change, the lack of supervision and in the absence of prevailing assumptions about a general adherence to those standards. These may range from the number of staff-organized frauds against funds held by the Public Trust Office on behalf of those with mental incapacity (PAC 1994c) to the Forward Civil Service catering department's attention to possible privatization that led to a failure to maintain financial control and allegations of deals with suppliers, massaged performance figures, fraud, conflict of interest and tax evasion (PAC 1993c). It embraces such as the controversies over a management buy-out of West Wiltshire District Council's software programmes activities and sale of council land, against a background of serious weaknesses in the Council's committee and decision making structures (Doig 1995c).

The Royal Commission of 1976 also recommended that the relevant 'government departments should review the bodies for which they are responsible', as well as NHS bodies, on issues such as disclosure of interests and codes of conduct (Salmon 1976, para. 162, p. 46). The Management and Personnel Office (1985) and the Treasury laid down a set of guidelines to establish formally the parameters of independence, autonomy and accountability within which new and existing NDBPs were expected to have 'good standards of management', including standards of conduct and internal management budget and information systems (NHS bodies and Next Steps agencies were later to be excluded from such a requirement). Sponsoring departments were expected to review management and control systems and practices, communicate information on ministerial priorities and policies, and to receive costed proposals for future work and the allocation of resources. But the prime responsibility for maintaining high standards of management in carrying out its functions rested with the relevant NDPB (Doig 1988). There was, however, a lack of attention given by sponsoring bodies to the parameters of NDPBs' independence, autonomy and powers. This led in some cases to the latter's embrace of governmental enthusiasm for managerial autonomy and entrepreneurialism. The Development Board for Rural Wales was criticized for unusual arrangements and expenditure relating to the retirement of its chief executive as well as the allocation of housing stock on the basis of unpublished rules and changes to car leasing arrangements (PAC 1992; 1994b). The Sports Council has been criticized for weakened accountability and control over publicly funded assets and services. This, according to the PAC (1995a), was made more serious by the lack of a clear arm's length relationship between the bodies forming the Council Group and by inadequate arrangements to prevent conflicts of duty following the creation of a number of trading companies with staff and members involved in the Council and its commercial companies. The Welsh Development Agency (WDA) was taken to task for, among other things, appointing a director of marketing who had previous convictions for deception. It was also taken to task for using public funds (concealed within the Agency's accounts) to pay consultants to consider options for the future of the Agency, including that of privatization (PAC 1993b). The Welsh Office was subsequently criticized by the PAC (1995b) for its failure to exercise effective authority over the WDA. Yet the Committee simply repeated the much earlier hope that: 'without undue interference in their sponsored bodies' policies and detailed conduct of business, the Welsh Office will pursue a more assertive role to provide a strong lead in helping to ensure the high standard of accountability and financial management that Parliament is entitled to expect in bodies largely supported by public funds' (PAC 1987, para. 32).

The 1976 Royal Commission's enthusiasm for the importance of responsible management in defining and determining standards presupposed the primacy of the public sector context, but one that the changes of the 1980s has significantly weakened. For example, the West Midlands RHA appointed a director to bring with him a new 'culture'. This led to the hiring of management consultants at substantial cost, allegedly at variance with standing orders and financial regulations. Allegations of 'grave weaknesses in management and accountability' were supplemented by further concerns over an unorthodox £7m consultancy contract to introduce an electronic trading system, a failed management buy-out underwritten by the Authority, loans to a company in financial difficulties, the employment of outside consultants for staff appointments, the withholding of funds owed to DHAs and various unusual arrangements concerning terms and conditions of service (PAC 1993d). In another case, the external auditor had submitted to the Wessex RHA and to the NHS Management Executive (NHSME) between February 1987 and August 1990 a series of reports detailing criticisms of the development of the IT strategy, the financial controls, the use of contract staff, the control of consultants, contract and procurement procedures, and project management. The NHSME told the PAC that they had sent the reports to senior management because Board members 'had not shown expertise in this complex field' (PAC 1993e, Q. 32). They had not intervened because it was not their role to run health authorities: 'the statutory arrangements and the lines of accountability' left the prime responsibility for what went wrong with the RHA (Q. 149).

Finally, the 1976 Royal Commission proposed as best practice the extension of internal financial audit into reviews of efficiency and the observance of procedural requirements, including safeguards against malpractice. Such safeguards would act as a deterrent against improprieties. Responsibility for ensuring the effectiveness of procedures and systems and for reporting on their utility in the prevention and detection of fraud or corruption has, however, not been realized in practice. In 1987 the Comptroller and Auditor General reviewed the comments made in 1981 by his predecessor about weaknesses in relation to the NHS internal audit, noting that 'most had not achieved the defined minimum acceptable level of audit coverage' (National Audit Office 1987b, para. 14). At the same time he also noted his predecessor's comments on internal audit in central government: 'the overall standard of internal audit in central government was substantially below the level needed to fulfil its recommended role. Weaknesses noted included lack of professionalism among staff; fragmented responsibility for duties, structuring and staffing; inadequate computer audit capability; and a general failure to appreciate the benefit of a strong internal audit' (NAO 1987a, para. 1). Again, five years later, he was reporting that, while the Internal Audit Development Division of the Treasury was bringing reform to internal audit and that internal audit staff were carrying out their work in a way that would reveal significant defects in internal control systems, departmental internal audit 'still have some way to go to achieve an adequate standard...' (NAO 1987a, para. 3.35). Thus the £9.4m MoD efficiency incentive scheme which should have benefited the defence community as a whole was used for high volume, low cost items of personal or social benefit because of a lack of guidance about how and for whom the money should have been spent (PAC 1993a). Wessex RHA's expenditure of over £40m on a sophisticated IT strategy led the district auditor to report that budgetary control was so weak that not until half way through the following financial year had it been possible to estimate with any accuracy the total commitment for the earlier year and that no internal audit work had been carried out between 1985-89 when £38m was spent (PAC 1993e).

Conclusion: back to basics – probity in public office

There is the tendency to dismiss the above examples as occurring at the periphery of government, reflecting the teething problems of change and therefore not representative of standards among mainstream government departments. But there are now 3,000 devolved units of recruitment monitored by the Office of the Civil Service Commissioners. Some two-thirds of all civil servants are working in Next Steps-type agencies and there are 150 pay bargaining units (see above, Chapter 5). This raises the question as to what is or will be the mainstream of the reformed but shrinking public sector (see above, Chapter 2). An equally important issue concerns internal accountability and officials' terms and conditions. While currently within the public service ethos, officials are more likely to begin to see themselves as the employees of a specific organization. While the Ibbs Report denied the concept of a unified civil service and blamed uniformity of pay and grading as a deterrent to effective management, the Next Steps concept militates against current patterns of movement, shared ethos and organizational cohesion. Instead, according to the Head of the Home Civil Service in 1988, the unifying framework would develop from the 'requirements of equity, accountability, impartiality and a wide view of the public interest' (Drewry and Butcher 1991, p. 237). But little thought was given as to how this would be achieved in a fragmented framework.

Those who have been criticized for serious failures in administrative and financial systems and for inadequate controls, be they within departments or in other public bodies, have often rushed to introduce or enforce the controls and procedures that should have existed in the first place. Such controls and procedures include the separation of duties, financial systems, training, tendering and contracts review and management, improved budgetary and financial control and improvements in the standard and style of reporting decisions. Similarly, supervising bodies like the NHS Executive or the Welsh Office have promised codes, procedures, controls, audit committees, compliance reviews and efficiency scrutinies. The real issue, however, is that, while there is no evidence of widespread fraud or corruption, the speed and direction of devolved managerial autonomy, together with the promotion of an entrepreneurial culture and of potential market testing or privatization as a goal for public sector organizations, have, when added to the various organizational, operational and procedural weaknesses identified in earlier decades, raised questions about the risk of misconduct among public sector officials and organizations. There have been further and related questions about the weakening of the public sector ethos and ethical environment, the impact of private sector perspectives within a public sector context, the inevitable balance between public service and personal benefit and about the implications of change on existing but ill-defined relationships of accountability, monitoring and control. The question then becomes: if personal standards of conduct are shown to have been wanting, if the socialization processes that would previously have ensured high standards of conduct prior to entering public service are shown to be weakening and if the various factors that are supposed to underpin those high standards are shown to be inadequate, ineffectual or irrelevent, then what should be introduced?

In responding to these questions there is a perceptible dichotomy between the pragmatists and the traditionalists. The Nolan Committee represents the latter, having been set up largely, though not entirely, because the traditional assumption of a consensual Commons approach to standards of conduct and the reliance on prudence, common sense and honour have been tested and found wanting in relation to those MPs who wished to use their parliamentary position for financial gain, or whose sexual proclivities appeared at variance with the government's 'back to basics' view of personal morality. It became very clear during the 1980s that what constituted a relevant financial interest in terms of registration and declaration had become the subject of elastic interpretation by MPs, especially where there was a correspondence between pursuit of personal financial interests and support for government policies. This elasticity began to affect the wider body of MPs, including the Select Committee on Members' Interests, the supervisory body which investigates alleged breaches of the rules. What individual MPs see as conflict of interest, corruption or, alternatively, as an acceptable way of representing an interest can vary substantially. As one observer put it: 'in cases of alleged conflict of interest the circumstances of the time, the form and place of the official's action, and the interpretation to be put on the action, as well as the intention of the official are all relative factors and opinion may reasonably differ as to the importance to be attached to each of them' (Williams 1985, p. 17). Without a shared understanding of relevance, honour, acceptable conduct and so on, research at the end of the 1980s suggested that, by continuing to allow MPs to depend on their own judgment and 'in the absence of the underlying ethical consensus it relies upon', there could develop 'a progressive legitimization of behaviour that is more and more removed from the original boundaries of probity' (Mancuso 1993, p. 181). Certainly, the conduct of senior Conservative MPs in relation to the receipt and disclosure of moneys offered in pursuit of sectional interests caused sufficient public concern, at a time of general disquiet over the private interests of those in public life (as well as those in the privatized utilities), to persuade the prime minister to establish the Nolan Committee in October 1994 (Ridley and Doig 1996).

The Nolan Committee's terms of reference required it: 'to examine current concerns about standards of conduct of all holders of public office, including arrangements relating to financial and commercial activities, and to make any recommendations as to any changes in present arrangements which might be required to ensure the highest standards of propriety in public life'. Its purview therefore embraced elected and appointed members and senior officials across the public sector. The Committee issued its first report in May 1995. After arguing that there was public anxiety about standards of conduct in public life, that cases of sexual misconduct were increasingly being reported by the media, that changes to the public sector had had an impact on conduct and that there appeared to be uncertainty over what was right and wrong in public life, it appeared to tread the well-worn path of championing personal standards of conduct as the key to a return to the high standards it believed once to have existed. It reflected the argument of the 1974 Prime Minister's Committee that 'Public life requires a standard of its own; and those entering public office for the first time must be made aware of this from the outset' (Cabinet Office 1974, para. 76) In similar vein the Nolan Committee (1995, para. 7) called for 'a degree of austerity' and a 'respect for the traditions of upright behaviour'.

To achieve this, it proposed seven principles of public life – selflessness, integrity, objectivity, accountability, openness, honesty and leadership. These were to be underpinned by codes of conduct, internal systems supported by 'independent scrutiny and monitoring' and 'guidance and education' in three areas: Parliament; ministers and civil servants; and NDPBs. The Committee accepted the tradition of paid employment for MPs, but recommended that there should be clearer information in the register as well as a ban on working for multi-client lobby firms. Integrity would be assured through a code of conduct and an independent commissioner for standards. There would be similar supervisory arrangements for appointments to NDPBs. Such appointments should, said Nolan, be made on merit, with political affiliations declared and, again, each NDPB should draw up a code of conduct. Codes were also called for in connection with ministers and civil servants, the former to be subject to rules similar to those already applicable to the latter upon seeking a move to the private sector within two years of leaving office.

To underpin its call for 'a degree of austerity' and respect for the traditions of upright behaviour in British public life the Committee also looked to other traditional means. It suggested that the media have 'a duty to enquire – coupled with a duty to do so responsibly – and in that way contribute to the preservation of standards in public life' (Nolan 1995, para. 5). Nolan further observed (para. 16) that 'internal systems must be supported by independent scrutiny and monitoring', part of which will be 'routinely performed by auditors', but which in certain circumstances would be the responsibility of an independent body to 'oversee the framework within which actions are taken and to monitor compliance... (as) an additional safeguard in maintaining public confidence'. Finally, the Nolan Committee set its faith in induction training, formulating key ethical standards, monitoring awareness and setting 'a good example' (para. 17).

This approach very much reflects a focus on the person. A more realistic approach would take a much more instrumental view of standards, focusing on the position or procedure. If the opportunity and incentive for misconduct exists, potentialy accentuated by the current climate of change, managerialism and uncertainty, and if the possibility of detection (and, even more so, of punishment) remains low (for the present), then the previous over reliance on individual discretion and judgement must become an area of vulnerability and risk. By contrast, the focus coming from the PAC, NAO and the Audit Commission is more the denial of opportunity and incentive, with an increased risk of detection and punishment, looking less to the individual than to the position and where the controls, procedures and supervision focuses on what is done and how it is done, rather than by whom it is done. This may be preferable to Nolan's faith in the principles of public life with all the attendant questions as to how they are to be achieved. Thus the PAC (1994a) report provides a checklist of controls that should be established. These include: proper, working financial systems; effective accounting and validating arrangements; procedure reviews; trained and experienced staff; supervision of NDPB activities together with clear guidance on accountability, expenditure and responsibility; avoidance of conflict of interest; open competition; transparency of necessary information and disciplinary procedures. Similarly the Audit Commission (1993) report on probity in local government reflects a range of intra- and inter-organizational initiatives that are not only procedure and audit based but which are amenable to verification and monitoring in a way that cannot be secured solely by a focus on the individual; while its 1994 report on probity in the NHS focuses on checks, 'data-mining' systems, audit committees, fraud and corruption response plans, risk assessment and improved liaison with the police (Audit Commission 1994). While this approach does not deny the value of personal standards of conduct, it does not make them the core or the predominant factor but rather a component, albeit an important one, within an ethical environment.

It is too early to say whether the Nolan or the auditors' approach will prevail. Of course, it must be remembered that nearly all the cases of misconduct highlighted in recent years have been discovered by either the National Audit Office or by District Audit. But the clearly announced enthusiasm for the latter agencies to pursue both the implementation of their recommendations as well as to make probity a major issue over the next few years seems likely to be more effective in achieving high standards of conduct in the new public sector than the wistful yearnings of the Nolan Committee for the return of the primacy of personal standards of conduct that would appear, like the baby, to have been thrown away with the bathwater of public sector reform.

8   Public interest immunity in criminal trials and public administration*

John McEldowney

Introduction

The Matrix Churchill trial collapsed in November 1992 (Leigh 1993; Sweeney 1993). This trial and the publication of the subsequent inquiry undertaken by Sir Richard Scott has directed attention to a complex and confusing area of law known as public interest immunity. The aim of this chapter is to consider the law of public interest immunity in the broader context of its relevance to public administration.

Public interest immunity is a ground for refusing disclosure of a document which is relevant and material to the determination of issues in either civil or criminal proceedings. The legal principles that cover public interest immunity have been developed by judges over the years. Increasingly, judges have been reluctant to view the Crown as a special category, exempt from civil liability. This has opened up the Crown to legal liabilities, including the availability of injunctive relief. There are signs that the courts are developing a similar approach to public interest immunity litigation. In a number of civil cases such as *Conway v Rimmer* (1968) and *Burmah Oil v Bank of England* (1979) the courts appear to have abandoned a rigid rule against

* Since the workshop this paper has been revised to take into account the publication of the five volume Scott Report. I am grateful for the help and advice I have received from the Vice-Chancellor, Sir Richard Scott, Deborah Turner and, in discussion, from Adam Tomkins, Professor Patrick McAuslan, Mike McConville and Geoffrey Wilson. The views expressed in this paper are personal to the author who alone is responsible for any errors.

the disclosure of a class of documents. Instead they have set out a less rigid rule in favour of a discretion to inspect documents and consider the balance of interests between the litigant and the public interest when considering whether to uphold public interest immunity. Documents may be considered as to their class as well as to their contents. In the case of a class claim for public interest immunity it is a matter for the courts, not an individual litigant, to weigh the competing claims of the litigant and the public interest. In the case of a contents claim the courts have a discretion to consider the contents of documents and whether they should be disclosed. In the Matrix Churchill trial the Attorney General claimed that ministers were under a duty to sign certificates upholding public interest immunity claims.

At the outset it is important to consider public interest immunity in the context of general concerns about the essential values of good government (see McEldowney 1994, 1995; Nolan 1995; HC Debs 6th Series, vol. 248, cols. 757-9 (25 Oct. 1994)). It is axiomatic that good government is the essential framework that facilitates social, economic and political progress. As the British Council (1995) explains:

> Good government cannot be precisely defined. It is a set of ideas about the legitimacy, competence and accountability of government, about respect for human rights and the rule of law, which together add up to what most people expect from those who rule over them.

This chapter analyses the law and practice relating to public interest immunity in criminal cases. First, consideration is given to the development of public interest immunity and how the doctrine has been developed in recent years by the judges. Second, the problems highlighted in the Matrix Churchill case are considered. This includes the use of public interest immunity certificates by the Crown, the role of the Attorney General and the procedures adopted for immunity certificates to be signed by ministers. Finally, there is consideration of the recommendations of the Scott inquiry and also the future direction of this area of the law. This will include recommendations for reform of the law and the implications of public interest immunity for the development of good government.

Public interest immunity: definition and procedures

Definition and importance

In civil litigation an action for the discovery of documents will often be necessary. This is where one party will ask the other party to produce documents that may be material to the issues in question in the case. Public interest immunity or Crown privilege is pleaded by the Crown as a means of resisting discovery proceedings. It has been described by Tomkins (1993, p. 650), as 'a doctrine of the law of evidence by which it is possible to seek to withhold material which would otherwise be disclosed during the course of litigation'. Crown privilege, when pleaded successfully, enables the Crown to refuse to disclose any documents on the grounds that it would be contrary to the public interest.

Some preliminary points should be made about the development of this area of law. The first point is that the law on public interest immunity has developed from a number of important appellate decisions raising issues arising out of civil proceedings[1]. Increasingly, however, public interest immunity has been pleaded in criminal proceedings. This has resulted in a difficult issue for the lower courts in establishing principles from civil cases that may also apply in criminal trials. A further difficulty is that the courts have not been guided by clear statements of the law from the appellate courts. Difficulties of interpretation of various *obiter dicta* in decided cases have inhibited the development of a consistent set of principles or clear statement about the law. Finally, this area of law is also governed by some statutory provisions such as section 28 of the Crown Proceedings Act 1947 and the Rules of the Supreme Court Order 24, rules 5 and 15 and Order 77 rule 12. These provisions are only of limited assistance when considering criminal matters. A further trend which appears relevant is the attitude of the courts to the Crown. Judicial self confidence has developed to the point that, in recent years, there has been increasing recognition by the courts that the Crown (meaning the government of the day) should not be granted any special immunities or privileges[2]. Thus ministers may be sued in the courts both in their official and in their private capacity[3], the Royal Prerogative is subject to judicial review[4] and there may be injunctions or damages granted by the court against the Crown or the government of the day[5].

The use of Crown privilege raises fundamental issues about the role of the courts and the confidentiality of government documents. There are important implications about the use of Crown privilege which may serve severely to restrict the availability of confidential documents that may be important to the trial of the main issues raised in the case. There is concern about the breadth and the extent of Crown immunity. The public interest

---

1 See: *Conway v Rimmer* [1968] A.C. 910, *Burmah Oil v Bank of England* [1980] A.C. 1090, *Air Canada v Secretary of State for Trade* [1983] 2 A.C. 394.
2 See: *R. v Secretary of State for Foreign Affairs ex p. World Development Movement Ltd.* [1995] 1 All ER 611.
3 See: *Racz v Home Office* [1994] 1 All ER 97.
4 *Council of Civil Service Unions v Minister for the Civil Service* [1985] A.C. 74.
5 See: *R. v Secretary of State for Education and Science ex p. Avon County Council* [1991] 1 Q.B. 558, *M. v Home Office* [1993] 3 All ER 537, *R. v Secretary of State for Transport ex p. Factortame Ltd (no. 2)* [1991] 1 A.C. 603.

may be defined by the interest of the government of the day. This is sufficiently broad to allow its use to cover material which may be politically sensitive or embarrassing but which may also be the most pertinent and relevant to the trial of the issues in a criminal or civil case. In criminal trials relevant evidence not made available to the defence and restricted from the trial judge or jury may contain the essential material that could determine the guilt or innocence of the accused.

Judicial development of public interest immunity

The modern law[6] relating to public interest immunity may be found in a number of cases decided after the landmark decision of the House of Lords in *Conway v Rimmer* ([1968] A.C. 910) (see also Craig 1994; Leyland *et al* 1994). *Conway v Rimmer* involved a civil action. The plaintiff was a former probationary police constable who initiated an action for malicious prosecution against his former superior officer. The secretary of state objected to the production of various documents, some of which fell within a class of privileged documents, claiming that publication would not be in the public interest. The House of Lords asserted the power of the courts to hold a balance between the public interest set out by ministers who may wish to withhold documents and the public interest in ensuring the proper administration of justice. How this balance may be struck is not clearly articulated in *Conway v Rimmer*. There is also debate over the interpretation to give to what their Lordships decided. There is one school of thought[7], largely drawing from principles developed earlier by the courts[8], that there will always be a class of document that should be excluded from disclosure. Examples of such documents are cabinet minutes, documents containing policy matters, or documents that may disclose the views of senior civil servants or ministers in confidential briefings. However, there is also sufficient discussion in the case to support the view that, potentially, all documents may be disclosed, based on the judgement of the courts on what constitutes the balancing of the various interests. In fact one of the difficulties arising from the *Conway v Rimmer* decision is that the courts have developed a broad discretion as to what constitutes the public interest and how a balance may be struck in the interests of justice. There is some evidence that the courts have not always followed a consistent line of reasoning.

Support for the view that the courts may be willing to take a more open approach and to include cabinet papers as potentially open to disclosure may be seen from some judicial decisions. For example the robust approach of the courts in the Crossman diaries case, allowing disclosure of the contents of cabinet discussion in the form of cabinet diaries written by a minis-

---

6   For a discussion of the old authorities see: *Duncan v Cammell Laird* [1942] A.C. 624.
7   See: Lord Reid [1986] A.C. 910, pp. 986-7.
8   See: *Duncan v Cammell Laird* [1942] A.C. 624.

ter while a member of the cabinet and published after leaving office[9]. The
increasing use of diaries and autobiographies of ministers, civil servants and
officials provides a different context for the discussion of principles in this
area of the law than was possible in the past. (There is also a movement in
favour of more open government, though this is not necessarily an effective
means of forcing the disclosure of confidential information.)

Equally, it is possible to see support for an opposing view which suggests
that the courts are reluctant to allow open access to information. This view
is that the courts have adopted a cautious approach to confidentiality and
are in fact willing to broaden its scope and content. In so doing the courts
are willing to recognize the need to protect sources and information in
defined circumstances where confidentiality is perceived as necessary for
the proper working of the system of public administration. For example in
Rogers v Secretary of State for the Home Department ([1973] A.C. 388) the Home
Secretary sought to prevent discovery of various documents written by a
chief constable to the Gaming Commission arising out of an application for
a gaming certificate. The applicant for the gaming licence was refused the
licence and wished to have available the contents of the letter. The House of
Lords refused an application for discovery. The public interest outweighed
the interest of the litigant.

The scope of the bodies able to claim public interest immunity was broad-
ened by the House of Lords in *D. v National Society for the Prevention of
Cruelty to Children* ([1978] A.C. 171). The NSPCC relies on information
received in confidence as part of its role in the investigation and monitoring
of child abuse. The House of Lords accepted that, because certain sources
needed to be protected, the identity of informants should be kept anonymous. The NSPCC was a body authorized by statute (the Children and
Young Persons Act 1969) to undertake care proceedings. Such a body was
authorized to obtain and receive information and was therefore within the
protection afforded by the courts in ensuring that confidential information
would remain confidential. Similarly, confidential information obtained
from the customers and clients of Alfred Crompton Amusement Machines
Ltd. by the Inland Revenue commissioners could be maintained as confidential and would not have to be disclosed[10]. The House of Lords held that
the disclosure of such confidential information could hinder the commissioners in the discharge of their functions.

The question of how the courts may evaluate such confidentiality is difficult to assess. In deciding whether public interest warrants disclosure, the
courts may consider the likely weight of the evidence in the documents and
their significance for the case. However, this task is itself a difficult one to

---

9 See: *Att-Gen. v Jonathan Cape Ltd.* [1976] Q.B. 752. In that case the diaries were published
   posthumously, after the death of Richard Crossman.
10 See: *Alfred Crompton Amusement Machines Ltd. v Customs and Excise Commissioners (no. 2)*
   [1974] A.C. 405.

perform. The reliability or accuracy of information cannot be tested. The parties who are the subject of the information are, by virtue of its confidentiality, not able to check on the accuracy of the information or challenge any assertions implied or made explicit in the confidential documents[11].

It is a mistake to believe that confidentiality is solely the work of government departments or an excessive preoccupation of government itself. Increasingly, confidentiality is part of the contracting mechanism of the state, required in commercial and industrial businesses and generally in the private sector, including the newly privatized public utilities. In a number of cases the courts have been confronted with the question of how commercial and financial institutions may demand disclosure of material from the government, even while acknowledging the confidentiality of the material. In *Burmah Oil v Bank of England* ([1980] A.C. 1090) the House of Lords accepted that it was important for the courts to inspect documents before deciding to disclose them or not. Such inspection may arise if there is a reasonable probability that the documents would help the applicant's case. The facts of that case arose when Burmah Oil was in financial difficulties. A rescue package was set up whereby Burmah Oil sold its British Petroleum (BP) shares to the Bank of England. At the time BP shares were low and it was hoped that in the future, when the price rose, the profits would be divided between the Bank and Burmah Oil. However when the shares did rise the government did not accept this arrangement. Burmah Oil sought to discover confidential documents which, it hoped, would support its allegations that the sale of the stock was unconscionable and unfair. The House of Lords, after considering various documents, rejected disclosure.

There remain a number of questions not clearly answered from the discussion of these cases. First, is there a class of documents which in law may never be disclosed? This question appears unresolved. In *Burmah Oil* it was suggested that no class of document was excluded from the court's discretion to consider when balancing the interests of the litigant with the interests of justice. However, this does not fully answer the question of whether different classes of document may be treated differently by the courts. Various confidential documents are placed into categories of confidentiality and there is a strong case for arguing that *prima facie* certain documents may fall within a category that ought never to be disclosed. The possibility remains that some documents, such as cabinet papers, appear automatically to attract public interest immunity.

Secondly, should the courts always inspect documents where public interest immunity is involved? Inspection may be made first to consider whether the documents fit within the category or class of document for

---

11 See: *Campbell v Tameside Metropolitan Borough Council* [1982] 3 W.L.R. 75. Documents disclosing psychological difficulties with a pupil were made available in a civil action by a teacher claiming negligence of the local authority in allowing a potentially violent pupil to attend school. The teacher had been attacked by the pupil and sustained injury.

which public interest immunity may be sought. Inspection may assist the court when deciding whether the case can be resolved on the grounds of cost. Inspection may arise when considering the balancing of interests between those of the litigant and the public interest. Inspection may allow documents to be considered by the courts prior to consideration of their release. In principle, it would appear to be a sound proposition that the courts should always take the opportunity to inspect documents. This principle provides the courts with a means to check whether there are sufficient grounds put forward by the person claiming public interest immunity for the claim to be upheld. It also helps to ensure that the courts are fully aware of the contents of the documents that are released, should this be the result of the case. Doubts as to whether all or only some of the documents are necessary to fall within the category of document for which immunity is claimed may be resolved by the courts. Finally, inspection provides an important check on the executive. This opens up discussion about public interest immunity to be a discretion to be applied by the courts and not simply a claim made by the Crown removed from judicial discretion. This point is considered below in further detail.

In *Burmah Oil* no clear consensus on these issues emerged. Lord Wilberforce considered that documents should not be inspected by the courts unless there was a strong positive case on behalf of the litigant justifying such inspection. On what basis may a strong case be tested? Lord Edmund-Davies ([1980] A.C. 1090, p. 1126) considered that a real likelihood test may be applied but Lord Keith (Ibid. pp. 1135-6) suggested that reasonable probability was sufficient. However, there are some reservations about the courts engaging in the exercise of inspecting various documents. In the *Jonathan Cape* case the court took the opportunity to read the Crossman diaries before determining whether or not the documents were to be confidential. Such inspection may not prove satisfactory when the parties to the action are excluded from any check on the accuracy of the information. The courts remain free to maintain a view that a certain class of document should never be made available. Indeed the courts may not provide workable principles as to when and when not to order inspection. It may prove difficult to maintain a consistency of approach in the lower courts. Thus the courts may wish to preserve discretion over when and when not to order inspection.

In *Air Canada v Secretary of State for Trade* the House of Lords decided not to inspect certain documents even when the issue of balancing the interests of the parties was under consideration ([1983] 1 All ER 910). The case arose because a number of airlines objected to the raising of landing charges by the British Airports Authority. The airlines argued that the motive behind the charges was to reduce public sector borrowing and that this was not permitted under the Airports Act 1975 as a basis to increase charges. The reluctance of the House of Lords to agree to inspect documents attracting public interest immunity has a specific rationale. It stems from identifying one group of documents that the courts would be reluctant to reveal or even inspect – namely, cabinet minutes and policy discussion between ministers involving matters of policy and public expenditure issues. Their lordships' reasoning put great emphasis on the need to prove a case showing why the documents ought to be released and inspected by the courts.

Recently there has been some shift in attitude about whether the courts should always inspect documents. In a lecture delivered before the House of Lords decision in *ex parte Wiley*, discussed below, Sir Simon Brown, now a Lord Justice of Appeal, noted how 'the court alone is responsible for carrying out the balancing exercise...' (Brown 1994, p. 579).

While there is no rule *requiring* the courts to inspect documents in every case, there is, since *Conway v Rimmer*, a judicial discretion to override a minister's certificate claiming immunity through the inspection by the court of the relevant documents. The fact that inspection by the court may take place does not guarantee that a litigant can surmount the hurdle that a case for inspection has to be made out. Often litigants are at a profound disadvantage because they do not have full or even partial access to the documents on which they must make out a case for the court to inspect.

Public interest immunity and the Matrix Churchill trial

The Matrix Churchill trial

This question of public interest immunity may be considered in the light of the Matrix Churchill trial, the House of Lords decision in *R. v Chief Constable of the West Midlands ex p. Wiley* ([1994] 3 All ER 420) which overruled three Court of Appeal decisions[12], and the findings of the Scott Report (Scott 1996).

An account of the events leading to the Scott inquiry was given above in Chapter 1. The Matrix Churchill case highlighted the fact that there was relatively little legal authority on the use of public interest immunity in criminal trials. The trial judge reviewed the existing authorities on public interest immunity and upheld the claim by the Crown that public interest immunity attached to the documents. However, he undertook an inspection of the documents and in one particular category of document considered that they should be disclosed. In other categories of document the judge refused disclosure on the grounds that the court was not really in a position to weigh the effect upon the public interest of a disclosure of information concerning

---

12 *Neilson v Laugharne* [1981] 1 All ER 829, *Hehiro v Comr. of Police of the Metropolis* [1982] 2 All ER 335 and *Makanjoula v Comr. of Police of the Metropolis* [1992] 3 All ER 617.

the security and intelligence services.

Two questions arise from the case. First, is a class of documents category automatically certified as falling within a public interest immunity protection? Second, what is the role of the Attorney General in the process of signing certificates of immunity? This latter question will be examined in more detail below.

The answer to the first question appears to be that in the Matrix Churchill trial and in various Court of Appeal cases, notably *Halford v Sharples* ([1992] 3 All ER 624), there is a class of document which might never be disclosed notwithstanding the question of the courts' powers to inspect and balance interests. This appears to be a mistaken view of the law. It is also arguable, in principle, that in criminal proceedings the courts should be free to exercise their discretion when inspecting documents and considering the balance of interests. Support for this interpretation may be found in the discussion above relating to the civil cases of *Burmah Oil* and *Conway v Rimmer*. In these it appears that there are *dicta* which suggest that even the highest category of document could be subject to the courts' discretion and that a class claim should not now exist in English law[13]. Indeed more recently in the House of Lords in *R. v Chief Constable ex p. Wiley*, a case involving civil proceedings, Lord Templeman has stated:

> If public interest immunity is approached by every litigant on the basis that a relevant and material document must be disclosed unless the disclosure will cause substantial harm to the public interest, the distinction between a class claim and a contents claim loses much of its significance.
> ([1994] 3 All ER 420, p. 424)

In the same case Lord Woolf noted that, in his opinion, establishing a class of case was never justified and a class claim in respect of the Police and Criminal Evidence Act 1984 was not generally available. The class claim tended to defeat the objectives of finding evidence under the Act. This suggests that the reasoning in a number of Court of Appeal cases is probably wrong when it was suggested that a class claim could be used automatically to attract protection[14].

The second question that arises is how the courts consider the question of the balancing of interests. The answer to this question in civil proceedings is provided by Lord Justice Woolf in *R. v Chief Constable ex p. Wiley*. First, in civil proceedings it is not desirable that such matters should be dealt with through collateral proceedings. It is more appropriate that the issue should be dealt with as part of the full proceedings. Second, in criminal proceed-

---

13 See: *Burmah Oil* [1980] A.C. 1090 and Lord Keith pp. 1134-5 and Lord Scarman pp. 1143-4.
14 See: *Neilson v Laugharne* [1981] 1 All ER 829, *Hehiro v Comr. of Police of the Metropolis* [1982] 2 All ER 335 and *Makanjoula v Comr. of Police of the Metropolis* [1992] 3 All ER 617.

ings, Lord Justice Mann in *R. v Governor of Brixton Prison ex parte Osman (No.1)* noted that '...the weight to be attached to the interests of justice is plainly very great indeed' ([1992] 1 All ER 108). This implies that the balance of interests will follow justice and that the courts will be likely to allow disclosure in order to ensure justice is upheld.

The role of the Attorney General and the duty on a minister to claim public interest immunity

The use of public interest immunity in respect of the Matrix Churchill trial raises the question of the existence, or not, of a duty on a minister to make a claim of public interest immunity. It appears from the government response to the Scott Report that the idea of a duty on ministers to sign public interest immunity certificates is of long standing:

> From the time of the decision of the House of Lords in *Conway v Rimmer* in 1968 until a change of approach signalled by the decision of the House of Lords in *R. v Chief Constable of West Midlands Police, ex parte Wiley* in 1994, it was the general understanding of those advising Government that, where a document fell within a PII class, the minister's duty was to assert the public interest in non-disclosure of that document.
> (Treasury Solicitor 1996, para. 2.1)

In the Matrix Churchill trial only one minister (Michael Heseltine) at first refused to sign a certificate. He reluctantly signed after persuasion from the Attorney General that, in law, ministers had no discretion in the matter but were under a duty to sign. The view argued by the Attorney General – that ministers were under a duty to sign certificates – arises from his interpretation of past practice and from the Court of Appeal decision in *Makanjoula*[15]. The key part of the Court of Appeal's reasoning is contained in the speech by Bingham LJ. This is critical to the interpretation of 'duty' provided by the Attorney General and it requires careful consideration.

> Where a litigant asserts that documents are immune from production or disclosure on public interest grounds *he is not (if the claim is well founded) claiming a right but observing a duty*. Public interest immunity is not a trump card vouchsafed to certain privileged players to play when and as they wish. It is an exclusionary rule, imposed on parties in certain circumstances, even where it is to their disadvantage in the litigation. This does not mean that in any case where a party holds a doc-

---

15 *Makanjoula v Comr. of Police of the Metropolis* [1992] 3 All ER 617.

ument in a class *prima facie* immune he is bound to persist in an assertion of immunity even where it is held that, on any weighing of the public interest, in withholding the document against the public interest in disclosure for the purpose of furthering the administration of justice, there is a clear balance in favour of the latter. But it does, I think mean: (1) that public interest immunity cannot in any ordinary sense be waived, since, although **one can waive rights one cannot waive duties**; (2) that where a litigant holds documents in a class *prima facie* immune, he should (save perhaps in a very exceptional case) assert that the documents are immune and decline to disclose them, since the ultimate judge of where the balance of public interest lies is not him but the court; and (3) that, where a document is, or is held to be, in an immune class, it may not be used for any purpose whatever in the proceedings to which the immunity applies and certainly cannot (for instance) be used for the purposes of cross-examination.

([1992] 3 All ER 617, p. 623) (Italics in bold added)

There is considerable difficulty in interpretation of this key passage. A further problem is that the *Makanjoula* case did not involve a government department and, further, it was a civil case not a criminal one. The interpretation offered by the Attorney General that there existed a duty on ministers to sign a public interest immunity certificate appears to follow from two interrelated propositions. First, that the existence of a class of documents that are *prima facie* to be excluded from disclosure means there is a duty on ministers to sign certificates to ensure exclusion. Second, that as a duty on ministers to sign does not guarantee automatically that the court will uphold exclusion from disclosure, ministers should see their duty as providing the courts with a discretion. If the minister fails to exercise a duty to sign, this in effect deprives the courts of their discretion in the matter.

The government's response to the Scott Report considers the existence of the duty claimed by the Attorney General. The implication is that 'duty' is some form of legal or binding obligation on ministers to sign certificates. But, as noted above, the existence of a legally binding duty on ministers is hard to justify. First, if there is a legal duty it appears unenforceable. What are the sanctions and how may they be applied? Second, it suggests that the duty applies automatically, leaving ministers with no discretion. This is odd. If the duty were automatic and in the form of a legal obligation, why should ministers feel it necessary to seek legal advice in cases where public interest immunity is claimed? There is also a generally accepted principle that ministers must decide while advisers advise. Legal advice is, of its nature, advice. It would be curious if legal advice were always binding on ministers. The key explanation as to what is the nature of the duty referred to by Lord Justice Bingham (see above) may be found in the phrase 'in the public interest'. The Scott Report (1996 Vol. III, para. G 18.52, p. 1505) makes this point in the following way:

> ...The existence of the duty to which Lord Justice Bingham was referring cannot be divorced from the view as to the public interest formed by the party whose responsibility it is to protect the public interest. If a Minister does not believe that disclosure to the defendant of the documents in question would be damaging to the public interest, how can it possibly be said that he is under a duty to claim PII for the documents?

It may be concluded that the better view is that a 'duty', if it exists, cannot mean a binding or legally enforceable legal obligation. A duty in this context can only mean a conventional duty and this may be waived at the discretion of the minister in the public interest.

Since the *Matrix Churchill* trial, the House of Lords has now accepted in *ex parte Wiley* a number of propositions about public interest immunity[16]. The view that there is a class of documents which may guarantee exclusion from disclosure is no longer tenable. Furthermore it is considered that in criminal cases the scales of justice have to be more keenly balanced to protect the accused. The House of Lords has also rejected the proposition that there is a duty on ministers to sign public interest immunity certificates. The House of Lords' interpretation of Bingham LJ's judgement when he speaks of a duty not a right is that this would appear to be a duty on ministers to bring to the attention of the court the need for public interest immunity and, therefore, from the Attorney General's analysis a duty on ministers to sign certificates. This appears to overlook the fact that there are many circumstances where public interest immunity may for practical purposes be waived voluntarily and those documents revealed to the defence (Smith 1993, p. 3). If there was a duty how could such documents reach the defence? It should be stressed that in criminal cases lawyers, including the Attorney General, owe a duty to uphold the interests of justice. In circumstances where there is material evidence affecting the guilt or innocence of the accused in a number of cases alleging miscarriages of justice on appeal, the appellate courts have shown willingness to quash convictions where relevant and material evidence is withheld by the prosecution authorities.

The discussion of duties and rights is qualified by the words set out in italics from the judgement of Lord Justice Bingham. These italicized words may be interpreted to mean that there is no obligation to persist with any duty when the interests of justice deem it unnecessary. This qualification

---

16 *R. v Chief Constable of the West Midlands ex p. Wiley* [1994] 3 All ER 420, p. 423.

would appear to run contrary to the Attorney General's interpretation. On the other hand, if the Attorney General's interpretation is to be followed, then the consequences that flow have severe implications for an accused person. The duty appears to be 'blind' – that is, no matter what the document may reveal the minister is obliged to sign. This has the potential consequence of excluding material which could ensure the acquittal of the accused.

From the above discussion, it may be concluded that the Attorney General's interpretation is unsound in principle and wrong in its potential effects on the accused.

Public interest immunity and criminal cases

The question of the use of public interest immunity certificates arises in both civil and criminal cases. The Matrix Churchill trial focused attention on their use in criminal cases. The higher appellate courts had, until *ex parte Wiley*, been mainly concerned with civil proceedings. The use of public interest immunity certificates in criminal cases has given rise to a clear difference of opinion on the part of the government's legal advisers and the Scott report on this issue. In the government's response the view of government advisers is as follows:

> The understanding of those advising Government was and is that the general principles of PII [Public Interest Immunity] apply in the same way in criminal proceedings as they do in civil proceedings. In each case both class and contents claims can properly be advanced; and in each case the public interest in non-disclosure falls to be balanced(at the material time, by the court) against the public interest in disclosure for the purposes of the administration of justice. The balance is much more likely to come down in favour of disclosure in criminal proceedings, and procedural differences exist, but the general principles are the same.
> (Treasury Solicitor 1996, para. 3.1)

The Scott Report views criminal proceedings as different from civil proceedings[17]. Two conclusions are reached:

> The recognition that some relevant and *prima facie* disclosable

---

17 The authority of *R. v Governor of Brixton Prison ex parte Osman* [1991] 1 WLR 281 is discussed in great detail in the Scott Report. The case involved an application for *habeas corpus* which for the purposes of the discussion of public interest immunity certificates was characterized as criminal proceedings.

documents appear to lack any potential to assist the defence is not, in my opinion, a sufficient reason for a continuance of the practice of making PII [Public Interest Immunity] claims in criminal cases. If contents claims cannot be justified PII should not, in my opinion, be claimed.
(Scott 1996, Vol. III, para. G 18.86, p. 1525)

There are some arguments that support the views put forward in the Scott Report. Different considerations arise when public interest immunity is considered in any criminal trial. This is apparent when the differences between civil and criminal procedure are considered. The most obvious difference between civil and criminal cases is that only in the latter does the possibility of imprisonment or heavy fine apply as a penalty on being found guilty. In the nature of criminal charges not only is there the potential for a more serious penalty, but also of incurring greater odium by society as a whole. Loss of reputation is potentially greater. Loss of business and financial confidence may also follow and the loss of self respect may be all the greater as a consequence.

In criminal trials different rules of evidence apply than in civil proceedings. The prosecution must prove the case against the accused person beyond a reasonable doubt whereas in civil cases the plaintiff must only establish a case on the balance of probabilities. In civil proceedings the relevance of a document depends on the issues between the parties established by written pleadings. This allows many issues to be dealt with[18]. The pleadings may be amended and exchanges of information may take place. In criminal proceedings there is currently no equivalent arrangement for written pleadings. As Lord Templeman explained:

Prosecution authorities know which documents are relevant to the prosecution but they cannot know for certain which documents will be relevant to the defence. ... In order to avoid criticism and a miscarriage of justice one way or the other, the police authorities now feel obliged to disclose documents of doubtful relevance and materiality[19].

In the light of these differences criminal cases involving public interest immunity claims have to be considered in a different context than cases where civil issues are resolved (Bradley 1992; Allan 1993; Ganz 1993).

The Scott Report proposed that documents protected by PII certificates should be disclosed in criminal trials if they 'might be of assistance to the defence'. This view is rejected by the government response on the grounds

---

18 See: *R v Chief Constable of the West Midlands ex p. Wiley* [1994] 3 All ER 420.
19 Ibid., p. 423.

that it may have '...serious repercussions for many criminal prosecutions' (Treasury Solicitor 1996, para. 5.3).

Conclusions: reform of public interest immunity

Following the House of Lords' decision in *R. v Chief Constable of the West Midlands ex p. Wiley* ([1994] 3 All ER 420) the courts appear to have accepted a number of principles concerning public interest immunity[20]. These principles include the following:

- The courts have the ultimate decision in assessing the balance of interests between the litigant and the public interest. Their discretion to inspect documents allows the courts the opportunity to consider how the balance may be struck.

- Generally, a class claim to public interest immunity does not automatically apply to documents. Any claim of public interest immunity is a matter for the court and not an individual litigant.

- It seems improbable that there is a duty on ministers to sign public interest immunity certificates. A duty that may appear to rest with ministers is a duty to consider whether the public interest in non-disclosure is outweighed on the facts of the particular case by the public interest in the administration of justice[21].

The recent decisions of the courts emphasize the public interest and the courts' role in deciding how to interpret the public interest. This places the courts in the invidious role of striking a balance with little guidance as to how such a balance may be struck. It is significant that, in the Matrix Churchill trial, the trial judge disclosed a number of documents but also upheld public interest immunity claims in a number of other important documents. Do judges have sufficient training or understanding of government and the work of the civil service to interpret documents when making their judgement as to how the balance is to be struck?

The Scott Report makes clear that there are a number of concerns arising out of the collapse of the Matrix Churchill trial. The role of the Attorney General is the most critical to the consideration of how public interest immunity operated at the trial. Clearly, confidentiality requires and the pub-

---

20 See: *Bennett v Metropolitan Police Comr.* [1995] 2 All ER 1.
21 This point is held in the judgement of Rattee, J. in *Bennett v Metropolitan Police Comr.* [1995] 2 All ER 1.

lic interest demands that many documents should, given their nature, remain confidential. Confidentiality may be justified in terms of national security – for example the names of informers or serving MI5 officers; or of financial or market sensitive information – for example, information that may cause the collapse of the currency, or a run on the liquidity of a major financial institution. It is therefore critical that the procedures adopted for protecting confidentiality should stand up to objective scrutiny and maintain the confidence of the general public.

In the Matrix Churchill case the advice that ministers must sign certificates appears misplaced. Doubts existed at the time about the accuracy of the legal advice that favoured that view. The role of the minister is surely to ensure that the public interest is upheld, even though in not every case will this mean signing a certificate. Distinguishing the interest of the government of the day from that of the public interest is a role that the Attorney General is expected to perform. As the government's legal adviser and senior law officer this may place upon the incumbent an impossible burden. This is especially so when the Attorney is an elected MP drawn from the ranks of the government's own party. Indeed that burden seems overwhelming when, by his own admission as in the Scott Inquiry, the Attorney has not read the documents at issue in the trial. Thus the Attorney must depend on the assistance of a relatively small number of legal advisers. This seems hardly satisfactory. In the British system of incremental development rather than radical reform the time has come for the development of a properly funded and managed Ministry of Justice, common among many other European countries. Such a ministry may help provide a better solution than the present arrangements as to how to balance the interests of justice. The Minister for Justice would separate out the political from the legal more clearly than the present arrangements allow.

The law on public interest immunity claims ought to be clarified. The distinction between civil and criminal proceedings is crucial and this must find a clear statement of principle in law. Class claims for immunity ought not to be made automatically but should require careful and detailed consideration by ministers, their legal advisers and the courts. There is also a strong case for including in criminal proceedings greater opportunity to answer and respond to documentary evidence. This is favoured by the police in terms of allowing the prosecution sight of the accused's defence in advance to allow time to reply. Correspondingly, there is a good case for more, not less, disclosure of the Crown's case. Admittedly, one important outcome of the Matrix Churchill case is that the defence are given much more information than hitherto. This is expensive and time consuming, leaving the prosecution with no option but to provide more voluminous documentation. It is arguably capable of giving the defence an unfair advantage in terms of tactics and delays.

Setting the framework for the protection of confidential information requires a view of the role of government. Good government should encourage more, not less, disclosure of information and good decision making is secured through better information rather than secrecy. (Recent examples in the privatization of electricity illustrate this point. The RPI-X formula applied by the regulator has had to be reviewed because Northern Electric had made greater profits than revealed to the regulator. The true state of the profits only became known when Trafalgar House attempted to make a take-over bid for Northern Electric.) The public interest does not justify confidentiality when it is used to prevent the government from being embarrassed or when at a criminal trial the accused is denied information that may be relevant to guilt or innocence.

The five volumes of the Scott inquiry provide an important insight into the internal workings of government. The lessons to be gained from such an inquiry are likely to be long lasting. The government's response takes an opposing view to the greater openness favoured by Sir Richard Scott, warning of the dangers of more open disclosure. Specifically it fears that:

> ...the recommendation [from the Scott report] that documents protected by PII (whether on a class or a contents basis) should be disclosed in criminal trials if they "might be of assistance to the defence" could have serious repercussions for many criminal prosecutions.
> (Treasury Solicitor 1996, para. 5.3)

In the final analysis it is for Parliament to decide the balance between the interests of the public and the government of the day. This is a matter that has wide implications for the relationship between ministers, civil servants and public trust. The Scott inquiry and the Matrix Churchill trial have raised matters that test the efficacy of the British constitution to its limits.

9 The accountability of ministers and civil servants

Peter Barberis

Introduction

At face value the formal, traditional notion of accountability in British government seems simple enough. It is that ministers alone are accountable to the public, via Parliament, for their own decisions and for the work of their departments. Civil servants are accountable internally – and only internally – to their political chiefs. This simple statement is both true and highly misleading. As a doctrine it remains broadly true insofar as it has never consciously been replaced by any other doctrine. In practice it is misleading because it tells only half the story and, in certain respects, it is honoured more in the breach than in the compliance. This is a particular handicap in a system which rests so heavily upon convention. The origins of the doctrine are, in any case, murkier than is often supposed and its applications have rarely been free from controversy. Some of the more recent developments analyzed in previous chapters – Next Steps, the Citizen's Charter and debates about standards of conduct – have brought new controversies and have given added piquancy to old ones.

The following discussion is organized into three sections. First, the traditional doctrine is examined to establish how and why it evolved and how, in practice, it has tended to work. The second section considers whether, to what extent and in what senses the doctrine and the reality of accountability have been prised further apart by developments of the 1980s and 1990s. The third section will then consider whether and, if so, how the gap between doctrine and reality may be bridged. There are three possibilities: accept the (growing) incongruence as a fact of life; bring reality back into closer conformity with (traditional) doctrine; change or reformulate the doctrine to meet the new realities. The latter may have the strongest attractions but would mean abandoning the Diceyan notion of parliamentary sovereignty – at least the idea that Parliament can be the nation's exclusive watchdog. It also requires modification of the notion that ministers alone can be held accountable for public services. The question is whether (and, if so, how) this can be done without impairing the democratic element of accountability.

Traditional doctrine examined

By 'traditional' is meant no more than the set of assumptions and practices by which, until fairly recently, notions about the accountability of ministers and civil servants were given meaning. In the absence of anything else, these assumptions and practices continue to provide the benchmark against which any discussion must be pitched. Many of these assumptions had become pretty well embedded by the third quarter of the nineteenth century, if not before (Parris 1969, p. 81). They may usefully be described by reference to some of the more influential commentators of the day and in the generations that followed.

AV Dicey (1835-1922) was among the foremost academic constitutional lawyers of late-Victorian and Edwardian England. He played no little part in formulating the conventions he described, his influence lingering long after his death. He gave two meanings to the notion of ministerial responsibility – quite simply '...the responsibility of Ministers to Parliament, or, the liability of Ministers to lose their offices if they cannot retain the confidence of the House of Commons' (Dicey 1959, p. 325). This, he said, entailed 'the legal responsibility of every Minister for every act of the Crown in which he takes part' (Ibid.). Within the department the minister is a sovereign power; neither the law nor the workings of the constitution acknowledge any other. Everything goes through the minister – or at least is done on behalf of the minister.

The notion that civil servants operate in the name of the minister became fundamental to the traditional doctrine. Its significance was recognized by successive generations during the late-nineteenth century and during the early and middle decades of the present century. As the American scholar A.L. Lowell (1856-1943) noted: '...the minister ought not to attribute blunders or misconduct to a subordinate unless prepared at the same time to announce his discharge... In short the permanent official, like the King, can do no wrong. Both are shielded by the responsibility of the minister' (Lowell

1908, Vol. I, pp. 122-3). Civil servants were to remain anonymous. Any arrangement at variance with the practice of anonymity could impair the democratic imperative. Another writer, Sidney Low (1857-1932), put it like this:

> ...ministers in the fulness of their power, are liable at any moment to be arraigned, not merely for their own acts, but for the acts of their subordinates, before the Assembly, which again is responsible to the people. This is the doctrine which is by many regarded as the main shaft and supporting pillar of the political edifice.
> (Low 1914, p. 138)

Representing a later generation of constitutional scholars Sir Ivor Jennings (1903-65) said:

> If the minister chooses... to leave decisions to civil servants, then he must take the political consequences of any defect of administration... He cannot defend himself by blaming the civil servant. If the civil servant could be criticised, he would require the means for defending himself. If the minister could blame the civil servant, then the civil servant would require the power to blame the minister... The fundamental principle of our system of administration is, however, that the civil servant should be impartial and, as far as may be possible, anonymous.
> (Jennings 1966, p. 149)

Such are the main tenets of traditional doctrine, as commonly understood among writers from the late-nineteenth to at least the middle of the twentieth century. Civil servants were anonymous to the public – not without influence but beavering away in the bowels of Whitehall. Whatever they did they did in the minister's name and with the minister's authority, for they had no other authority – or, as it would be expressed many years later: 'the civil service, as such, has no constitutional personality or responsibility separate from the duly constituted Government of the day' (HM Treasury 1993, Section 4. Annex A, para. 3). Civil servants can neither be blamed nor directly brought to account, except within the confines of Whitehall. They are accountable only through their ministers, rather like a child through its parents. This is partly a matter of convenience for Parliament, partly a device to preserve or legitimize the democratic 'chain of being'. Governments are democratically elected; governments comprise a collection of ministers each heading a department whose work they 'control', and for which they are responsible. If Parliament is dissatisfied with the work and policy of a department, it is from the minister that it seeks retribution.

In fact this seemingly neat set of maxims was by no means universally understood and certainly did not reflect deeply ingrained practice, even in the nineteenth century. Anonymity was a mantle adopted by top officials only gradually and in some cases uneasily (Clark 1959; Barberis 1996, pp. 6-11). Some statutes gave specific powers other than to ministers, as with the factory inspectors. Schools inspectors had no statutory independence from ministers, but custom permitted their reporting directly to Parliament. It was a confusion about the prerogative of a minister to adulterate the report of a school inspector and of a minister's responsibility vis-à-vis officials which precipitated the resignation of Robert Lowe in 1864 as President of the (Education) Committee of the Privy Council. Many semi-independent boards became ministerial departments or were brought within the embrace of a department headed by a minister who was an MP (Willson 1955; Parris 1969, pp. 82-93). But the relationship between ministers and Parliament was not as straightforward as may be imagined. Even down to the 1920s it was technically necessary for an MP to seek re-election upon taking a paid position within the government. As Maitland (1908, p. 396) put it: 'far from wishing to have ministers there to answer for their doings, the House struggled to exclude them'. It is also easy to overstate the unanimity among contemporaries of the period. For example, Sidney and Beatrice Webb (1920, p. 170) wanted to abandon the notion of ministerial responsibility, believing it to be 'illusory as an instrument of democratic control'. Sidney Low lamented: 'It is practically impossible to bring a minister to book unless the House is prepared to sacrifice the whole Cabinet to punish him' (Low 1914, p. 148). In any case, ministers were as likely to be thrown out of office on account of wider political factors. Thus, Low went on: 'A Minister will not refrain from governing ill lest he be "hung", since he must feel that he is quite likely to be hung even if he governs well' (p. 152).

Low's despair, not to say his cynicism, may seem strikingly modern. In truth, even as it evolved the doctrine of ministerial responsibility was spun within the web of political reality. The practice may have preceded the formulation of the doctrine (Birch 1964, p. 65). Yet doctrine was never the product solely of experience and precedent. Dicey, for example, was no historian. He did not ignore empirical evidence but he (and others) abstracted what were considered to be the salient principles and in the light of broader precepts about the sovereignty of Parliament and the rule of law. The doctrine of ministerial responsibility has come to have the status of a constitutional convention. And, like most conventions, it is 'somewhat vague and slippery' (Marshall 1986, p. 54). Nowhere is this better illustrated than in the ability (or inability) of Parliament to apply the ultimate sanction – enforced resignation.

Parris (1969, p. 101) cites the resignation of Robert Lowe in 1864 as being 'the earliest arising out of a minister's responsibility for those under him, as distinct from his responsibility for advice to the Crown'. Parris acknowledges that it took a further ten years for the notion to become the broad assumption. It may be wondered whether, in the absence of any fully established principle, Lowe was really obliged to resign at all. A select committee subsequently appointed to investigate the case absolved him personally and concluded that his resignation had been unnecessary. Thus Woodhouse (1994, p. 35) claims that the resignation was not 'an acceptance of "vicarious" responsibility for the actions of his officials but a relinquishing of office by a minister who considered his honour had been impugned by the accusations made in the House'. The classic modern vicarious resignation – that of Sir Thomas Dugdale over the Crichel Down case in 1954 – has been subject to similar reinterpretation. For many years it was customary to cite his resignation as exemplifying the ultimate acknowledgement of ministerial responsibility – loss of office on account of the acts of officials. Dugdale had resigned as Minister for Agriculture seemingly on account of maladministration within the Ministry in carrying out (or subverting) a policy formulated long before his appointment as minister. But more recent research has shown that he had failed to take the opportunity to remedy or at least to ameliorate wrongdoings; that he had confirmed the original decision and had no qualms about the behaviour of his civil servants (Nicolson 1986, pp. 191-3; Griffith 1987). His resignation was an attempt to assuage back benchers in his own party. This reinterpretation gives further strength to the classic thesis that resignations have been 'rare... arbitrary and unpredictable... whether a Minister is forced to resign depends on three factors, on himself, his Prime Minister and his party' (Finer 1956, p. 393).

More recently Marshall (1986, p. 65) has claimed that the resignation in 1982 of Lord Carrington over events leading to the Falklands war was in acknowledgement of errors within the Foreign Office in which he was implicated. On the other hand, Jordan (1994b, pp. 229-30) sees it as the product of back bench unease and as 'a lightening conductor to deflect criticism from the Cabinet'. The same may be said about the resignation of (Sir) Leon Brittan in 1986 over the Westland affair. These few cases suffice to show that the precise reasons for some of the more celebrated resignations are open to interpretation. It is difficult to deduce the consistent *application* of any constitutional principle. And even the principle itself, as distinct from its application, was in the past often upheld more conditionally than is commonly supposed. In words which have since been widely quoted Herbert Morrison famously said that ministers were responsible for all the acts of their officials, 'for every stamp stuck on an envelope' (HC Debs 1953/54, 5th Series, vol. 530, col. 1274). This point he made in a speech on the floor of the Commons following Dugdale's resignation over Crichel Down. He went on to say (col. 1275) that 'it may be right, in exceptional circumstances, for the

Minister publicly to criticise his civil servants'. This, Morrison acknowledged, was a delicate matter and was not to obscure the fact that if the
House wanted somebody's head, it should be that of the minister.

Morrison did not claim to be changing or modifying the constitutional
doctrine (Morrison 1964, p. 333). Nor was he. He was simply expounding
upon the existing doctrine, expressed in greater detail shortly afterwards by
the Maxwell Fyfe Report. This report confirmed that ministers need not
resign on account of errors, unknown to them, made by officials. They were
supposed to take any necessary corrective action upon being apprised of
such errors, failure to do so being a legitimate ground for ministerial resignation. And, of course, ministers alone were supposed to come before
Parliament by way of making explanation, if nothing else.

The Vehicle and General (V and G) affair of the early 1970s added a further twist. The collapse of the V and G Company had left many policy-hold-
ers uninsured. In fact its decline had for some time been known about within the Department of Trade and Industry whose supervisory capacity on
behalf of the public was therefore called into question. The ensuing inquiry
named and blamed officials. This was not without precedent: the investigation following Crichel Down had done that. Nor was it novel to absolve
ministers in recognition of their having neither known nor having had reason to have suspected malfunctioning (James 1972, para. 61). The new element was that ministers were not even required to give testimony. There
was probably little to gain from questioning ministers who had little or no
direct knowledge of events. It was not a parliamentary inquiry but a tribunal headed by a judge. The fact remains that there arose no question of
ministers being obliged to come forward with an explanation, though the
prime minister did make a statement in the House of Commons.

It is obvious that ministerial responsibility must be seen not as a one-
dimensional but as a multi-dimensional doctrine. Resignation is but one and
perhaps not even the main plank (Turpin 1994, pp. 109-10). The dimension
of resignation, or sacrificial responsibility, must be distinguished from the
dimensions of supervisory, remedial and explanatory responsibility. The
occasional resignation may still give focus, without which the concept of
accountability loses its bite. But supervisory, remedial and (especially)
explanatory responsibility provide the ballast.

Such may be said of the traditional doctrine. Yet, as has been shown, it
has never been set in stone. Rather it has evolved, gathering added refine-
ment and conditionality. It is less straightforward, less firmly grounded in
either theory or empiricism, yet more circumstantial and even controversial
than is often supposed. It is important to establish this as the base from
which more recent practice has allegedly deviated. Neither in its application
nor perhaps even in the abstract did the traditional doctrine mark a fixed
and immutable boundary between the acceptable and the unacceptable. At

all times the traditional doctrine has worked through the medium of the political system. In what senses, then, has the traditional doctrine been challenged by the developments of the 1980s and 1990s?

The challenges of the 1980s and 1990s

To deny the existence of any static 'golden age' is not to deny that traditional doctrine provided the touchstone, the prevailing ethos to which practice was thought to conform or at any rate ought to conform. Nor is it to deny the possibility of further subsequent slippage. The force of the argument so far is that slippage from the common understanding as annunciated by the likes of Dicey, Low or, later, Jennings has been gradual and long term – in certain senses having its origins almost as they were writing. The Crichel Down case, the V and G affair and other moments of temporary crisis simply provided the occasion to flesh out (or to pare down) some of the elements implicit in the traditional doctrine. In so doing the traditional doctrine became more finely calibrated but no less and in fact more readily open to interpretation. Cabinet Secretary Sir John (Lord) Hunt was merely saying what might have been said twenty, thirty or even forty years earlier when he told a Commons' select committee: 'The concept that because somebody whom the minister has never heard of has made a mistake means that the minister should resign is out of date, and rightly so' (Expenditure Committee 1977, Vol. II (part II), Q. 1855).

Have the events of the 1980s and 1990s brought any new dimension of working practice or in any way heralded any further evolution of the traditional doctrine? A number of developments have implications for the traditional doctrine of ministerial responsibility and for the accountability of officials. Managerial and related developments within and affecting Whitehall are well known and are more fully documented elsewhere in this volume and in other sources. They include: Whitehall's greater transparency and the loss of anonymity for many senior officials; the changing role of accounting officers; accountable management; and the implications of Next Steps and contracting out. To these one could add the growth of *ad hoc* bodies or QUANGOs as having circumscribed the parameters of accountability within ministerial departments, the focus of the present chapter.

For all the secrecy it retains Whitehall is now more transparent. More is known about what officials (and ministers) do and about the way in which they work. Civil servants down to and occasionally below grade 5 appear before parliamentary select committees. To MPs and to those who care to find out they are no longer, to use Churchill's phrase, 'slaves of the lamp concealed from the public in the deeper recesses of Whitehall'. Greater transparency is built into the system. In public officials still appear strictly on behalf of their ministers, as critics of the Osmotherly Rules have been wont to point out. To this there is one formal exception – that of accounting officers. It has long been accepted that accounting officers are accountable to the Commons' Committee of Public Accounts (PAC) in their own right, not on behalf of their ministers (Barberis 1996, pp. 62-7). If an irregularity surfaces it is the accounting officer who, in extremis, may be surcharged. He or she may have been unable to prevent the minister from proceeding with a dubious expenditure proposal but will have had the authority to issue a note of reservation, so absolving them from subsequent blame. In recent years there have been two main changes affecting these arrangements. First, there are now more accounting officers, most notably with the inclusion of agency chief executives. Second, notes of dissent may now be issued not only in cases of possible irregularity but also where a proposal is considered by the accounting officer not to represent value for money. This clearly broadens the responsibilities of accounting officers. It was largely under this remit that (Sir) Tim Lankester, then Permanent Secretary at the Overseas Development Administration, triggered controversy over British financial support for the Malaysian Pergau Dam project.

The notion of value for money lies at the heart of accountable management, an idea given expression by the Fulton Committee. By accountable management Fulton meant (1968, para. 191): 'forms of organisation and principles... by which individuals and branches can be held responsible for objectively measured performance'. It was Fulton's best shot at something original and, not surprisingly, brought perhaps the heaviest criticism. The worry was that if civil servants were more accountable ministers would be less so; that to make accountable anyone other than elected politicians was a threat to the system of democratic institutions. Similar dissent was registered when, twenty years later, the Ibbs Report called for a redefinition of the traditional doctrine (Efficiency Unit 1988, Annex A, pp. 17-9). But by now Management Information Systems for Ministers (MINIS) and the Financial Management Initiative (FMI) had been introduced and were beginning to bed down. Replete with mission statements, performance targets, performance related pay, micro cost centres and the like these initiatives were supposed now to equip ministers and top officials with more finely tuned mechanisms for supervision and control within their departments (see above, Chapter 3). At the same time structures have become more variegated, more fragmented. Of this, Next Steps agencies have been the most visible manifestation. It was the deliberate intention that they should become semi-independent. They now have a good deal of latitude to determine their own pay and grading arrangements. Agency chief executives present their own annual reports to Parliament. They field many of the initial enquiries made by MPs on behalf of their constituents.

What difference has all this made? Greater transparency does not in itself destroy the traditional canons of accountability, unless anonymity is held either to be an integral element of the doctrine or to be necessary for its sustenance. It is true that, until a generation or so ago, this was the assumption. It was partly a matter of political and administrative culture. It is doubtful if the loss of anonymity has itself brought any diminution in the theory and practice of accountability – provided everybody, including civil servants themselves, understands that they make public appearances on behalf of their ministers, certainly where policy is concerned. Nor has the special position of accounting officers – at least not according to the Treasury and Civil Service Select Committee (TCSC 1986 Vol. I, para. 3.7). The value for money element increases the scope for interaction between accounting officers and the PAC though, again, it does not in itself introduce any new dimension of accountability. But it may create friction between accounting officers and ministers, especially when the former are invited by the PAC to explain differences of opinion. It may be difficult in such circumstances to maintain the notion that civil servants are only representing the minister.

Accountable management, too, as it has developed during the 1980s and 1990s, has made this a difficult line to hold. On some occasions it has suited ministers who have been happy to push civil servants into the limelight, especially when something has gone wrong. This has been made easier by the existence of published performance targets, 'operational contracts' and so forth by which the work of civil servants may be judged and culprits identified. This might have happened without the advent of executive agencies. But their existence has sharpened the battle lines, strengthening what Gray and Jenkins (1985, p. 158) describe as 'a new code of *administrative accountability* where responsibility and answerability have increasingly shifted from ministers to officials'.

Ministers may feel that this is justified. In strictly managerial terms it is no doubt justifiable. Senior officials are entrusted with the day-to-day running of departments and agencies on behalf of ministers. They have less occasion than formerly to claim ignorance as to what is expected of them, at least in terms of performance outcomes. More generally, it may be said that as functions become detached or semi-detached from central government, then ministers need no longer take it on the chin when something goes wrong. This is true at least inasmuch as the traditional doctrine of responsibility (especially the obligation to resign) rested upon the ability of ministers to control their departments (Turpin 1994, p. 111; Woodhouse 1994, pp. 34-5). On this reading, if the sheer scale, complexity and fragmentation of modern government have reduced the control which ministers can reasonably be expected to exercise within their departments then they may to that extent feel at liberty to plead diminished responsibility.

Against this there are counter-arguments. First, the notion of internally accountable management is intended, among other things, to give ministers greater overall control of their departments. It ought, in principle, to allow better strategic direction, ensuring a closer correspondence between policy input and operational outcome. This may be offset by such fragmentation as has occurred, though the official line is that no greater fragmentation has taken place. There should be less occasion for wayward malfunctioning unconnected with official policy. We may therefore assume that malfunctioning is more likely to be the result of policy. Second, it is doubtful if even the ministerial control alluded to by the likes of Low or Jennings and upon which responsibility (sacrificial) was supposed to be conditional ever equated to direct, detailed supervision. There was surely an implicit 'chain of being' by which the 'mind of the minister' permeated the department. This did not require the minister personally to supervise the pulling of all the levers by which policy is transmitted. It did and does require that senior officials pass on the ministerial baton, so to speak. Thus ministers are able to direct affairs well beyond the orbit of their immediate supervision. This certainly was and probably remains the working assumption of accountability in its remedial and explanatory dimensions. The sacrificial dimension is more difficult, though it may not be possible completely to disconnect it from the other two. The case of Home Secretary Michael Howard in 1995 illustrates the point. Howard had come under increasing pressure to resign following a number of highly publicized escapes by prisoners from high security gaols. He was able to claim that he had discharged the obligation of remedial responsibility in sacking the head of the Prison Service, now an executive agency. One of the prison governors had already resigned. Howard accepted that he personally was responsible to Parliament for policy and accountable (i.e. answerable) for the Prison Service generally. But, he said, the agency framework document had placed upon the Director General of the Prison Service a specific responsibility for operational matters (HC Debs 1994-95, 6th Series, vol. 252, col. 40). He went on to say that the distinction between policy and operations had long preceded the creation of executive agencies. In this he was correct. His predecessors Kenneth Baker, William Whitelaw and Roy Jenkins were among those who had successfully resisted calls for their resignations following similar, albeit more isolated, escapes from gaols. But Howard's denials that shortcomings were in any way the result of Home Office (i.e. his) policies were much more difficult to sustain. They could only be sustained if he was also to say (which he did not) that the Prison Service had been driven by independently generated policies other than those of the Home Office. This was probably untrue but, even if true, would have required either a public confession of failure in internal management or an assertion of wilful subversion somewhere down the line. Alternatively, it could be said that there had been some purely technical, localized malfunctioning. But there had been more than one gaol escape in more than one place. Moreover, the Director General of the Prison

Service pleaded that the malfunctioning *was* the consequence of the Home Secretary's policies, an allegation which eventually resulted in an out of court (financial) settlement to the benefit of the sacked official. None of this is to say that the Home Secretary was under any *constitutional* obligation to resign, though the tide must have come pretty near to the threshold. There is no *a priori* specification which in practice requires sacrificial accountability. There is no constitutional tariff. There is only the negative precept that ministers do not and (apart from Robert Lowe long ago and unnecessarily) have not resigned except on matters over which they have or might reasonably have exercised some direction. The rest is pure party politics.

This leads to the third point in the argument. It rests upon consideration of two questions. First, can the sacrificial dimension of accountability be divorced from the other dimensions? Second, if not, then can a constitutional principle be maintained indefinitely in the absence of its activation, or where its activation is uncertain and even capricious?

Ministers who avoid resignation (or sacking) when something has gone seriously wrong rarely escape unscathed. There is usually an immediate embarrassment and occasionally long-term blight upon their political careers. On one account, this provides 'symbolic, if not actual, accountability' (Woodhouse 1994, p. 174). The sacrificial dimension of accountability is certainly different from the explanatory or the remedial. But 'different from' is not the same as 'unconnected with'. Would it not be better to see sacrificial accountability not as some far flung and detached meteor at loose within the conceptual universe but as forming a constellation with the explanatory and remedial elements, all three moving in some observable relationship? This may be asking too much. But the bottom line of sacrifice must, in principle, remain visible and generally understood in order to give guts to the other dimensions of accountability. This need imply no more than a long-stop sanction – but one which sets a clear marker. The one thing to emerge clearly in the fracas following the publication of the Scott Report was that there is no answer to the question 'what does a minister have to do to resign?'

The second and connected question, then, is whether, even on the long-stop assumption, sacrificial accountability can be maintained in principle if it never operates except where there is self-confessed culpability and then only through the capricious medium of political exchange. There are laws against murder, burglary and countless other felonies. That these laws are often broken is no reason to remove them from the statute book. Here we are, of course, concerned not with criminal law but with the 'laws' or 'conventions' of the constitution, to use Dicey's terminology. Dicey himself said (1959, p. 26, note 4) that some conventions have 'only a slight amount of custom in their favour'. There comes a point, though, at which the abstraction then becomes little more than a caricature and when, finally, it loses

touch with reality and becomes meaningless. When this happens the mechanisms of accountability lose their credibility.

Developments of the 1980s and '90s have brought few if any completely
new challenges to traditional notions of accountability. In certain respects
they may even offer opportunities to strengthen traditional mechanisms,
though in practice they seem to have had the effect or to have been given
the effect of exacerbating existing fault-lines. Some of these fault-lines are of
long standing. Mechanisms for accountability are far from dead. Yet in an
age which perhaps expects more they seem to offer less. In particular there
is growing confusion about the respective responsibilities of ministers and
civil servants. As more have gravitated to the latter, there has occurred an
increasing disparity between the doctrine and the reality of accountability.
What, then, is to be done?

What is to be done?

Logically, there are three distinct responses to the g   wing disparity
between doctrine and reality: do nothing and live with it; ! "ing reality back
into line with doctrine; or develop a new doctrine which better fits the reality. Each has its attractions and its drawbacks. One of the obstacles is the
tight constitutional skein within which the doctrine of accountability exists –
in particular the twin sovereignties of ministerial accountability to
Parliament and of Parliament as the nation's watchdog. By modifying (but
not abandoning) these shibboleths it may be possible to work towards
arrangements which, while lacking the elegance demanded by the purist,
may have virtues wholly befitting the British tradition of empiricism, prag-
matism and common sense. Let us look at each in turn of the three options.

Option one: do nothing and live with the present disparity

That there is and always has been some disparity between the doctrine and
the reality of accountability should be no cause for surprise. There need be
no perfect congruence. A certain amount of 'play' is inevitable and even
desirable in a 'living' constitution. This has obvious attractions for politicians, especially government ministers. The *status quo* gives them almost
(not quite) free rein to decide when and how to apply constitutional doctrine. But this should not be sufficient to satisfy the student of politics, public administration or constitutional law. For some of the reasons offered in
the last section it is difficult to sustain a doctrine when it stands increasingly
at variance with reality and when it simply has no answer to some of the
questions that have been raised about its application. It may be possible to
keep the show going as a matter of day-to-day, practical government. It can

be done – but only at some cost to the fabric of the broader body politic in a society which claims to be liberal democratic and to be governed by genuinely representative institutions subject to the rule of law.

Option two: bring reality into line with doctrine

If the facts do not fit the theory, then so much the worse for the facts! This is not to trivialize a position which has something to offer. With varying degrees of enthusiasm, it also has its supporters (Jones 1987; Judge 1993, p. 140). If there has been 'slippage', then it may be desirable to bring the offending practices back into line with (traditional) doctrine. To pursue the earlier analogy, the response to an increasing murder rate ought to be to introduce such measures as will prevent or reduce the incidence of the crime, not to ignore the problem or to redefine murder. This kind of option is attractive to those who think that the traditional canons of accountability have been violated either without proper acknowledgement of the fact or with hurried and unseemly attempts by ministers (and others) to neutralize or redefine the problem out of existence. The earlier analysis suggests that this has indeed been going on – and for much longer than we often care to admit.

The superficial attractions of option two are nevertheless overshadowed by a number of drawbacks. First, as has been noted, there were often elements of ambiguity, interpretation and even controversy surrounding the traditional doctrine of accountability. It is by no means clear as to exactly what ideal state we ought to return. Second, again to repeat, there has always been some disparity between doctrine and reality. There never was a golden age when the constitution worked in sweet harmony with the textbooks. This leads to the third and further point that it is difficult to see how contemporary government could be brought to conformity with a traditional doctrine which evidently proved too much for governments of the past. In the nature of the British system it is almost impossible to compel governments to adhere to specific arrangements, even those to which they profess still to subscribe. Even if the constitutional spirit is willing the political flesh is often weak at the vital moment. In short, there are times when it will suit ministers to deny or limit their responsibilities. This piece of realpolitik may seem a poor reason for denying option two. But there is a fourth and final point. It may simply not be wholly desirable, even if it were possible, to secure adherence to the traditional precepts. What would it involve? Allowing for some of the ambiguities alluded to above, it would mean ministers assuming full responsibility, in all aspects of the term, for their own acts and for those of their officials. For civil servants it could mean a return to greater anonymity, a loss of much of such transparency as there has been in recent years, perhaps the withdrawal of the presently published targets and other appurtenances of the Citizen's Charter. These are some of the possible and likely, if not inevitable, consequences. They are certainly among the characteristics formerly *thought* to have been necessary to uphold the traditional doctrine. The knock-on effects may not be quite what proponents have in mind when they seek a return to basics.

Option two is therefore unrealistic as a matter of practical politics and not without its drawbacks. As an ideal it need not be sunk without trace: indeed some elements are worthy of retention. But without modification it will take us no further forward and must be laid aside for the moment.

Option three: a doctrine to fit the reality

If we cannot live with the present incongruence and if we cannot or do not wish to establish conformity with traditional doctrine then we should try to formulate a new doctrine of accountability which better fits the modern realities. This is to assume the inductive approach: doctrine emerges from, thus reflects, the observation of accumulated facts or realities. What central realities would have to be reflected? Do we now have to condone murder?

Perhaps the most fundamental reality is that accountability has its practical application through the medium of political exchange. There are no constitutional tablets of stone, merely a collection of assumptions, sometimes ambiguous, often flexible in their interpretation. This is so in the absence of a written constitution. It bears upon all aspects of accountability, especially the sacrificial dimension. There is a residual constitutional notion of ministerial resignation, but the government and its supporters usually decide when it should come into play. Civil servants may be sacrificed if ministers decide they should be sacrificed. This may be done either quietly or more publicly, showing that ministers have taken things seriously and by way of remedy. Parliament and the public can huff and puff but, provided government supporters hold the line, it is ministers who parcel out the blame. This, of course, deals only with the more spectacular but less common instances where there is a serious call for the resignation of ministers or civil servants. Much more common is explanatory accountability. Here, too, the load is now borne by civil servants as well as by ministers. Whatever the doctrine may say, this is the brute reality. Given the sheer volume of business it is probably inevitable. If this responsibility were to be discharged solely by ministers through Parliament there would be a log-jam. In practice civil servants do answer to Parliament, most visibly through select committees. This is squared with 'traditional doctrine' by virtue of their representing ministers rather than themselves or the civil service as an institution which, it is said, has no personality aside from the government of the day. But ministers have given the official machine a personality by making certain of its members publicly (and sacrificially) accountable for operations. This has been underscored by all the paraphernalia of accountable management – not only the mechanisms of internal control but the outer face of greater transparency, annual reports to Parliament, the Citizen's Charter and so forth.

The seemingly inescapable thrust of all this is towards a doctrine which explicitly acknowledges the direct accountability of civil servants. As the Treasury and Civil Service Committee (1986, Vol. I, para. 3.17) put it:

> If Crichel Down is dead and ministers are not accountable to Parliament for some activity of their officials, then who is? Not to put too fine a point on it, who ought to resign or be penalised if mistakes are made? If it is not ministers, it can only be officials.

This is not to deny that ministers should also be held accountable and occasionally sacrificed in serious cases of failure. It is rather to suggest that the accountability of ministers need not preclude that of civil servants. It may be better to mark out and lay bare certain clearly defined areas, or zones, in which civil servants will usually be held to account than to pretend that ministers are accountable when increasingly they are less so. Otherwise there will be continued confusion and obfuscation with the result that, on occasion, no one really seems to be responsible.

Such clarity, bringing a deliberate shift towards officials, may seem to suit ministers. It is, as has been seen, implicit in some of the ministerial disclaimers about responsibility for operations. But while ministers are happy to make disclaimers on the odd occasions when something has gone seriously wrong they have been unwilling to develop the principles implicit therein into any more general formulation. Nor have opposition parties been keen to press the point. This is because any such formulation would run counter to the twin sovereignties of ministerial accountability to Parliament and of Parliament as the nation's sole watchdog. Connected to both is the notion of the 'great chain of democracy'.

The great chain of democracy implies the transmission of an impulse issuing from the people, via representatives elected to a legislative assembly. In Britain some of these representatives become ministers who have, in addition, another role as members of the executive. When the legislative assembly (Parliament) tries to bring the executive to account it does so through ministers and ministers alone. It speaks only to its own kind, as it were. At the same time the business of bringing ministers to account belongs formally to Parliament and to Parliament alone. The knitting together of these two threads creates the 'constitutional loop'. If either thread is broken the other is weakened and the loop is destroyed. The chain of democracy is thus impaired.

It is as well to remember that the notion of exclusive ministerial responsibility evolved during the late-nineteenth century both to recognize and to strengthen the democratic underpinning of accountability. This it tried in effect to do by insisting that only those who had been elected could be held to account and that they should account only to others who had also been elected. To suggest any modification here may be to risk unravelling the constitution and the edifice of representative government. The stakes are high: we must proceed with care. Can the constitutional loop be interposed without it being broken? The answer is that it is possible, provided we are prepared to modify but not to abandon the twin sovereignties of ministerial and Parliamentary supremacy. That there need be no damage to the fabric of democratically accountable government is the no less contentious suggestion.

Implicit in much of the earlier argument is the assertion that ministers are not *de facto* exclusively responsible for their departments. In many ways the notion of exclusivity has been subverted, little by little. Ministers are no longer wholly accountable for everything, though Parliament is prepared formally to recognize no other. Parliament, for its part, remains the watchdog of the nation but is not fully equipped to perform the task satisfactorily on its own. Ministers pay lip service to Parliament's sovereignty while misleading it, manipulating its procedures and sometimes explicitly effecting its circumvention. This they have done not perhaps routinely but at any rate when it has been to their advantage in escaping from a tight corner. If and when exposed, such practices have usually been justified in the cause of the national interest or of commercial confidentiality. Such was the government's defence in having withheld information from Parliament over the sale of arms to Iraq during the 1980s. Different aspects of the official inquiry into this matter – the Scott Report – are dealt with elsewhere in this volume (see chapters 1 and 8). Here suffice it to note that Scott (1996, Vol. I, para. D4.56, p. 502) accepted that there have been and always will be subjects about which full information cannot be made public. These would include national security or imminent changes in interest rates or in exchange rates. But Scott did not agree that the sale of arms fell into this category, suggesting that the government had acted so as to avoid embarrassment. He held that the statements made to Parliament by the government 'failed to discharge the obligation imposed by the constitutional principle of ministerial accountability' (Vol. I, para. D4.63, p. 507). Such failure, he concluded, 'undermines... the democratic process' (Vol. IV, para. K8.3, p. 1801).

Parliament is simply not able effectively to act alone as the nation's watchdog. It has done and can do much in this area, but alone it is inadequate. To continue as if it were alone adequate would be further to undermine the very process of democratic accountability that Parliament is supposed to sustain. It is therefore time to modify the purist, Diceyan notion of parliamentary sovereignty – at least inasmuch as this demands that

Parliament be the only body to which ministers can be brought legitimately to account. It is also time to legitimize the direct accountability of officials, both to Parliament and to other authorities and in carefully specified areas beyond those for which accounting officers are already responsible. In connection with the latter, the value for money dimension has in any case taken things further along. There is no good reason, in principle, why the apparatus of the Citizen's Charter could not be developed to create a network of 'tribunals' in which officials were brought to account in the explanatory sense and as a 'first stop' in connection with the activities of their own agencies or units.

Proposals of this kind do more than provide a new doctrine to meet prevailing realities: they go beyond the existing realities. Similar ideas have met official resistance as constituting a threat to Parliament (Cabinet Office 1993b, para. 4.21). This is sheer evasive disingenuity. Such objections were raised to initial proposals for the establishment of the ombudsman, even to the extension of the select committee system. Most would now agree that these institutions operate on behalf of and to the enhancement of Parliament. If Parliament were further to 'sub-contract' some of its accountability functions its overall capacity could be further strengthened, not diminished.

Clearly, much careful thinking needs to be done and without which any stumbling attempt at reform could be detrimental rather than helpful. Taking up the earlier analogy, we may then find ourselves forced to condone (constitutional) murder. Certain safeguards are requisite if the outcome of any such reforms were to be for good rather than ill. It is important that Parliament continues to bring ministers to account; that ministers are never able to get away with saying that accountability is none of Parliament's business; and that the location of responsibility is not reduced to yet further confusion. It is important that the notion of ministerial responsibility and of Parliament's role in bringing the executive to account be retained as a 'long-stop', procedurally integrated with other mechanisms. But there is no reason why it should begin and end with ministers and with Parliament and every reason now why it should not. No one supposes that the authority of the House of Lords as the supreme court in the land is diminished on account of there being a network of subordinate courts. Supplementary mechanisms could be devised to bring to account, on behalf of Parliament, people other than ministers – i.e. civil servants.

In connection with civil servants it would be necessary to avert two possible dangers. First, there is the danger that, in being brought to account, civil servants may either unwittingly or deliberately, in order to save their skins, betray confidences with which they have been entrusted and which are necessary to the efficient conduct of government. It is important that the policy advice given by civil servants to ministers should remain confidential. Not all would agree, but confidentiality is a prerequisite to free and frank exchange between officials and ministers. It is also important that senior officials, including agency chief executives, do not get themselves publicly identified as partisan supporters of particular policies. Otherwise they will not command the confidence of an incoming government or even of a new minister within an existing government. The naked politicization of the civil service would be but one small step away and the impartiality of the civil service lost – a serious loss for those (the majority) who still think it a virtue. This is a possible but far from inevitable outcome of the kind of model suggested here. It seems not to have been a problem to civil servants when appearing before select committees, albeit at present technically on behalf of their ministers. There would need to be clearly established ground-rules as to what exactly civil servants are and are not accountable for in relation to ministers. Osmotherly Mark II (or III) is surely not beyond the wit of Whitehall! Second, it is possible that, if held to account in their own right on certain matters, civil servants may assume and even demand some measure of independence from their ministers. If they think they may have to take the rap officials could be more inclined to say 'no' – or at least to cover themselves with notes of dissent similar to those sometimes issued by accounting officers. Ministers may have to work harder to 'permeate' their departments. If it went too far this could become an impediment to democratic government. But provided it did not go too far it could enhance the quality of government, ministers having to offer better reasons to justify policies and hopefully producing better policies. Ministers would by no means lose the initiative. And to the extent that there are dangers it is something which ministers ought to bear in mind when they proclaim that malfunctioning is purely operational – indeed to the point at which critics feel that ministers are no longer prepared to recognize anything as being a policy-related failure. If ministers go much further in this direction it is possible that civil servants (certainly the FDA) and other interested parties will begin more vigorously to agitate for a reappraisal of both doctrine and practice.

The ideas sketched out here rest upon a view of accountability rather different from that of the simple 'great chain of democracy' type. As it exists in Britain the 'great chain' model is rather one-dimensional, incorporating what is described above as the 'constitutional loop'. It is not necessary to destroy, merely to interpose and augment the loop. This requires what Spiro (1969, pp. 83-110) calls a multicentric rather than a command model of bureaucratic accountability. By this he means accountability 'to different authorities, for different purposes, to different degrees and in terms of different, though mutually complementary standards' (p. 98). It is surely appropriate to the multicentric forms of administration that have developed more strongly in recent years. As such it would go some way towards resolving the problem of incongruity, though it also reaches beyond present realities. It is not without its potential dangers. The dangers outlined above are avoidable but only, it must be emphasized, if things are done properly. Otherwise option two remains an attractive ideal, though with little chance of fulfilment and even then not without its drawbacks. That leaves option one. This is increasingly unsatisfactory but may be no worse than a botched up option three. In any case, as the likeliest outcome, though for bad reasons rather than good, the hot money is on option one.

10 Conclusions: into the twenty-first century

Peter Barberis

Introduction

In a public lecture Sir Robin Butler (1992b, p. 1) once said that, if asked where the civil service ought to be in ten or twenty years' time, his answer would have to be: 'where the political and economic environment of the time requires us to be'. It would have been unwise for him to have engaged in naked prescription or indeed in any such prediction as might have pre-empted either his present or future political masters. Even without the constraint of constitutional propriety, firm prediction is often an unprofitable pursuit. Things move quickly in a changing world – and not always in the direction that one would expect. As a rule, the further into the future we look the greater the chances of our being confounded. It can be like trying to pick a Derby winner from the Doncaster yearling sales! Yet without mortgaging our credibility beyond redemption we can make certain projections, given the present drift of events. If we cannot be sure where exactly current events are leading or that there will be no seismic reorientation, we can usually identify some of the broad issues that seem likely to command the agenda for the next half generation. We are usually able to outline the context and to specify the range of possibilities, some seeming stronger than others from the perspective of the present.

With these points in mind this concluding chapter offers not a set of predictions but a sketch of the main issues likely to bear upon the civil service as the new millennium approaches and begins to unfold. It considers, first, the changing nature of the state and the corresponding role of the bureaucracy. At this fairly general level the discussion necessarily remains at times on a more abstract plane, setting the broad context within which patterns of change will be determined. Second, it will analyse the civil service within the changing constitution. Almost unnoticed and with little or no apparent direction of effort the British constitution is wont to transmute itself, shifting (however slightly) the ground upon which the state bureaucracy finds itself encamped. Beyond this there have in recent years been numerous calls for deliberate and more or less radical reconstruction. The character of some of these proposals is explored, together with the implications for the civil service. Third and finally the chapter prognosticates upon some of the organizational, management and personnel matters that have defined the present era of change and which have featured in this volume.

The state and the role of the bureaucracy

Britain seems destined to remain a liberal democracy. It is difficult to detect the seeds of any revolution, Marxist or otherwise, which would disturb this state of affairs in the foreseeable future. Indeed there has been made the much bolder claim that liberal democracy represents the final form of government in which the individual may achieve both 'social' recognition and reasonable satisfaction of material desires (Fukuyama 1992). The contradictions and impediments of earlier epochs have, it is asserted, been overcome, so facilitating an Hegelian type 'realization of spirit'. Needless to say, this partial and highly controversial championing of (capitalist) liberal democracy has had its critics, Marxist and non-Marxist alike (Townshend 1996, pp. 256-8; Gellner 1996). But for the moment, liberal democracy continues to flourish.

The imperatives of a market economy, the rule of law and representative institutions provide the compass points, together with certain conceptions of freedom and responsibility. These are the outer perimeters, allowing much latitude and a good deal of 'play'. The state may be more or less passive or interventionist; responsive or proactive; permissive or coercive; secular or moralistic – all within the skein of liberal democracy. It may beget various forms of government, differing institutional arrangements and distinct interpretations of political principle (Crick 1973; Finer 1970; Dunleavy and O'Leary 1987; Ham and Hill 1993). This is certainly so among the liberal democracies that exist today. Within any one country, such as Britain, patterns and inflections may change over time, sometimes within quite a short period. Such indeed has been the evidence presented in this volume. Over the last ten, fifteen and twenty years there has been a broad shift from collectivism to individualism; from universality to selectivity; from comparatively integrated structures to more variegated, 'customized' forms. Alongside all this there has been the transformation of the state from that of direct provider to that of enabler.

There is and will always be scope for interpretation as to what exactly is the role of the state, the nature of its activities and the character of its institutions. Historians have debated whether the mid nineteenth century state was essentially *laissez-faire* or interventionist, or some more complicated compound (Hobsbawm 1968, Ch. 12; Roberts 1960; Lubenow 1971). The leeway for interpretation arises at least as much from the inherent and sometimes contrived ambiguities of role as from the differing perspectives of the historians themselves. In truth there is for any one state at any given time much scope as to what it does and how it does those things, what it entrusts to other institutions and how it interacts with those institutions. This is not to imply that the state has unlimited discretion or that it is an entirely free agent. It has some autonomy but is increasingly constrained by the incursions of supranational institutions, by the global economy and even by its own internal logic. As some nations rise, others fall (Olson 1982; Kennedy 1987). Strong states may become enfeebled by their own actions (Hall and Ikenberry 1989, p. 13). Perhaps the nation state as an entity is doomed, hanging on like dinosaurs waiting to die. This is certainly a view held by some (Hoffman 1995; Ohmae 1995), though others are much more circumspect (Dunn 1995; Boyer and Drache 1996). It is an extreme scenario, unlikely to happen in the foreseeable future and, as such, beyond our present concern. Still, the changing character of the state and of its activities bears heavily upon the state bureaucracy.

If there is a distinct, directional change in the character of the state there will be implications for the role of the state bureaucracy. Again, there is no simple, deterministic relationship. Britain's so-called 'night-watchman' state of the nineteenth century engendered a bureaucracy of high ideals, service to society and, in some respects, of paternalistic autarky (see above, Chapter 6). In this there was perhaps a certain anomaly if not open contradiction. At the same time, the activities of the state in the last century and in this century no less have, in part, been driven by the bureaucracy itself (Finer 1952; MacDonagh 1961; Davidson 1985; Lowe 1986, 1993).

It is difficult to know whether the bureaucracy has been an essentially active or passive agent amidst the changes surveyed in this book. Senior mandarins seem to have presided over a redefinition and perhaps a diminution in their own ability to shape events. They have, according to some, largely saved their own skins. But this serves only to illustrate that they have been less able to effect much purchase on the broader forces which have swayed the bureaucracy, be they economic or political, national or international. For some this is a mercy, while for others it is a cause for regret. It is a cause for regret especially among those who see no end to the more utilitarian, target-chasing temper which, they say, now pervades Whitehall. By contrast, the quasi-detachment, the concern for higher morality with a suggestion of other-worldliness may be seen as qualities necessary among senior officials if the bureaucracy is to maintain its integrity. Some see these qualities as having been under threat in recent years. It may prove difficult for the mandarinate of the future to recapture and reassert the high-minded, public spiritedness of former years.

Britain's civil service is generally acknowledged to be politically impartial. This impartiality is the product of the late eighteenth and early nineteenth century 'settlement' from which there emerged a permanent constitutional bureaucracy (Parris 1969). As politicians come and go, civil servants stay in their posts. This does not render the bureaucracy strictly neutral. If the state (as distinct from this or that particular party in office) bears a certain inclination then, to a greater or lesser extent, so too will the bureaucracy. Indeed in order adequately to serve the elected government of the day it may be necessary for the bureaucracy to assume, to some minor degree, the coloration of the party in office (Part 1990, p. 107). As one party yields office to its political opponents, so the (pale) coloration assumed by the bureaucracy must change. The bureaucracy must never become so imbued with the party currently in office as to render it incapable of transferring its allegiance immediately upon a change of government. This is one reason why it has been thought inappropriate and unwise for mandarins to become publicly associated with government policies – at least not as advocates or apologists. If they did it may be difficult for them to claim the confidence of a new government with new and different policies.

Such is the British notion of impartiality. It has been linked with notions of fairness, justice and equity – links acknowledged by British governments (see Chapter 1). It continues to command quite wide support, but has nevertheless attracted increasing criticisms and misgivings. At the purely abstract level one may wonder, first, whether and, if so, in what senses impartiality is connected with 'fairness' and 'justice' (Rawls 1972, pp. 183-92; MacIntyre 1988; Barry 1995). Second, one may question the reality of the bureaucracy's political impartiality, even on traditional assumptions. If the bureaucracy is unable in practice to transfer its allegiance and is unable adequately to serve one government without placing in jeopardy its ability to serve another then the notion of impartiality may become less appealing, even among some of its staunchest advocates. The price to be paid for its retention – excessive secrecy, undue caution and lack of imagination, according to the critics – may be considered too high. Very limited proposals for politicization have been made by some, partly in the belief that covert and mild forms of politicization have already taken place and that it would be better to make a clean breast of things (Plowden 1985; Jay 1985). It has been more difficult to sustain the potentially more serious charge that a long period of one party domination after 1979 left the civil service incapable of serving other than a Conservative government. But there is a third argument. Formerly associated with the left it has resurfaced during the 1990s more on the radical right, though there may also be a secular impulse. It asserts that, whatever the present reality, the civil service ought to be more overtly partisan. The belief is that while it is possible to maintain traditional postures of impartiality the very effort in so doing prevents the bureaucracy from placing its full energies at the service of the incumbent government. The obvious remedy is to introduce a greater number of political appointees, either to work alongside or to replace the existing permanent mandarinate.

To date, such proposals have remained on the periphery or have taken only mild form. They are unlikely to claim centre stage unless it were to become clear that the civil service was unable to serve with due loyalty an elected government of certain political persuasion. Allegations to this effect have been made from time-to-time but have not enjoyed widespread support. The credibility of such allegations has suffered in part from the fact that they have emanated from both ends of the political spectrum. Both sides cannot be correct, it may be said. There is, nevertheless, some strength in the belief that if the bureaucracy has a position it is a centrist one. So long as there remains a measure of consensus among the leaders of the main political parties, there is unlikely to be a strong enough impetus for a heavily politicized bureaucracy. Such an impetus could gather momentum, though, if there were to be a lurch towards the political polarization of the early 1980s.

There is, in any case, a secular trend. One of the legacies of the 1980s is a mandarinate which *appears* to be less influential and which has certainly lost some of its former stranglehold over the supply lines of policy advice to ministers. The so-called 'managerialization' of the higher civil service is a jibe often heard and sometimes overstated. It is nevertheless one which reflects an essential truth. If the role of the bureaucracy continues to be more managerial and less policy orientated then the virtues of political impartiality may lose some of their appeal, except as a plea for the return to days gone by. These virtues may come to seem less appropriate to the world of the administrator technician than to the philosopher ruler. It is a logical implication of Thatcher's preference for the less reflective, head-down, can-do type of senior official. It may – though it need not – imply the appointment of party political partisans to fill the upper echelons of the bureaucracy. It would almost certainly sound the death knell for a politically impartial civil service as it has been commonly understood.

This is a possible if by no means inevitable development. For there have arisen growing calls to enshrine the semi-independence and impartiality of the civil service in a code or Act of Parliament, or in a written constitution.

The question of impartiality is thus linked with the role of the bureaucracy in the constitution.

The civil service and the constitution

Elsewhere in this volume there has been occasion to note and to consider some of the consequences of the fact that Britain does not have an integrated written constitution. At no point has there been any attempt to redefine the ways in which all the different organs of state fit together. It has been said that the British constitution is 'a continuing historical process rather than a matter of fixed points or legal settlements that hold until they are consciously undone or remade' (Hennessy 1995, p. 29). This is not quite true. There have been certain moments of reappraisal, such as those following the Crichel Down affair in the 1950s (see Chapter 9) or the Parliament Act of 1911 in the aftermath of the People's Budget. It remains to be seen whether the Scott inquiry will result in any reappraisal of roles and responsibilities – for example those of the Attorney General in the issue of public interest immunity certificates (see Chapter 8). Still, things are rarely clear cut and even these examples illustrate the tendency to introduce formality only to serve that which was previously assumed to have existed at the level of common understanding. In recent years, though, common understandings seem to have become rather less common. In consequence we have seen the introduction of written codes for MPs, civil servants and ministers, the latter in the form of *Questions of Procedure for Ministers*, made public in 1992 and revised in 1996 (see Chapters 1 and 7). With these formalizations, prompted by the Treasury and Civil Service Committee (now the Committee for Public Service) and the Nolan Committee, Britain may be edging towards some sort of written constitution. This has encouraged those who want to see a comprehensive written constitution.

Calls for a written constitution rest partly upon the belief that the executive has assumed too much power; that Britain has become excessively centralized; and that the system of checks and balances needs reinforcement (Jenkins 1995; Marr 1995). In the absence of a written constitution it is tempting to paraphrase Herbert Morrison's dictum about the Labour Party and socialism – in other words to say that the British constitution is what the government of the day says it is, or at any rate that it works in the way that the government of the day deigns that it should work. This is not quite true either, though in some areas, such as ministerial responsibility, the government is often able to determine how traditional 'conventions and understandings' will apply in a particular case – so long as its own back benchers remain satisfied or feel obliged to toe the line (see Chapter 9). For some, this only reinforces the need to establish a set of rules by which all governments would be bound and which could not be changed at the whim of any one government which happened to find the rules an inconvenience.

What would a written constitution amount to and what would be its implications for the civil service? It is a moot point as to whether a written constitution would, in the event, simply enshrine all existing elements and understandings; or whether it would attempt to establish new relationships between the various organs of state. The latter is clearly the preferred option among most of those who currently want a written constitution. They would expect to see some statement about the role of the civil service – something which goes well beyond the Armstrong Memorandum or the Civil Service Code. The 1994 white paper *Continuity and Change* stated that 'the civil service is not the property of any single Administration' (Cabinet Office 1994a, para. 1.8). To whom or to what, then, should it belong? It could be held to belong to the Crown, but what exactly does this imply? It has been described as being the bulwark or as providing the ballast of the constitution. But this offers few solutions when disputes arise, say, as to when civil servants may legitimately call upon higher authority (what higher authority?) to help restrain a government from engaging in an act of illegality or constitutional impropriety.

These difficulties seem to strengthen the anti-constitutionalists' case – that is those who oppose a formal, written constitution. As Enoch Powell said of the Nolan Committee, it is neither appropriate nor even desirable to 'define the undefinable and reduce to a set of rules that which cannot be so treated' (*The Times* 19 May 1995). The Civil Service Code shows both the strengths and the weaknesses of this proposition. The code establishes a set of procedures, including mechanisms for appeal, to protect individual civil servants who feel that they are being inveigled by ministers to behave improperly. It does not specify what constitutes improper behaviour and it may be that any attempt so to do would be to 'define the undefinable'. But it is possible in the very broadest sense to specify categories of impropriety. This the Civil Service Code does, in effect, with references to breaking the law; to misleading Parliament; and to violating international agreements. That it provides no further specification perhaps reflects the shortcomings of the code rather than the futility of any attempt to establish more precise definition.

There are certainly those who think that a more detailed civil service code is both possible and desirable. It may be that the maintenance of probity and good standards of conduct demands stronger mechanisms of supervision, remedy and deterrence (see Chapters 6 and 7). Many who hold such views nevertheless agree that formal measures are unlikely to operate to full effect unless the standards and values they are designed to safeguard are also internalized by participants. This connects with the notion of the public service ethic. It is difficult to know to what extent, if any, the public service ethic has been weakened or is likely (further) to be weakened in the future. The 1994 white paper *Continuity and Change* and its 1995 sequel, *Taking Forward Continuity and Change*, contained in their opening paragraphs strong endorsements of the traditional civil service values. Unconfirmed rumours had it that these paragraphs were inserted at the behest of the bureaucracy and in the face of resistance from ministers. If so, it may bode well or it may bode ill for the future. It bodes well inasmuch as it shows that senior mandarins remain sensitive to traditional values and that they are prepared to battle in defence of those values should they feel them to be under any threat. Officials have not, as some of the critics claim, stood by helplessly as politicians play fast and loose with the constitution. On the other hand it bodes ill inasmuch as it implies that politicians, left to themselves, cannot be relied upon to respect the conventions of engagement. The bureaucracy is not entirely safe in their hands. This is a handicap in a system which yields considerable scope to the political executive. The sense of foreboding is underlined to the extent to which the civil service may have withered as a recognizable entity (see Chapter 2). For if this is so then it may become more difficult to sustain the core values which have given the civil service its special character. This is certainly possible and indeed increasingly likely though, again, it is by no means an inevitable outcome. It brings us to the questions of organization, management and personnel.

Organization, management and personnel

It may be useful at this juncture to explain one or two points arising from the discussion so far which may otherwise seem confusing and even contradictory. Reference has been made to the state's diminishing autonomy. It has also been suggested that greater centralization and a weakening of traditional checks and balances have served to strengthen the executive. But the bureaucracy, it has been said, seems to have lost some of its independence. At first sight, these statements appear to rest rather uneasily alongside one another. In fact they are not difficult to reconcile. The state has indeed lost some of its former autonomy. Much of the loss has been to the international community – groups of states (EU) and the more nebulous artefact of the global economy. At the same time there has in Britain been a shift of initiative to the executive and a ratcheting up from local to central government institutions. The executive has gained, largely at the expense of Parliament and, perhaps, of the citizenry. Within the executive there has been a further shift from the permanent, or official, to the political element, though how much is difficult to say. Central government has tried with some success to shape and reshape the activities of sub-national institutions. But it has not itself remained static. It has reshaped its own structures. For sure it has tried to maintain control. This it has done with a greater emphasis upon arm's length supervision in favour of the more traditional, hierarchical command. The resulting processes have been variously described as the 'hollowing out' of the state, the de-Sir Humphreyfying of the Westminster model and as the federalization of the civil service (Rhodes 1994; Hood 1991b; Pyper 1995).

Four distinct types of manoeuvre have been taking place. First, the state has relinquished its involvement in certain activities. This is seen most clearly in the programmes of privatization and contracting out. Here the state has removed itself from the heart of the action, retaining only the toehold of regulation or, in the case of contracting out, the discretion to transfer its favours from one private contractor to another. Second, direct responsibility for the performance of some functions has been taken away from central government departments as direct agents and placed upon specialist bodies, collectively known as QUANGOs. Most QUANGOs operate under the tutelage of a 'sponsor' government department, though the respective responsibilities of QUANGOs and their departments have not always been clear in practice. Third, the arm's length principle has had purchase within the organizational territory of central government itself. It has had its clearest expression in the creation of executive agencies. Next Steps agencies remain part of central government. Those who work within them continue to be civil servants. Some enjoy a good deal of independence from their respective core departments, others less so (see Chapter 3). Fourth, there has been greater delegation and evidence of disaggregation within the core departments. Matrix styles of management have tended to replace hierarchical structures, inasmuch as such 'ideal types' can ever adequately represent complex realities.

Are these developments likely to continue their march, or even to accelerate in their momentum? Or is there reason to believe that they will calcify or recede? Here it is necessary to repeat the earlier warning about predictions. It would be unwise to make any firm forecast. That said, it looks for the moment as if privatization has gone about as far as it is likely to go, yet with little prospect of unwinding, whatever party is in office. Contracting out could make further inroads, depending upon the political climate. Like contracting out QUANGOs have been at the centre of political controversy, though for longer and for rather different reasons. It is nevertheless unlikely that they will disappear or that there will be a heavy 'cull'. They will probably be brought under closer supervision but not within the organizational embrace of ministerial departments. Next Steps agencies enjoy the support, in principle, of the main political parties. They are likely to remain on the scene for the foreseeable future and perhaps for a long time to come. How much further they will move in the direction of semi-detachment and how much more autonomy they will claim or be granted is less certain. They are beginning to enjoy some of the freedoms initially promised but sometimes granted only grudgingly by the core and central departments – for example in determining pay and service conditions (see Chapter 5). It remains to be seen whether these freedoms would survive a bout of sustained high inflation. Indeed it may be wondered whether at some future date the whole process of federalization could be halted and thrown into reverse. There is no sign of this at present and, even if such were to be the objective, it would be interesting to see whether the centrifugal forces now in motion could be contained and reined back. The same apples to the greater transparency, further loss of anonymity and shifting patterns of accountability which have been characteristic of the recent era of change.

Willingly or otherwise civil servants may be on the verge of assuming responsibility in public for certain aspects of the bureaucracy's work and functions. This has implications for the system of accountability and for the respective responsibilities of officials and their ministers (see Chapter 9). Initiatives such as the Citizen's Charter (see Chapter 4) are designed to increase the transparency of the civil service. Whether Whitehall will (or should) ever open its doors to the extent demanded by critics of the mid 1990s let alone those of the future is a moot point. But inasmuch as the cloak of anonymity has been lifted, it has probably been lifted for ever. Sir Robin Butler's successor as head of the home civil service is much more likely to act the role of Butler Mark II than of a reincarnated Sir Edward Bridges or Sir Warren Fisher. Yet in one respect alone a revival of the Fisher portfolio seems on the cards. There have been calls for a merger of the home civil service and of the foreign service – or at least for a unified headship as during the Fisher years. At the same time, it is by no means obvious that the headship of the (home) civil service will remain linked to the cabinet secretaryship. It has been so linked on a regular basis only since the early 1980s. Critics have seen the combined roles as placing an excessive burden upon one individual and, on occasion, as being incompatible. These charges are by no means unanswerable but they may prove decisive. There have been calls, too, for a strengthening of the central machinery of government. Proposals have included the creation of a Prime Minister's Department, a stronger central co-ordinating agency, a reincarnated Civil Service Department and, again with shades of the 1960s, for a new economic ministry to work alongside the Treasury. These are among the possible but far from inevitable patterns of future organizational change. They are more in the nature of fashions that come and go than of any sustained trend.

Of particular interest is the thesis that the Whitehall model of state administration has had its day (Campbell and Wilson 1995). By 'Whitehall model' is meant a strong, integrated, permanent career civil service offering ministers frank, fearless policy advice. According to Campbell and Wilson this system has simply failed to produce the advantages often claimed for it

– that is that it provides sound policy advice and effective, well co-ordinated implementation. The British administrative state has become more centralized yet without the capacity to formulate and deliver appropriate and workable programmes. The Poll Tax and other apparent policy failures have been cited as examples of the rotten fruits of systemic malfunctioning (Butler, Adonis and Travers 1994; Dunleavy 1995). Yet some of these failures – most notably the Poll Tax – can as easily be adduced as evidence in support of the Whitehall model. If the Whitehall model had been working properly, might this policy disaster have been averted? On the other hand, it is not clear that the Whitehall model is dead, merely that it has changed. What is even less clear is by what model it is supposed to have been replaced or as to what model will in future take its place. Viva Whitehall! Rise again, Sir Humphrey, your country still needs you – for the time being at least.

This brings us back to the question of the *corps d'elite*, the senior civil service as it is now officially called. The fact that it has been so designated since April 1995 is itself testimony to Whitehall's desire to maintain some sort of cohesive group at the heart of the government machine. Popular prognostications about the death of Sir Humphrey and about the dissolution of the traditional administrative elite may or may not find fulfilment. The roles played by senior officials have already changed. They are now less policy-oriented, more managerial. The importation of more outsiders and semi-careerists has given a further jolt to what critics have seen as the cosy (if busy) world of the 'Whitehall womb'. Britain's administrative elite is less homogenous and perhaps less self-assured than formerly. It is more difficult to know to what extent these changing characteristics are the cause or the consequence of its changing role – or indeed whether separate and independent factors are at work. Whatever the case, it is tempting to say that, even as it changes and even if some of these changes are the products of extraneous factors, Britain's administrative elite will always take care of itself.

This may be to assume a degree of control by the mandarinate over its own destiny that it no longer possesses. Already, as we have seen, its role at the centre of things is less secure than once it was. There are those who would give the process of further diminution a helping hand, with their talk about the need for more 'production engineers' (Kemp 1993). More importantly, ministers are unlikely to allow the permanent mandarins to reclaim any near-monopoly over policy advice. Still, aside from the occasional skirmishes, most ministers most of the time seem to value the support they get from their senior officials. They may not be too anxious to see it dissipated.

For the moment, then, there is likely to remain a recognizable *corps d'elite* at the heart of Whitehall. A sharper demarcation between it and the general non-elite is a plausible possibility, especially as the latter becomes a more amorphous, disaggregated body than at any time in living memory. Such disaggregation could become the long-term fate of the elite, too, if the process of departmental recruitment were driven to its ultimate conclusion. Whitehall seems uncertain as to whether to retain 'fast stream' recruitment. Its total abandonment would be a blow to the identity of the elite corps, though not necessarily a mortal blow. Whatever the arrangements for recruitment, 'Oxbridge' is likely to retain a share that is disproportionate numerically if not in relation to the quality of its output. Such is the nature of the education system. In absolute terms, Oxbridge may in future be less heavily represented among the upper echelons of the civil service, if only on account of Whitehall's increasing propensity to fill senior posts from outside its own ranks. In any case the Oxbridge product of the future may be of different hue from that of the present or recent past. This will have implications for Whitehall – not in the short-term but in the medium and long-term.

Beyond this it would be unwise to speculate. At the beginning of this volume there was some discussion about whether the last 15-20 years will come to be seen as a special era in the history of the civil service. If nothing else we should by, say, 2010 have a clearer idea as to the significance of the changes that have taken place during the 1980s and 1990s. It is possible that the next fifteen years will see the launch of yet more dramatic initiatives – or the unfolding of changes that are less dramatic but equally telling. In this case the recent era will not be regarded as special. On the other hand, there is no compelling reason to suppose that the present momentum will be or can be sustained indefinitely. A period of quieter consolidation is possible. In that case we may well look back upon the 1980s and 1990s as a special era of change.

Bibliography

Adjudicator's Office (1995a) *How to Complain About the Inland Revenue*, The Adjudicator's Office, London.

Adjudicator's Office (1995b) *The Adjudicator's Office Annual Report 1995*, The Adjudicator's Office, London.

Adonis, A. (1995a) 'Advisers outbid each other to show billions saved', *Financial Times*, 23 May.

Adonis, A. (1995b) 'Foreboding pervades corridors of power', *Financial Times*, 23 March.

Adonis, A. (1995c) 'Minister seeks more civil service savings', *Financial Times*, 10 January.

Allan, T.R.S. (1993) 'Public interest immunity and ministers' responsibilities', *Criminal Law Review*, pp. 660-8.

Armstrong, W. (1969) Television interview, 13 April. Quoted in R.A. Chapman, *The Higher Civil Service in Britain*, Constable, London, 1970, p. 141.

Audit Commission (1993) *Protecting the Public Purse: Probity in the Public Sector: Combating Fraud and Corruption in Local Government*, HMSO, London.

Audit Commission (1994) *Protecting the Public Purse II: Ensuring Probity in the NHS*, HMSO, London.

Barberis, P. (1995) 'The civil service from Fulton to Next Steps and beyond: two interpretations, two epistemologies', *Public Policy and Administration*, vol. 10 no. 2, pp. 34-51.

Barberis, P. (1996) *The Elite of the Elite: Permanent Secretaries in the British Higher Civil Service*, Dartmouth, Aldershot.

Barry, B. (1995) *A Treatise on Social Justice: Vol. II – Justice as Impartiality*, Clarendon, Oxford.

Benefits Agency (1991) *Framework Document*, Benefits Agency, London.

Benefits Agency (1993) *Customer Charter: Renewing Our Commitment to You*, Benefits Agency, Leeds.

Benefits Agency (1995) *95/96 Business Plan*, Benefits Agency, Leeds.

Birch, A.H. (1964) *Representative and Responsible Government: An Essay on the Constitution*, George Allen and Unwin, London.

Birkinshaw, P., Harden, I. and Lewis, N. (1990) *Government by Moonlight: The Hybrid Parts of the State*, Unwin Hyman, London.

Blackstone, T. and Plowden, W. (1988) *Inside the Think Tank: Advising the Cabinet 1971-1983*, Heinemann, London.

Blau, P.M. (1956) *Bureaucracy in Modern Society*, Random House, New York.

Bolger, A. (1995) 'Merger creates largest union for civil service', *Financial Times*, 20 September.

Boyer, R. and Drache, D. (eds.) (1996) *States Against Markets: The Limits of Globalization*, Routledge, London.

Bradley, A.W. (1992) 'Justice, good government and public interest immunity', *Public Law*, pp. 514-21.

Bridges, E. (1950) *Portrait of a Profession: The Civil Service Tradition*, Cambridge University Press, London.

Brindle, D. (1994) 'Benefits system in crisis', *The Guardian*, 6 September.

British Council (1995) *Good Government* (Exhibition organized by the British Council), British Council, Manchester.

Brown, S. (1994) 'Public interest immunity', *Public Law*, pp. 579-95.

Burns, T. (1992) 'Researching customer service in the public sector', *Journal of the Market Research Society*, vol. 34, no. 1, pp. 53-60.

Butler, D., Adonis, A. and Travers, A. (1994) *Failure in British Government: The Politics of the Poll Tax*, Oxford University Press, Oxford.

Butler, R. (1990) 'New challenges or familiar prescriptions' (Redcliffe-Maud Memorial Lecture), PA Consulting Group/Royal Institute of Public Administration, London.

Butler, R. (1992a) 'The new public management: the contribution of Whitehall and academia', *Public Policy and Administration*, vol. 7, no. 3, pp. 4-14.

Butler, R. (1992b) 'The future of the civil service', *Public Policy and Administration*, vol. 7, no. 2, pp. 1-10.

Cabinet Office (1970) *The Reorganization of Central Government* (Cmnd. 4506), HMSO, London.

Cabinet office (1974) *Report of the Prime Minister's Committee on Local Government Rules of Conduct* (Redcliffe-Maud Committee) (Cmnd 5636), HMSO, London.

Cabinet Office (1988) 'Service to the public', *Cabinet Office Occasional Paper*, Cabinet Office, London.

Cabinet Office (1991) *The Citizen's Charter: Raising the Standard* (Cm. 1599), HMSO, London.

Cabinet Office (1992a) *The Citizen's Charter: First Report* (Cm. 2101), HMSO, London.

Cabinet Office (1992b) *Questions of Procedure for Ministers*, Cabinet Office, London.

Cabinet Office (1993a) *Next Steps Agencies in Government: Review 1993* (Cm. 2430), HMSO, London.

Cabinet Office (1993b) *Open Government* (Cm. 2290), HMSO, London.

Cabinet Office (1994a) *The Civil Service: Continuity and Change* (Cm. 2627), HMSO, London.

Cabinet Office (1994b) *Next Steps Agencies in Government: Review 1994* (Cm. 2750), HMSO, London.

Cabinet Office (1995a) *The Civil Service: Taking Forward Continuity and Change* (Cm.

2748), HMSO, London.

Cabinet Office (1995b) *The Citizen's Charter: The Facts and Figures. A Report to Mark Four Years of the Charter Programme* (Cm. 2970), HMSO, London.

Cabinet Office (1995c) *The Government's Response to the First Report from the Committee on Standards in Public Life* (Cm. 2931), HMSO, London.

Cabinet Office (1996) *Next Steps Agencies in Government: Review 1995* (Cm. 3164), HMSO, London.

Campbell, C. and Wilson, G.K. (1995) *The End of Whitehall: Death of a Paradigm?*, Blackwell, Oxford.

Chapman, L. (1978) *Your Disobedient Servant*, Chatto and Windus, London.

Chapman, R.A. (1968) 'Profile of a Profession: The Administrative Class of the civil service', in *The Civil Service, Vol. 3 (2): Surveys and Investigations – Evidence Submitted to the Fulton Committee*, HMSO, London, pp. 1-29.

Chapman, R.A. (1970) *The Higher Civil Service in Britain*, Constable, London.

Chapman, R.A. (1983) 'The rise and fall of the CSD', *Policy and Politics*, vol. 11, pp. 41-61.

Chapman, R.A. (1988) *Ethics in the British Civil Service*, Routledge, London.

Chapman, R.A. (1991) 'The end of the civil service?', *Teaching Public Administration*, vol. 7 no. 2, pp. 1-5.

Chapman, R.A. and Greenaway, J.R. (1980) *The Dynamics of Administrative Reform*, Croom Helm, London.

Chapman, R.A. and O'Toole, B.J. (1994) 'The heroic approach to the historiography of public administration in the United Kingdom', *Jahrbuch Fur Europaische Verwaltungsgeschicte*, pp. 65-77.

Civil and Public Services Association (CPSA) (1994) *Response of the CPSA to the Government's Civil Service White Paper 'Continuity and Change'*, CPSA, London.

Civil and Public Services Association (CPSA) (1995) Research department update: 1995 pay negotiations, brief no. 5, NEC/218/43 (unpublished).

Civil Service Commissioners (1991) *Civil Service Commissioners' Report, 1990-91* (124th Report), Office of the Civil Service Commissioners, London.

Civil Service Commissioners (1995a) *Civil Service Commissioners' Recruitment Code*, Office of the Civil Service Commissioners, London.

Civil Service Commissioners (1995b) *Civil Service Commissioners' Report, 1994-95* (128th Report), Office of the Civil Service Commissioners, London.

Civil Service Department (1972) *Civil Service Statistics*, HMSO, London.

Civil Service Department (1976) *Civil Service Statistics*, HMSO, London.

Clark, G.K. (1959) 'Statesmen in disguise: reflections on the history of the neutrality of the civil service', *Historical Journal*, vol. 2, pp. 19-39.

Clarke, M. (1981) *Fallen Idols: Elites and the Search for the Acceptable Face of Capitalism*, Junction Books, London.

Committee of Public Accounts – *see* Public Accounts Committee (PAC).

Common, R., Flynn, N. and Mellon, E. (1992) *Managing Public Services: Competition and Decentralization*, Butterworth-Heinemann, London.

Connelly, J. (1992) 'All customers now? Notes on consumerism in the public services', *Teaching Public Administration*, vol. 12, no. 2, pp. 29-32.

Consumers' Association (1995) 'Paper Promises', *Which?* (September), pp. 48-51.

Cookson, C. (1995) 'Unsettled outlook', *Financial Times*, 25 August.

Corby, S. (1994) 'How big a step is "Next Steps"? Industrial relations developments in civil service executive agencies', *Human Resource Management Journal*, vol. 4, no. 2, pp. 52-69.

Corcoran, L. (1995) 'Trade union membership and recognition: 1994 Labour Force Survey data', *Employment Gazette*, (May), pp. 191-203.

Craig, P.P. (1994) *Administrative Law*, 3rd edn., Sweet and Maxwell, London.

Crick, B. (1973) *Basic Forms of Government: A Sketch and a Model*, Macmillan, London.

Croom-Johnson, D.P. (Crown Agents Tribunal) (1982) *Report of the Tribunal Appointed to Inquire into Certain Issues Arising out of the Operations of the Crown Agents as Financiers on Own Account in the Years 1967-74* (Chaired by Sir D.P. Croom-Johnson), Session 1981-82, HL 149, HC 364.

Dale, H.E. (1941) *The Higher Civil Service of Great Britain*, Oxford University Press, Oxford.

Davidson, R. (1985) *Whitehall and the Labour Problem in Late-Victorian and Edwardian Britain*, Croom Helm, London.

Deakin, N. (1994) 'Accentuating the apostrophe: the Citizen's Charter', *Policy Studies*, vol. 15, no. 3, pp. 48-58.

Delafons, J. (1982) 'Working in Whitehall: changes in public administration 1952-1982', *Public Administration*, vol. 60, pp. 253-72.

de Leon, P. (1993) *Thinking About Political Corruption*, M.E. Sharpe, New York.

Department of Social Security (DSS) (1989) *Our Business is Service*, DSS, London.

Dicey, A.V. (1959) *An Introduction to the Study of the Law of the Constitution*, 10th edn. (first publ. 1885), Macmillan, London.

Doern, B. (1993) 'The UK Citizen's Charter: origins and implementation in three agencies', *Policy and Politics*, vol. 21, no. 1, pp. 17-29.

Doig, A. (1984) *Corruption and Misconduct in Contemporary British Politics*, Penguin, Harmondsworth.

Doig, A. (1988) 'Advice, guidance and control: non-departmental public bodies and standards of conduct', *Teaching Public Administration*, vol. 8, no. 2, pp. 1-23.

Doig, A. (1992) 'Retreat of the investigators', *British Journalism Review*, vol. 3, no. 4, pp. 44-50.

Doig, A. (1995a) 'Mixed signals? Public sector change and the proper conduct of public business', *Public Administration*, vol. 73, pp. 191-212.

Doig, A. (1995b) 'Changing public sector approaches to fraud', *Public Money and Management*, vol. 15, no. 1, pp. 19-24.

Doig, A. (1995c) 'Continuing cause for concern? Probity in local government', *Local Government Studies*, vol. 21, pp. 99-114.

Dolan, L. (1995) 'Number is up for the taxman', *The Times*, 4 February.

Dowding, K. (1995) *The Civil Service*, Routledge, London.

Drewry, G. and Butcher, T. (1991) *The Civil Service Today*, 2nd edn., Blackwell, Oxford.

Dunleavy, P. (1995) 'Policy disasters: explaining the UK's record', *Public Policy and Administration*, vol. 10, no. 2, pp. 52-70.

Dunleavy, P. and Hood, C. (1994) 'From old public administration to new public management', *Public Money and Management*, vol. 14, no. 3, pp. 9-16.

Dunleavy, P. and O'Leary, B. (1987) *Theories of the State: The Politics of Liberal Democracy*, Macmillan, Basingstoke.

Dunn, J. (ed.) (1995) *Contemporary Crisis of the Modern State*, Blackwell, Oxford.

Dunsire, A. (1993) 'Ethics in governance: the United Kingdom 1979-1990', in R. Thomas (ed) *Teaching Ethics: Government Ethics*, Centre for Business and Public Sector Ethics, Cambridge, pp. 315-34.

Dynes, M. and Walker, D. (1995) *The Times Guide to the New British State: The Government Machine in the 1990s*, Times Books, London.

Earl, M. and Khan, B. (1994) 'How new is business redesign?', *European Management Journal*, vol. 12, no. 1, pp. 20-30.

Efficiency Unit (1988) *Improving Management in Government: The Next Steps – Report to the Prime Minister*, HMSO, London.

Efficiency Unit (1991) *Making the Most of Next Steps: The Management of Ministers' Departments and their Executive Agencies* (Fraser Report), HMSO, London.

Employment Service (1995) *Annual Reports and Accounts 1994-95*, HC 638 (Session 1994-95).

Expenditure Committee (1977) *Eleventh Report, Session 1976-77: The Civil Service, Vol. I – Report; Vol. II – Minutes of Evidence*, HC 535 – I and II.

Fairbrother, P. (1994) *Politics and the State as Employer*, Mansell, London.

Finer, S.E. (1952) *The Life and Times of Sir Edwin Chadwick*, Methuen, London.

Finer, S.E. (1956) 'The individual responsibility of ministers', *Public Administration*, vol. 34, pp. 377-96.

Finer, S.E. (1970) *Comparative Government*, Allen Lane, London.

Finkelstein, D. (1993) Foreword in Kemp, P., *Beyond Next Steps: A Civil Service for the 21st. Century*, Social Market Foundation, London.

Fitzwalter, R. and Taylor, D. (1981) *The Web of Corruption: Full Story of John Poulson and T. Dan Smith*, Granada, London.

Flynn, R. (1992) *Structures of Control in Health Management*, Routledge, London.

Franklin, B. and Murphy, D. (1991) *What News? The Market, Politics and the Local Press*, Routledge, London.

Fredman, S. and Morris, G. (1989) *The State as Employer: Labour Law in the Public Services*, Mansell, London.

Fry, G.K. (1969) *Statesmen in Disguise: The Changing Role of the Administrative Class of the Home Civil Service, 1853-1966*, Macmillan, London.

Fry, G.K. (1995) *Policy and Management in the British Civil Service*, Prentice Hall/Harvester Wheatsheaf, Hemel Hempstead.

Fryer, R.H. (1989) 'Public service trade unionism in the twentieth century', in R. Mailly, S.J. Dimmock and A.S. Sethi (eds), *Industrial Relations in the Public Services*, Routledge, London, pp. 17-67.

Fulton (1968) *The Civil Service – Vol. I: Report of the Committee 1966-68* (Fulton Report) (Cmnd. 3638), HMSO, London.

Fukuyama, F. (1992) *The End of History and the Last Man*, Hamish Hamilton, London.

Ganz, G. (1993) 'Matrix Churchill and public interest immunity', *Modern Law Review*, vol. 56, pp. 564-8.

Gellner, E. (1996) 'The rest of history', *Prospect* (May), pp. 34-8.

Gladden, E.N. (1972) *A History of Public Administration* (2 vols.), Frank Cass, London.

Goldsworthy, D. (1991) *Setting up Next Steps: A Short Account of the Origins, Launch and Implementation of the Next Steps Project in the British Civil Service*, HMSO, London.

Goldsworthy, D. (1993) 'Efficiency and effectiveness in public management: a UK perspective', *Administration*, vol. 41, no. 2, pp. 137-48.

Goodsell, C. (1994) *The Case for Bureaucracy: A Public Administration Polemic*, 3rd. edn., Chatham House Publishers Inc., Chatham, N.J.

Gray, A. and Jenkins, W.I. (1982) 'Policy analysis in British central government: the experience of PAR', *Public Administration*, vol. 60, pp. 429-50.

Gray, A. and Jenkins, W.I. (1985) *Administrative Politics in British Government*, Harvester Wheatsheaf, Brighton.

Greenaway, J.R., Smith, S. and Street, J. (1992) *Deciding Factors in British Politics: A Case-Studies Approach*, Routledge, London.

Greer, P. (1994) *Transforming Central Government: The Next Steps Initiative*, Open University Press, Buckingham.

Greer, P. and Carter, N. (1995) 'Next Steps and performance measures' in B. O'Toole and G. Jordan (eds), *Next Steps: Improving Management in Government?*, Dartmouth, Aldershot, pp. 86-96.

Griffith, J.A.G. (1987) 'Crichel Down: the most famous farm in British constitutional history', *Contemporary Record*, vol. 1, no. 1, pp. 35-40.

Guillemard, L. (1937) *Trivial Fond Records*, Methuen, London.

Hall, J.A. and Ikenberry, G.J. (1989) *The State*, Open University Press, Milton Keynes.

Ham, C. and Hill, M. (1993) *The Policy Process in the Modern Capitalist State*, 2nd. edn., Harvester Wheatsheaf, New York.

Harrow, J. and Gillett, G. (1994) 'The proper conduct of public business', *Public Money and Management*, vol. 14, no. 2, pp. 4-6.

Heclo, H. and Wildavsky, A. (1981) *The Private Government of Public Money: Community and Policy Inside British Politics*, 2nd. edn., Macmillan, London.

Heiser, T. (1994) 'The civil service at a crossroads?', *Public Policy and Administration*, vol. 9, no. 1, pp. 14-26.

Hencke, D. (1995) 'Sweeping Whitehall sell-off', *Guardian*, 28 September.

Hennessy, P. (1991) 'Traditional language backed by "exocets"', *The Independent*, 7 October.

Hennessy, P. (1995) *The Hidden Wiring: Unearthing the British Constitution*, Victor Gollancz, London.

Hepple, B.A. (1982) 'Labour law and public employees in Britain', in Lord Wedderburn of Charlton and W.T. Murphy (eds.), *Labour Law and the Community: Perspectives for the 1980s*, Institute of Advanced Legal Studies, London, pp. 67-83.

HM Treasury (1952) *Handbook for the New Civil Servant*, HM Treasury, London.

HM Treasury (1961) *Control of Public Expenditure* (Plowden Report) (Cmnd. 1432), HMSO, London.

HM Treasury/OPSS (1992) *Guide to Departments*, HM Treasury, London.

HM Treasury (1993) *Civil Service Management Code*, HM Treasury/Cabinet Office, London.

HM Treasury (1994) *Civil Service Statistics*, HMSO, London.

HM Treasury (1995) *Code of Best Practice for Board Members of Public Bodies*, HM Treasury, London.

Hobsbawm, E.J. (1968) *Industry and Empire: An Economic History of Britain since 1750*, Weidenfeld and Nicolson, London.

Hoffman, J. (1995) *Beyond the State*, Polity, Cambridge.

Holland, G. (1995) 'Alas! Sir Humphrey – I knew him well', *Royal Society of Arts Journal*, vol. 143, no. 5464 (November), pp. 39-51.

Hood, C. (1991a) 'A public management for all seasons?', *Public Administration*, vol. 69, pp. 3-19.

Hood, C. (1991b) 'De-Sir Humphreyfying the Westminster model of bureaucracy: a new style of government', *Governance*, vol. 3, pp. 205-14.

Hood, C. (1994) *Explaining Economic Policy Reversals*, Open University Press, Buckingham.

Hood, C. (1995) 'Contemporary public management: a new global paradigm?', *Public Policy and Administration*, vol. 10, no. 2, pp. 104-17.

Hughes, O.E. (1994) *Public Management and Administration*, Macmillan, Basingstoke.

Incomes Data Services (IDS) (1995) *Pay in the Public Services: Review of 1994, Prospects for 1995*, IDS, London.

Industrial Relations Services (IRS) (1995) 'Agencies wrestle with delegated pay', *Industrial Relations Review and Report (Pay and Benefits Bulletin No. 371)* (March).

Ingraham, P.W. (1995) 'Reinventing the American federal government: reform redux or real change', Maxwell School of Citizenship and Public Affairs, Syracuse University, New York.

Institution of Professionals, Managers and Specialists (IPMS) (1995a) 'Audit office clears Forward sell-off', *IPMS Bulletin*, 2/95 (February).

Institution of Professionals, Managers and Specialists (IPMS) (1995b) 'Union gears up for 200 pay talks', *IPMS Bulletin*, 4/95 (April).

Institution of Professionals, Managers and Specialists (IPMS) (1995c) 'Transfer Unit out of work', *IPMS Bulletin*, 1/95 (January).

Institution of Professionals, Managers and Specialists (IPMS) (1995d) 'Membership swaps win backing', *IPMS Bulletin*, 6/95 (June).

James, A. (1972) *Report of the Tribunal Appointed to Inquire into Certain Issues in Relation to Circumstances Leading up to the Cessation of Trading by the Vehicle and General Insurance Company Limited* (Hon. Justice James – James Report), 1971/72, HL 80 (HC 133).

Jay, P. (1985) 'Pontius or Ponting: public duty and public interest in secrecy and disclosure', in Royal Institute of Public Administration (ed) *Politics, Ethics and Public Service*, RIPA, London, pp. 69-92.

Jenkins, S. (1995) *Accountable to None: The Tory Nationalization of Britain*, Hamish Hamilton, London.

Jennings, I. (1966) *The British Constitution*, 5th edn., Cambridge University Press, Cambridge.

Johnston, M. and Wood, D. (1985) 'Right and wrong in public and private life' in R. Jowell and S. Witherspoon (eds), *British Social Attitudes: The 1985 Report*, Gower, Aldershot, pp. 121-47.

Jones, G.W. (1987) 'Stand up for ministerial responsibility', *Public Administration*, vol. 65, pp. 87-91.

Jordan, G. (1994a) 'Reinventing government: but will it work?', *Public Administration*, vol. 72, pp. 271-9.

Jordan, G. (1994b) *The British Administrative System: Principles versus Practice*, Routledge, London.

Judge, D. (1993) *The Parliamentary State*, Sage, London.

Kemp, P. (1993) *Beyond Next Steps: A Civil Service for the 21st Century*, Social Market Foundation, London.

Kennedy, P. (1987) *The Rise and Fall of the Great Powers: Economic Change and Military Conflict from 1500 to 2000*, Random House, New York.

Kessler, I. and Purcell, J. (1992) 'Performance-related pay: objectives and application', *Human Resource Management Journal*, vol. 2, no. 3, pp. 16-33.

Kinnie, N. (1987) 'Bargaining within the enterprise: centralised or decentralised?', *Journal of Management Studies*, vol. 24, pp. 463-77.

Kuhn, T.S. (1970) *The Structure of Scientific Revolutions*, University of Chicago Press, Chicago, Ill.

Labour Research (1995) 'When bargaining goes local', *Labour Research*, vol. 84, no. 11 (November), pp. 17-18.

Leigh, D. (with Norton-Taylor, R.) (1993) *Betrayed: The Real Story of the Matrix Churchill Trial*, Bloomsbury, London.

Leith-Ross, F. (1968) *Money Talks: Fifty Years of International Finance*, Hutchinson, London.

Levi, M. (1993) 'The investigation, prosecution and trial of serious fraud', *Royal Commission on Criminal Justice Research Study No. 14*, HMSO, London.

Lewis, N. (1993) 'The Citizen's Charter and Next Steps: a new way of governing?',

Political Quarterly, vol. 64, pp. 316-26.

Leyland, P., Woods, T. and Harden, J. (1994) *Textbook on Administrative Law*, Blackstone Press, London.

Low, S. (1914) *The Governance of England*, revised edn.,T. Fisher Unwin, London.

Lowe, R. (1986) *Adjusting to Democracy: The Role of the Ministry of Labour in British Politics 1916-1939*, Clarendon, Oxford.

Lowe, R. (1993) *The Welfare State in Britain Since 1945*, Macmillan, Basingstoke.

Lowell, A.L. (1908) *The Government of England*, (2 vols.), Macmillan, New York.

Lubenow, W.C. (1971) *The Politics of Government Growth: Early Victorian Attitudes Toward State Intervention, 1833-1848*, David and Charles, Newton Abbot.

Lynn, P. (1992) *Public Perceptions of Local Government: Its Finance and Services* (Department of the Environment), HMSO, London.

MacDonagh, O. (1961) *A Pattern of Government Growth 1800-60: The Passenger Acts and their Enforcement*, MacGibbon and Kee, London.

McEldowney, J.F. (1994) *Public Law*, Sweet and Maxwell, London.

McEldowney, J.F. (1995) 'Ethics and standards in public life', unpublished evidence submitted to the Committee on Standards in Public Life (Nolan Committee).

MacIntyre, A. (1988) *Whose Justice? Whose Rationality?*, Duckworth, London.

Mackenzie, W.J.M. and Grove, J.W. (1957) *Central Administration in Britain*, Longmans, London.

McKinney, J.B. and Johnston, M. (eds) (1986) *Fraud, Waste and Abuse in Government*, ISHI Publications, Philadelphia, Penn.

MacPherson, S. (1987) 'Department of Health and Social Security', in A. Harrison and J. Gretton (eds), *Reshaping Central Government*, Policy Journals, Hermitage, Berks, pp. 131-44.

Maitland, F.W. (1908) *Constitutional History of England*, Cambridge University Press, Cambridge.

Management and Personnel Office (MPO) (1983) *Review of Personnel Work in the Civil Service: Report to the Prime Minister* (Cassels Report), HMSO, London.

Management and Personnel Office (MPO)/HM Treasury (1985) *Non-Departmental Public Bodies: A Guide for Departments*, HMSO, London.

Mancuso, M. (1993) 'The ethical attitudes of MPs: a typology', *Parliamentary Affairs*, vol. 46, pp. 179-91.

Marginson, P. (1988) 'Centralised control or establishment autonomy?', in P. Marginson, P.K. Edwards, R. Martin, J. Purcell and K. Sisson (eds), *Beyond the Workplace*, Blackwell, Oxford, pp. 183-226.

Marr, A. (1995) *Ruling Britannia: The Failure and Future of British Democracy*, Michael Joseph, London.

Marshall, G. (1986) *Constitutional Conventions: The Rules and Forms of Political Accountability*, Clarendon, Oxford.

Massey, A. (1988) *Technocrats and Nuclear Politics: The Influence of Professional Experts on Policy-Making*, Gower, Aldershot.

Massey, A. (1993) *Managing the Public Sector: A Comparative Analysis of the UK and the USA*, Edward Elgar, Aldershot.

Massey, A. (1995a) 'Civil service reform and accountability', *Public Policy and Administration*, vol. 10, no. 1, pp. 16-33.

Massey, A. (1995b) 'After Next Steps'. Report to the Office of Public Service and Science, OPSS, London.

Massey, A. (1995c) 'Public bodies and Next Steps'. Report to HM Treasury and the Office of Public Service and Science, HM Treasury/OPSS, London.

Massey, A. (1995d) 'Ministers, the agency model and public ownership', *Public Policy and Administration*, vol. 10, no. 2, pp. 71-87.

Megaw (1982) *Inquiry into Civil Service Pay: Report of an Inquiry into the Principles and the System by which the Remuneration of the Non-Industrial Civil Service Should be Determined – Vol. I: Findings* (Megaw Report) (Cmnd 8590), HMSO, London.

Metcalfe, L. and Richards, S. (1990) *Improving Public Management*, 2nd edn, Sage, London.

Millward, N., Stevens, M., Smart, D. and Hawes, W.R. (1992) *Workplace Industrial Relations in Transition*, Dartmouth, Aldershot.

Ministry of Housing and Local Government (1967) *Management of Local Government – Vol. I, Report of the Committee* (Maud Report), HMSO, London.

Ministry of Reconstruction (1918) *Report of the Machinery of Government Committee* (Haldane Committee) (Cd. 9230), HMSO, London.

Moodie, M., Mizen, H., Heron, R. and Mackay, B. (1988) *The Business of Service: The Report of the Regional Organization Scrutiny*, DHSS, London.

MORI (1995) *FDA Staff Survey*, MORI, London.

Morrison, H. (1964) *Government and Parliament: A Survey From the Inside*, 3rd edn., Oxford University Press, London.

National Audit Office (1987a) *Internal Audit in Central Government*, HC 313 (Session 1986-87).

National Audit Office (1987b) *Internal Audit in the National Health Service*, HC 314 (Session 1986-87).

National Audit Office (1988) *Department of Health and Social Security: Quality of Service to the Public*, HC 451 (Session 1987-88).

National Audit Office (1994) *HM Customs and Excise: Prevention and Detection of Internal Fraud*, HC 244 (Session 1993-94).

Nicolson, I.F. (1986) *The Mystery of Crichel Down*, Clarendon, Oxford.

Nolan (1995) *Standards in Public Life: First Report of the Committee on Standards in Public Life* (Nolan Report), (Cm. 2850-I), HMSO, London.

Norton-Taylor, R. (1985) *The Ponting Affair*, Cecil Woolf, London.

Office of the Minister for the Civil Service (OMCS) (1991) *The Next Steps Initiative: The Government Reply to the Seventh Report from the Treasury and Civil Service Committee, Session 1990-91, HC 496* (Cm 1761), HMSO, London.

Office of the Parliamentary Commissioner for Administration (1993) *Sixth Report, Session 1992-93: Delays in Handling Disability Living Allowance Claims*, HC 652.

Office of the Parliamentary Commissioner for Administration (1994) *Third Report, Session 1993-94: Annual Report for 1993*, HC 290.

Office of Public Service (OPS) (1995) 'Mobility within the civil service', *Consultation Paper, Issue 3*, OPS, London.

Office of Public Service and Science (OPSS) (1994a) *The Citizen's Charter: Second Report* (Cm. 2540), OPSS, London.

Office of Public Service and Science (OPSS) (1994b) *Next Steps Briefing Note No. 7* (December), OPSS, London.

Office of Public Service and Science (OPSS) (1995) *Public Bodies 1994*, HMSO, London.

O'Halpin, E.J. (1989) *Head of the Civil Service: A Study of Sir Warren Fisher*, Routledge, London.

Ohmae, K. (1995) *The End of the Nation State: The Rise of Regional Economics*, Harper Collins, London.

Oliver, D. (1991) *Government in the United Kingdom: The Search for Accountability, Effectiveness and Citizenship*, Open University Press, Buckingham.

Olson, M. (1982) *The Rise and Decline of Nations: Economic Growth, Stagflation and*

Social Rigidities, Yale University Press, New Haven, CT.

Osborne, D. and Gaebler, T. (1992) *Reinventing Government: How the Entrepreneurial Spirit is Transforming the Public Sector*, Addison-Wesley, Reading, Mass.

O'Toole, B.J. (1989) *Private Gain and Public Service: The Association of First Division Civil Servants*, Routledge, London.

O'Toole, B.J. (1990) 'T.H. Green and the ethics of senior officials in British central government', *Public Administration*, vol. 68, pp. 337-52.

O'Toole, B.J. (1993) 'The loss of purity: the corruption of public service', *Public Policy and Administration*, vol. 8, no. 2, pp. 1-6.

O'Toole, B.J. (1994) 'The civil service in the 1990s'. *Fifth Report from the Treasury and Civil Service Committee, Session 1993-94: The Role of the Civil Service – vol. III*, HC 27-III, Appendix 34, pp. 123-6.

O'Toole, B.J. (1995) 'Accountability in the civil service now', *Public Policy and Administration*, vol. 10, no. 4, pp. 1-3.

O'Toole, B.J. and Jordan, G. (eds) (1995) *Next Steps: Improving Management in Government?*, Dartmouth, Aldershot.

Overman, E.S. and Boyd, K.J. (1994) 'Best practice research and postbureaucratic reform', *Journal of Public Administration Research and Theory*, vol. 4, no. 1, pp. 67-83.

Painter, C. (1995) 'The Next Steps reforms and current orthodoxies', in B.J. O'Toole and G. Jordan (eds), *Next Steps: Improving Management in Government?*, Dartmouth, Aldershot, pp. 17-36.

Parker, A., Rose, A. and Taylor, J. (1986) *The Administration of Standards of Conduct in Local Government: A Research Report*, Charles Knight Publishing, Newton Abbot.

Parker, G. and Kampfner, J. (1995) 'Unions warn of public service breakdown', *Financial Times*, 29 November.

Parris, H. (1969) *Constitutional Bureaucracy: The Development of British Central Administration Since the Eighteenth Century*, George Allen and Unwin, London.

Part, A. (1990) *The Making of a Mandarin*, André Deutsch, London.

Peters, T.J. and Waterman, R.H. (1982) *In Search of Excellence: Lessons From America's Best-Run Companies*, Harper and Row, New York.

Phillips, A. (1988) 'Is the market mentality a licence for greed?' (BBC Hibbert lecture), *The Listener*, 28 February, pp. 10-11.

Phillips, H. (1993) 'The professional ethic of the home civil service of the United Kingdom', in R. Thomas (ed), *Teaching Ethics: Government Ethics*, Centre for Business and Public Sector Ethics, Cambridge, pp. 48-66.

Plato (Trans. F.M. Cornford, 1941) *The Republic of Plato*, Clarendon, Oxford.

Plowden, W. (1985) 'What prospects for the civil service?', *Public Administration*, vol. 63, pp. 393-414.

Plowden, W. (1994) *Ministers and Mandarins*, Institute of Public Policy Research, London.

Pollitt, C. (1993) *Managerialism and the Public Services*, 2nd edn., Blackwell, Oxford.

Ponting, C. (1985) *The Right to Know: The Inside Story of the Belgrano Affair*, Sphere Books, London.

Price Waterhouse (1993) *Executive Agencies: Facts and Trends: Edition 6*, Price Waterhouse, London.

Price Waterhouse (1994) *Executive Agencies: Facts and Trends: Edition 8*, Price Waterhouse, London.

Priestley (1955) *Report of the Royal Commission on the Civil Service 1953-55* (Priestley Report) (C. 9613) P.P. 1955-56, xi.

Prime Minister's Office (1980) *Report on Non-Departmental Public Bodies* (Cmnd. 7797), HMSO, London.

Prior, D. (1995) 'Citizen's charters', in J. Stewart and G. Stoker (eds), *Local Government in the 1990s*, Macmillan, Basingstoke, pp. 86-103.

Public Accounts Committee (PAC) (1987) *Fifteenth Report, Session 1986-87 – Sponsorship of Non-Departmental Public Bodies: Department of the Environment, Welsh Office*, HC 38.

Public Accounts Committee (PAC) (1992) *Eleventh Report, Session 1992-93 – Development Board for Rural Wales: Retirement Settlement to Former Chief Executive*, HC 144.

Public Accounts Committee (PAC) (1993a) *Twenty-Eighth Report, Session 1992-93 – Ministry of Defence: Irregular Expenditure Under an Efficiency Incentive Scheme*, HC 348.

Public Accounts Committee (PAC) (1993b) *Forty-Seventh Report, Session 1992-93: Welsh Development Agency Accounts 1991-92*, HC 353.

Public Accounts Committee (PAC) (1993c) *Forty-Eighth Report, Session 1992-93: Irregularities in the 1991-92 Accounts of Forward Civil Service Catering*, HC 558.

Public Accounts Committee (PAC) (1993d) *Fifty-Seventh Report, Session 1992-93 – West Midlands Regional Health Authority: Regionally Managed Services Organisation*, HC 485.

Public Accounts Committee (PAC) (1993e) *Sixty-Third Report, Session 1992-93– Wessex Regional Health Authority Regional Information Systems Plan*, HC 658.

Public Accounts Committee (PAC) (1994a) *Eighth Report, Session 1993-94: The Proper Conduct of Public Business*, HC 154.

Public Accounts Committee (PAC) (1994b) *Twenty-Third Report, Session 1993-94 – Development Board for Rural Wales: Allocation and Sale of Housing and Car Leasing Scheme*, HC 182.

Public Accounts Committee (PAC) (1994c) *Thirty-Ninth Report, Session 1993-94: Looking After the Financial Affairs of People with Mental Incapacity*, HC 308.

Public Accounts Committee (PAC) (1995a) *Second Report, Session 1994-95 – The Sports Council: Initiatives to Improve Financial Management and Control and Value for Money*, HC 93.

Public Accounts Committee (PAC) (1995b) *Twenty-Ninth Report, Session 1994-95 – The Welsh Development Agency*, HC 376.

Pyper, R. (1995) *The British Civil Service*, Prentice Hall/ Harvester Wheatsheaf, Hemel Hempstead.

Quinlan, M. (1994) 'Changing patterns in public business', *Public Policy and Administration*, vol. 9, no. 1, pp. 27-34.

Rawls, J. (1972) *A Theory of Justice*, Oxford University Press, Oxford.

Rhodes, R.A.W. (1994) 'The hollowing out of the state', *Political Quarterly*, vol. 65, pp. 138-51.

Richardson, R. and Marsden, D. (1991) 'Does performance pay motivate? A study of Inland Revenue staff', LSE, London.

Ridley, F.F. and Doig, A. (eds) (1996) *Sleaze: Politics, Private Interests and Public Reaction*, Oxford University Press, Oxford.

Roberts, D. (1960) *Victorian Origins of the British Welfare State*, Yale University Press, New Haven, CT.

Roethlisberger, F.J. and Dickson, W.J. (1939) *Management and the Worker*, Harvard University Press, Cambridge, Mass.

Roseveare, H. (1969) *The Treasury: The Evolution of a British Institution*, Allen Lane, London.

Royal Institute of Public Administration (RIPA) (1987) *Top Jobs in Whitehall: Appointments and Promotions in the Senior Civil Service. Report of an RIPA Working Group*, RIPA, London.

Russell, M. (1993) 'Standards of conduct in the Foreign and Commonwealth Office and the Diplomatic Service' in R. Thomas (ed) *Teaching Ethics: Government Ethics*, Centre for Business and Public Sector Ethics, Cambridge, pp. 1-19.

Salmon (1966) *Report of the Royal Commission on Tribunals of Inquiry* (Salmon Report) (Cmnd. 3121), HMSO, London.

Salmon (1976) *Report of the Royal Commission on Standards of Conduct in Public Life 1974-76* (Salmon Report) (Cmnd. 6524), HMSO, London.

Salter, A. (1961) *Memoirs of a Public Servant*, Faber and Faber, London.

Scott, R. (1996) *Report of the Inquiry into the Export of Defence Equipment and Dual-Use Goods to Iraq and Related Prosecutions* (Scott Report) (5 vols), HC 115 (Session 1995-96).

Select Committee on the Parliamentary Commissioner for Administration (1992) *Second Report, Session 1991-92 – The Implications of the Citizen's Charter for the Work of the Parliamentary Commissioner for Administration*, HC 158.

Select Committee on the Parliamentary Commissioner for Administration (1994a) *Second Report, Session 1993-94 – Report of the Parliamentary Commissioner for Administration for 1992*, HC 64.

Select Committee on the Parliamentary Commissioner for Administration (1994b) *First report, Session 1994-95: Maladministration and Redress*, HC 112.

Smith, A.T.H. (1993) 'Public interest immunity in criminal cases', *Cambridge Law Journal*, vol. 52, part 1 (March), pp. 1-3.

Spiro, H.J. (1969) *Responsibility in Government: Theory and Practice*, Van Nostrand Reinhold Co., New York.

Stewart, J. and Walsh, K. (1992) 'Change in the management of the public services', *Public Administration*, vol. 70, pp. 499-518.

Storey, J. (1992) *Developments in the Management of Human Resources*, Blackwell, Oxford.

Sweeney, J. (1993) *Trading with the Enemy*, Pan Books, London.

Taylor, R. and Kelly, J. (1995) 'Revenue to cut 25% of staff and close half its offices', *Financial Times*, 3 February.

Thain, C. and Wright, M. (1995) *The Treasury and Whitehall: The Planning and Control of Public Expenditure 1976-1993*, Clarendon, Oxford.

Theakston, K. (1995) *The Civil Service Since 1945*, Blackwell, Oxford.

Theobald, R. (1990) *Corruption, Development and Underdevelopment*, Macmillan, London.

Thomas, R. (ed) (1993) *Teaching Ethics: Government Ethics*, Centre for Business and Public Sector Ethics, Cambridge.

Tomkins, A. (1993) 'Public interest immunity after Matrix Churchill', *Public Law*, pp. 650-68.

Tomkinson, M. and Gillard, M. (1980) *Nothing to Declare: Political Corruptions of John Poulson*, John Calder, London.

Tomlin (1931) *Report of the Royal Commission on the Civil Service 1929-31* (Tomlin Report) (Cmd. 3909), P.P. 1930-31, x.

Townshend, J. (1996) *The Politics of Marxism: The Critical Debates*, Leicester University Press, London.

Treasury and Civil Service Committee (TCSC) (1984) *Eighth Report, Session 1983-84 – Acceptance of Outside Appointments by Crown Servants*, HC 302.

Treasury and Civil Service Committee (TCSC) (1986) *Seventh Report, Session 1985-86 –*

Civil Servants and Ministers: Duties and Responsibilities – Vol. I, Report; Vol. II,
   Annexes, Minutes of Evidence and Appendices, HC 92 – I and II.
Treasury and Civil Service Committee (TCSC) (1989) *Fifth Report, Session 1988-89* –
   Developments in the Next Steps Programme, HC 348.
Treasury and Civil Service Committee (TCSC) (1990) *Eighth Report, Session 1989-90* –
   Progress in the Next Steps Initiative, HC 481.
Treasury and Civil Service Committee (TCSC) (1993) *Sixth Report, Session 1992-93:*
   The Role of the Civil Service, Interim Report – Vol. I, Report; Vol. II, *Minutes of*
   Evidence and Appendices, HC 390 – I and II.
Treasury and Civil Service Committee (TCSC) (1994) *Fifth Report, Session 1993-94: The*
   Role of the Civil Service – Vol. I, Report; Vol. II, *Minutes of Evidence;* Vol. III,
   Appendices to the Minutes of Evidence, HC 27 – I, II and III.
Treasury Solicitor (1996) *Public Interest Immunity: Government Response to the Scott*
   Report (PII Consultation Group), Treasury Solicitor's Department, London.
Trollope, A. (1858) *The Three Clerks* (The World's Classics Edition, 1907), Oxford
   University Press, Oxford.
Trosa, S. (1994) *Next Steps: Moving On. An Examination of the Progress to Date of the*
   Next Steps Reform Against a Background of Recommendations Made in the Fraser
   Report, Office of Public Service and Science, London.
Turpin, C. (1994) 'Ministerial responsibility', in J. Jowell and D. Oliver (eds) *The*
   Changing Constitution, 3rd edn., Clarendon, Oxford, pp. 109-51.
Waldegrave, W. (1993) *Public Service and the Future: Reforming Britain's Bureaucracies*,
   Conservative Political Centre, London.
Walker, D. (1993) 'Taxed by sweeping change', *The Times*, 23 September.
Wass, D. (1985) 'The civil service at the crossroads', *Political Quarterly*, vol. 56, pp.
   227-41.
Webb, S. and B. (1920) *A Constitution for the Socialist Commonwealth of Great Britain*,
   Longmans, Green and Co., London.
West, A. (1908) *One City and Many Men*, Smith Elder, London.
West, M. and Shaeff, R. (1994) 'Back to basics', *Health Service Journal*, vol. 104, no.
   5391 (24 February), pp. 26-9.
Williams, R. (1987) *Political Corruption in Africa*, Gower, Aldershot.
Williams, S. (1985) *Conflict of Interest: The Ethical Dilemma in Politics*, Gower,
   Aldershot.
Williamson, O.E. (1975) *Markets and Hierarchies: Analysis and Anti-Trust Implications*,
   Free Press, New York.
Willman, J. (1994) 'Private managers of public services "surprised at scrutiny"',
   Financial Times, 2 February.
Willmore, N. (1992) 'The Citizen's Charter brings out the cynics', *The Times*, 20
   October.
Willson, F.M.G. (1955) 'Ministries and boards: some aspects of administrative devel-
   opment since 1832', *Public Administration*, vol. 33, pp. 43-58.
Willson, M. (1991) 'Contracting corruption', *Local Government Studies*, vol. 17, no. 3,
   pp. 1-6.
Wilson, E. and Doig, A. (1996) 'The shape of ideology: structure, culture and policy
   delivery in the new public sector', *Public Money and Management*, vol. 16, no.
   2, pp. 53-61.
Woodhouse, D. (1994) *Ministers and Parliament: Accountability in Theory and Practice*,
   Clarendon, Oxford.
Zifcak, S. (1994) *New Managerialism: Administrative Reform in Whitehall and Canberra*,
   Open University Press, Buckingham.

Index